Enjoying Jazz

Consulting Editor: Gerald Warfield

Enjoying Jazz

HENRY MARTIN

SCHIRMER BOOKS
A Division of Macmillan, Inc.
NEW YORK

Schirmer Books
A Division of Macmillan, Inc.
866 Third Avenue, New York, N.Y. 10022

Collier Macmillan Canada, Inc.

Library of Congress Catalog Card Number: 85-27819

Printed in the United States of America

printing number
1 2 3 4 5 6 7 8 9 10

Library of Congress Cataloging-in-Publication Data

Martin, Henry.
   Enjoying jazz.

   Bibliography: p.
   Includes index.
   1. Jazz music—Analysis, appreciation. I. Title.
ML3506.M35   1986   785.42'01'5   85-27819
ISBN 0-02-873130-1

for Lonni Sue

contents

preface and acknowledgments

Enjoying Jazz is a general introduction and guide to the music called jazz. It is intended for the reader who seeks a systematic presentation of jazz styles and its greatest players.

Enjoying Jazz is more concerned with the music itself than with the detailed aspects of jazz history. Although the most important historical events are covered, the book focuses primarily on a small number of outstanding recordings and musicians. These recordings are examined in considerable detail to demonstrate differences and similarities among the various jazz styles. Brief biographies of the principal musicians precede discussions of their music.

Part One provides the reader with an introduction to jazz and its structural basis. Chapter 1 attempts to impart something of the personality of jazz. After a brief examination of jazz history, Chapter 1 concludes with some comments on jazz aesthetics. Chapter 2 discusses the European, African, and Afro-American origins of the music. The reader should not assume that because the European background is discussed first that it is thought to be more important. The order is based on a progression from larger-to-smaller-scale aspects of structure, so that the European contribution (form, large-scale rhythm, and harmony) logically precedes the African and Afro-American contributions (small-scale rhythm, melody, and spirit). Thematic material and improvisation are described in Chapter 3.

Part Two examines various jazz recordings, first in a general manner, then in more detail. Chapter 4 begins with a presentation of the small jazz group, the most important vehicle for performance throughout jazz history. This chapter is presented in reverse chronological order because more recent music is likely to be more familiar to most listeners. That is, King Oliver and the music of the 1920s might not at first appeal to a listener whose taste for jazz has been whetted on jazz-rock. Beginning in Chapter 5 with the big band, reverse chronological order is abandoned since that procedure makes it more difficult to analyze changes in style.

The remaining chapters of Part Two examine the major improvisational styles of the important jazz instruments and musicians. Few of the comments necessitate the use of musical notation, but for those readers with an ability to read or follow a melody, several transcriptions are provided in the Appendices. More detailed musical comments sometimes accompany the transcriptions. Since it would be impossible to cover all the major artists, the selection of music in Part Two is based on presenting a range of important performers for the various jazz styles. Hence, the emphasis is placed on well-known jazz performers whose historical importance is undisputed.

Whenever possible, recordings from the *Smithsonian Collection of Classic Jazz* (SCCJ) are used throughout Part Two. Such recordings are identified at the first mention of the title.

After the music has been heard in Part Two, Part Three will help the reader place jazz in a broader cultural perspective. Chapter 11 evaluates the present state of jazz and shows how its development has been analogous to the development of Western fine-art music. Chapter 12 lists important artists (other than jazz musicians) whose work has been influenced by jazz and some of their most important contributions.

Five appendices are provided for the reader. The first is a list of transcriptions. Next is a discography of some of the best jazz records. This small group of recordings could serve as the basis for a jazz record collection. Next, a glossary presents terms found in jazz and music theory. A chronological chart follows that correlates events in fine-art music, popular music, and cultural history with events in jazz history. Finally, an annotated bibliography is provided with suggestions for further reading. The books listed are the ones that have been the most useful to me in exploring jazz and music theory.

This book has grown out of my experience with jazz on a variety of levels: as a classroom teacher trying to impart the excitement of the music to college students, as a private teacher working with individual students on music theory and improvisation, as a pianist talking with other musicians about our discovery and admiration of particular artists, as a theorist who has studied jazz theory and has written about it in his doctoral dissertation, and as a composer who attempts to incorporate the language and feeling of jazz into his music. Throughout the book I rely mainly on my own observations of the music and the recordings, though at times, especially when discussing history, my debt to other authors' books will be evident (see Bibliography).

I would like to thank Don Jamison, Ed Johnson, Maggi Johnson, and Aline Johnson for helpful suggestions on earlier drafts. Robert Sadin and I have had many long discussions on both the music of jazz and its culture; many of the ideas presented in Part Three arose from these discussions. Mr. Sadin also suggested many useful improvements on earlier drafts. I thank him gratefully for all his help. Thanks also to Michael J. Budds, whose careful and critical reading of earlier drafts saved me from a few errors and helped improve the overall flow and design of the book.

I would like to thank Gerald Warfield and Tren Anderson for conceiving of this project and for suggesting many changes and improvements. I am also very grateful to Maribeth Anderson Payne and Joan Pitsch for the attention and help I received at Macmillan.

From my first days of banging on the piano, my parents, Mary and Henry Martin, always encouraged me to listen to and love not just jazz, but music of all kinds. To them I owe my life-long dedication to music. I would especially like to thank my wife, Lonnie Sue Johnson, for her marvelous illustrations on the book's cover and throughout the text. I cannot acknowledge adequately her continued moral support, encouragement, and inspiration. This book is dedicated to her.

part one

setting up

chapter
one

main
themes
in
jazz

the background of jazz

The term "jazz" is remarkably ambiguous, connoting many distinct performers, situations, and musical styles. The large range of styles, perhaps more than any other single factor, prohibits us from precisely defining "jazz." Nevertheless, let me suggest a general description: jazz is a twentieth-century music originated in America by black Americans and characterized by improvisation and a strong projection of rhythm.

As you may know, improvisation, probably the most important feature of jazz, is a technique of playing during which the musician, working within certain constraints and conventions, composes his part as he goes along. Because he improvises his music in "real time" (while the piece is proceeding), he never plays anything exactly the same way again. While most other forms of Western music emphasize a distinction between the performer and composer, the jazz musician is both at once.

Some contemporary critics and jazz musicians avoid using the term "jazz" because they believe that it has become obsolete, describing a past performance practice, not a specific type of contemporary music. Before jazz splintered into numerous styles and substyles during the 1950s, the term designated a specific type of music somewhat more exactly. Moreover, many critics object to the term "jazz" itself because of its sexual implications.

Jazz was developed in the eighteenth and nineteenth centuries by black Americans, who were the first to combine the heritages of African and European music. To understand how this cultural mix came about, it is necessary to recall the early history of blacks in America.

In the eighteenth and early nineteenth centuries, most black Americans were slaves, leading lives perhaps unimaginable to those of us who have known only relative freedom. The slave, who was entirely at the mercy of his master, could only envision days of endless work with little or no chance for freedom or future improvement. Under such difficult conditions, it is not surprising that the repressed feelings of the black people found an outlet in music, one of the only opportunities for personal expression permitted. Furthermore, it was necessary for them, a subjugated people in a foreign country, to perform their own music, African in origin, on instruments of European design or on clever, homemade instruments (based on African models) such as the washtub bass and the banjo.

4

Once converted to Christianity, the slaves learned Protestant hymns and other religious songs. These pieces helped to acculturate the slaves to the conventions of European music. As a result, the slaves' own music took on both European and African characteristics. Jazz, one of the descendants of these early hybrid musics, achieved distinction as a style by the end of the nineteenth century or in the first decade or so of the twentieth century.

Although the innovators of jazz have been primarily black artists, jazz has remained the Afro-American musical style with the largest number of well-known white performers and fans. Jazz, among all the musical styles associated with black Americans, seems to balance its European and African elements most evenly.

Because the black population in the United States was at first largely rural and concentrated in the South, jazz probably began its development as a country folk music. After Emancipation, the slow urbanization of the black population resulted in the music, born on the plantation, maturing in the city. New Orleans, Kansas City, Chicago, and New York in particular were centers for the development of jazz as a cohesive style.

Jazz is now rarely, if ever, thought of as a rural music. Since the 1950s at least, it has become thoroughly urban, most often heard in nightclubs, jazz clubs, and concert halls. Yet, despite its urbanization, jazz preserves some of its rural heritage, especially in connection with the blues form. **Blues** has to some extent remained a black rural music, despite the important presence of urban blues in the last few decades.

Because jazz was developed by black musicians, many of them consider it to be an expression of their culture. Yet, many brilliant white musicians have played and continue to play jazz. During the years of segregation throughout the South and overt discrimination throughout the country, only all-black or all-white bands could perform in public. The white bands were treated much better. For example, black musicians were paid only about half the wages received by whites; blacks often were not allowed to patronize the very clubs where they worked as entertainers; and when touring the South they frequently experienced humiliating incidents in which they were denied lodging or food in segregated hotels.

White bands, in general, achieved much greater popular acclaim, that is, acclaim among white audiences. These bands were able to build greater reputations despite the fact that they were often "outplayed" by the black groups who had innovated the new styles. Since the 1970s, white players, asserting that they have been discriminated against by black jazz musicians, have complained of "reverse racism," sometimes called "Crow Jim." Sometimes these controversies obscure the main point, namely that black musicians have innovated practically all the major jazz styles. Of course, there are many outstanding white musicians as well.

Jazz embodies features of both popular and fine-art music. After some contemplation one realizes that this is quite remarkable, if not unique. Any given piece of art, whether it is an example of music, painting, writing, or dance, can be categorized according to its potential audience and intrinsic complexity. Folk art is usually very simple, since it is created by nonprofessionals, often in rural areas, for their own enjoyment or for their friends and family. Popular art may also be simple, but it is usually more polished, created by professionals to appeal to a more urban and "sophisticated" population. Fine art, created by professionals for connoisseurs, tends to be more complex, to activate a wider emotional response, and to engage highly developed critical faculties. I should point out that complexity is no measure of value—a musical community may rightfully prefer a beautiful folk song to a badly written symphony.

The popular jazz styles, which will be described more fully in the next section, include, for example, **dixieland** and **swing,** both of which attracted huge crowds of listeners and dancers in their day. Quite often jazz styles are promoted by popular performers, for example, Stevie Wonder and Donald Fagen often feature improvisation on their records. Moreover, in the professional world of popular music, one meets many musicians who would rather be playing jazz but cannot earn a living doing so.

Other jazz styles, such as **bop** and **free jazz,** should be classified as fine art. Classically trained musicians have been attracted to jazz since the late 1920s, and many modern jazz musicians, such as Cecil Taylor and Herbie Hancock, reflect much of their fine-art backgrounds in the kind of jazz they play. Furthermore, many jazz substyles share the techniques and aesthetic aims of contemporary fine-art music.

The jazz musicians and fans of the 1920s would have found it hard to believe that today jazz would be studied as both an artistic and scholarly discipline. Yet, despite the number of students who have studied performance in university jazz programs and jazz schools, a great many jazz musicians begin their training as popular musicians who gradually acquire the skill to improvise creatively. Some of these same musicians continue working with rock bands and dance orchestras, and doing studio recording sessions to earn a living.

The complexities of jazz culture can be best understood by examining its history. Because this field is continually being studied by scholars and jazz lovers, the amount of historical detail is always increasing. However, an accurate overview of jazz can be achieved by listening to as well as reading about a representative selection of its greatest recordings.

Despite my concentration on the best-known musicians, the reader should bear in mind that much jazz has been and is still played by more obscure musicians who remain generally underrecorded, underrated, and underpayed. By listening to the recordings suggested in the Appendix, as well as to lesser-known artists both on record and in live performance, the reader will acquire a more profound understanding of this great musical culture.

a brief history of jazz

In tracing the development of music through the course of Western history, we find that new musical styles do not usually arise from scratch—a new style is more commonly formed when previously developed styles meet and influence each other under the proper circumstances. In particular, jazz, one of the more recent musical events in the long span of Western cultural history, merges the European traditions of the white Americans with the African traditions of the slaves and their descendants. The long years of musical gestation that eventually gave birth to jazz stretched over more than two centuries and can be thought of as its prehistory. Jazz history itself begins around 1910-1915, as that is when the first groups calling themselves "jazz bands" began to perform.

black nineteenth- and early twentieth-century music

Throughout the eighteenth and nineteenth centuries, various forms of black music evolved that were rooted in the African tradition but revealed elements of the European tradition as well. Slaves who were called upon as musicians to entertain whites became proficient on traditional European instruments. As mentioned in the last section, numerous slaves learned to sing hymns and religious songs characteristic of the European tradition. Moreover, classified advertisements in the newspapers of the time sometimes referred to slaves as highly skilled musicians. From this and other evidence surviving from the eighteenth and nineteenth centuries, it seems clear that the slave population soon assimilated European music into their own culture.

The Afro-American music of the eighteenth and early nineteenth centuries is largely unknown today, for it was based on an oral tradition in which there was no need for musical notation. Instead, the songs and instrumental pieces were taught by one individual to another and played by ear. Passed along from person to person over many years, this music and its performances probably underwent gradual stylistic change, but historians, working today without hard evidence, are unable to document this development in any detail.

In any event, the slaves certainly performed both secular and sacred music. Their own secular songs, more African in nature, would have included work songs, field hollers, and occasional songs. The occasional songs accompanied various aspects of slave life, such as playing games or celebrating holidays. The work songs often accompanied field labor and were generally very rhythmic, a feature that enabled the workers to synchronize their tasks and movements: a group leader would sing out the main phrases while the rest of the workhands would respond together in time with their work. This procedure is known as

7

call-and-response singing, a stylistic trait of African music that was to become prominent centuries later in jazz.

The early secular slave songs probably led to the development of the blues, a type of folk music that crystallized after the Civil War and later contributed many of its features to jazz. The feeling of the blues is unique, projecting sadness, guilt, and sometimes even despair, but at the same time transcending worldly and vulgar concerns. Of especial significance is the concept of a **blue note,** whose varying pitch frequency occasionally places it outside the standard 12-note chromatic scale.

Country blues flourished in the late nineteenth and early twentieth centuries. It was characterized by earthy, gutsy solo performances of rural blues tunes. The singers usually accompanied themselves on guitar. Many of the better country blues singers such as Huddie Ledbetter ("Leadbelly") (1885-1949) and "Blind Lemon" Jefferson (1897-1930) were not recorded until the 1920s and 1930s, so it is difficult to speculate on how this music sounded during the late 1800s.

A later, more fully documented development in the history of the blues occurred with the development of **classic blues.** This substyle, which flourished from roughly 1920 to 1940, was created by professional singers, mostly women, who often performed with shows that toured the country. These singers were generally accompanied by bands and solo pianists. Among the classic blues performers were such outstanding vocalists as Gertrude "Ma" Rainey (1886-1939), Bessie Smith, and Mamie Smith (1890-1946). The stupendous success of the first blues record, *Crazy Blues,* recorded by Mamie Smith in 1920, motivated record companies to begin issuing jazz and blues.

In the late nineteenth century, various Southern black bands adopted marches from the white repertory for performance at parades and concerts. These bands, forerunners of the first jazz bands, served as training ensembles for many of the early jazz musicians. Moreover, the marches themselves influenced the development of **ragtime,** the most important prejazz style and an extremely popular fad from the late 1890s until World War I. Rags—lively, syncopated, and usually lighthearted pieces—reveal the same musical design or layout as marches. In fact, rags, though principally written for solo piano, sound like embellished marches. They are so similar that many composers, including Scott Joplin, named some of their rags "marches" or indicated "march tempo" as the speed and rhythm of the work.

The sacred music of the Afro-Americans in the nineteenth century consisted of many well-known hymns borrowed from the white Protestant repertory as well as compositions modeled on them, such as spirituals. The close kinship between spirituals and white European music is suggested by the European approach to form and harmony observable in much black sacred music. In addition to performing these popular spirituals, preachers in many black churches would often engage the congregation in singing a more informal music based on the call-and-response format. At times, their singing would burst into a frenzied uproar, the congregation shouting key phrases and dancing to the driving rhythms, mainly created by hand-clapping. Both ecstatic congregational singing and the more tranquil hymns and spirituals contributed stylistic features to jazz.

Blacks trained in European fine-art music helped to cross-fertilize the separate cultures as well. Among the several fine black concert artists in the nineteenth century, soprano Marie Selika and violinist Walter Craig were especially well known. Composer Louis Moreau Gottschalk (1829-1869) was highly respected, with a style of nineteenth-century salon music that incorporated harmonic and melodic devices from black folk music. These artists helped blacks and whites more fully appreciate each other's musical traditions.

white nineteenth-century music

The music of the white Americans in the eighteenth and nineteenth centuries was very similar to the European music from which it was derived. Like the Afro-American music of the time, it can be divided into various secular and sacred genres. Much of this music was notated. Accordingly, it is somewhat easier to trace its stylistic development, although its exact performance practices still elude historians. Throughout music history, popular music is always less specifically described than art music, and so as an era becomes more distant, its performance practices are gradually forgotten. (The difference between notation and performance in popular song can be appreciated by comparing the sheet music to the actual record of practically any uptempo top-40 hit of today.)

In the eighteenth and nineteenth centuries, white secular American music included popular songs by such composers as Stephen Foster (1826-1864), folk songs, minstrel tunes, dance music, marches, and European fine-art music. Because fine-art music was rarely performed or appreciated outside of the major cities, popular music affected the development of jazz far more critically. The songs and songlike melodies of the popular music, usually based on standard harmonies and rhythms, were simple and unpretentious in character.

Like black sacred music, white sacred music consisted mostly of hymns, religious songs, and occasional call-and-response singing. If the congregation or the preacher himself were sufficiently moved by the spirit, the singing might become highly exuberant, even leading to wild dancing and shouting. Although ecstatic religion was practiced by both black and white churches, the black churches more directly influenced the early black jazz groups to incorporate uninhibited expression into their music.

nineteenth-century entertainment

Aside from the music itself, several entertainment vehicles contributed to the mix of the African and European traditions, the most important of these being the minstrel show. Throughout the nineteenth century white troupes in blackface, and later authentic black companies toured the country and Europe performing shows patched together with songs, dances, comedy routines, and short plays. Stereotyped black characters such as the city slicker, sometimes called the "Zip Coon," or the lazy, shiftless Jim Crow were lampooned by both black and white companies.

Despite the initial exclusion of blacks from minstrelsy and the pejorative light in which blacks were portrayed, minstrel shows introduced many whites to black music, helped popularize various black dances, and later provided employment for black as well as white actors, dancers, and musicians. Among the most memorable of the dances were the cakewalk and the soft shoe, both of which achieved some popularity with whites, too. In the late nineteenth century, minstrelsy was replaced by vaudeville, a touring entertainment form like minstrelsy, but with less racial stereotyping and with songs and comedy more like those of today's entertainment. Great vaudeville performers, such as blues singer Bessie Smith, helped popularize jazz in its early years.

Black vocal ensembles, another important form of entertainment, traveled throughout the country in the late 1800s performing gospel songs and spirituals. These ensembles, trained in the European tradition, brought worldwide acclaim to black American culture and featured such beautiful works as "Carry Me Back to Old Virginny," the most famous of black composer James Bland's (1854–1911) many fine songs. Stylistically, spirituals and gospel songs contained harmonic and melodic features that were later to become standard in jazz.

Concert performances of spirituals required singers well versed in European fine-art music. In New Orleans, many Creoles, who were among the founders of New Orleans jazz, reflected such training. These people, a mixture of French or Spanish and African descent, had regarded themselves as an indigenous ethnic group positioned on a somewhat higher social plateau than blacks, but later in the nineteenth century their status was lowered to that of blacks. Ironically, the Creoles had at one time disdained blacks as musically illiterate, but the enforced association of the two populations resulted in the inevitable mixing of their somewhat disparate cultures.

early jazz

Much of the stylistic strength of early New Orleans jazz can be seen as arising from the cultural mix of the blacks and Creoles. All of the first great jazz musicians from New Orleans were either Creoles, like pianist Jelly Roll Morton and clarinetist Sidney Bechet (1897-1959), or blacks like cornet players Louis Armstrong and Joe "King" Oliver.

Concerning early jazz (ca. 1910-1920), a significant and ongoing controversy has arisen among historians. Some contend that jazz definitively crystallized in New Orleans. Other scholars argue that jazzlike styles were evolving throughout the country, but that New Orleans musicians were perhaps the first to break through with the **dixieland** style that became widely imitated and defined in the 1920s as jazz. To put it another way, some historians define early New Orleans style as the beginning of jazz, while others define it as the first jazz style to achieve national prominence. Neither position seems to present the complete picture.

In any event, the second position is bolstered when one considers that jazz styles were developing in New York and Kansas City, at the very least, not to mention other urban centers where musicians would have naturally taken jazzlike liberties with ragtime and the other popular music of the time. Since recording is the decisive step toward national prominence for an artist and the popularizing of his style, records may have presented historians with a distorted view of how early jazz crystallized: bands that were physically present near the recording centers of New York and Chicago would naturally have had the opportunity to record first. Moreover, some early jazz musicians refused to record since they were afraid of having their solos and arrangements stolen by other musicians! Still, the only hard evidence remaining is the recordings. Insufficient as they are, they alone must arbitrate matters of historical opinion, since memoirs and interviews are notoriously inaccurate, and there was little serious writing about jazz at the time.

Although they were never recorded, popular musical groups from New Orleans had been touring the country for at least two decades, as, for example, the early important bands of pianist-composer Jelly Roll Morton and cornetist Freddy Keppard (1889-1933). It is possible that if some of these earlier jazz groups had made records, their manner of playing would today be considered the seminal jazz style.

A few important developments associated with the city of New Orleans contributed significantly to the rise in popularity of its jazz style. The mixing of blacks and Creoles helped unite African-oriented music and the traditional music of Europe. Musicians of both ethnic groups performed together in the brothels of Storyville, New Orleans' red-light district, as well as on the riverboats that traveled the Mississippi River. In 1917, the secretary of the navy, Josephus Daniels, ordered Storyville closed. Traditionally, it is thought that this act encouraged the unemployed musicians to carry dixieland jazz up the Mississippi to Chicago. There, King Oliver, leader of the first great jazz band, achieved his fame. He also made the first jazz records still taken seriously today, and on them featured some of the finest New Orleans musicians of the time. In particular, his second cornet player was Louis Armstrong.

new orleans and chicago styles (dixieland)

Credit for the first jazz record goes to the Original Dixieland Jazz Band (ODJB), who recorded *Livery Stable Blues* and *Dixieland Jass Band One-Step* on February 26, 1917. This was not their first recording, but it is generally considered to be their first jazz recording. (Note the early spelling "jass": there were several variants before the current spelling was standardized in the early 1920s.) Although the band is competent and plays well together in New Orleans style, the inspired playing of the early King Oliver recordings is lacking. The records of the ODJB, while entertaining, are of doubtful musical value, especially when they feature squeaking, howling, horse neighing, and other dated effects. The ODJB was a white ensemble, but jazz novelty records were issued by both black and white groups throughout the 1920s.

Since jazz in the 1920s was dominated by New Orleans musicians playing and recording in the Chicago area, the music of that time is sometimes classified as New Orleans-Chicago style jazz, but is also sometimes called "dixieland." Its uptempo, raucous quality is usually referred to as **hot** to separate it from the more staid, smoother style known as **sweet.**

Great hot bands dominated jazz in the early 1920s. In addition to the brilliant King Oliver ensemble, Jelly Roll Morton led a fine studio group known as the Red Hot Peppers. He was one of the greatest pianists of his day and one of the first to write skillful and effective jazz arrangements. In Chicago, a group of white musicians now known as the Austin High School Gang achieved prominence especially after they were joined by the brilliant cornet player Bix Beiderbecke. Beiderbecke recorded great cornet solos as early as 1924.

early big band jazz

In addition to the smaller dixieland ensembles, larger bands of eight or more pieces were influenced by the "hotter" sound of the dixieland musicians. For example, Fletcher Henderson's polite society dance orchestra soon evolved into a hot jazz band. The influential Duke Ellington band, playing at New York's Cotton Club, gradually acquired some of the jazz feeling first heard in the midwest groups, too. Meanwhile, Louis Armstrong, working in Chicago with his own band and in New York with Fletcher Henderson, recorded his best work, which includes some of the greatest solos in jazz history.

In viewing the decade of the 1920s as a whole, we find that the development of early big band jazz (ca. 1924-1930) was centered in New York and Chicago. Until perhaps the 1950s, artists required exposure in New York, the main base of the recording industry, to achieve national prominence. Yet, a unique jazz style flourished in Kansas City too, which at the time was considered the regional capital or focus of the southwestern portion of the country.

As a regional center dominated by the notorious Pendergast political machine, Kansas City developed into a town well known for its many jazz night spots. The jazz style maturing there was more oriented toward improvisation and the blues, as is evident from the recordings of the Benny Moten and Buster Smith bands. Regional bands such as these helped propel the development of hot jazz from the New Orleans-Chicago style into the more relaxed, smoother style known as swing.

Throughout the 1920s, various popular dances such as the Charleston and eventually the Lindy hop became associated with jazz. These popular jazz dances were frequently performed during the 1920s and 1930s, the decades in which jazz was sometimes synonymous with American popular music.

swing

The music of the 1930s (ca. 1930-1945) is usually referred to as **swing,** but the documentation of its style development is marred by the dramatic decrease in record production during the Depression. Victor, partly because of its fortunate merger with RCA, was among the very few record companies to avoid bankruptcy. When records became more numerous again after 1932, swing had replaced dixieland as the dominant jazz style. Essentially, swing is the Kansas City jazz style spiced with New Orleans intensity and structured by the solid arranging techniques of Fletcher Henderson and Duke Ellington.

With a less harsh, silkier surface than the New Orleans and Chicago styles, swing brought jazz to the forefront of American consciousness. A uniquely popular era in jazz history, swing was oriented toward dancing and used the popular song form. Swing era musicians brought great technical proficiency to their art. Many of them, such as Benny Goodman, Duke Ellington, Count Basie, Fats Waller, Coleman Hawkins, and Glenn Miller (1904-1944), were widely admired.

The latter part of the swing era was dominated by the **big bands,** highly popular ensembles of 14 or more players. Among the best were the bands of Benny Goodman, Count Basie, Tommy Dorsey, Duke Ellington, and Jimmy Lunceford (1902-1947).

bop

World War II and the record ban of 1942, initiated by the musicians' union because of disagreements with the record industry, critically affected the history of jazz. After the invasion of Pearl Harbor, many of the big band musicians were drafted; the nation turned its attention from music and entertainment to war and industrial production. Even after the conclusion of the war and the settlement between the musicians union and the recording industry, musical life could not return to its customary patterns because of the inevitable changes in the country and its need for a corresponding change of musical style. Moreover, a dance hall tax law passed in 1948 greatly increased the expense of hiring big bands and hastened their almost complete extinction.

Swing music itself had reached an evolutionary plateau where it became more and more difficult to sound fresh within the usual stylistic norms. In the early 1940s, a group of black musicians in New York City began experimenting with new musical ideas that eventually coalesced into a style of jazz known as **bop, bebop,** or **rebop** (ca. 1942-1950). The innovators **jammed** (that is, played together informally without music or prior rehearsal) in the early 1940s at Minton's Play House and Monroe's Uptown House in Harlem where, after hours, such musicians as Charlie Parker, Dizzy Gillespie, pianist-composer Thelonious Monk, and drummer Kenny Clarke (1914-1985) were often heard. Later, around 1944 or so, the activity shifted to the various jazz clubs along 52nd Street where the style became more widely known.

The first bop records, produced around 1944, featured a music that was considered strange and difficult to follow by many listeners, exciting and progressive by still others. Some bop innovators claim to have developed the new style to discourage dancing and exclude other musicians, who were not sufficiently versed in its methods, from **sitting in** (playing along). Not only were the catchy melodies and smooth rhythms of the swing bands avoided, but the beat was also too fast, and occasionally too slow, for popular dancing. Whereas swing had depended on the use of a familiar tune as a main theme to insure communication with the mainstream audience, bop substituted themes (known as **heads**) that were as angular, dense, and improvisational as the solos themselves. Avoiding the flashy arrangements of the swing bands, bop focused attention on the individual creativity of the solo improviser. With bop and the modern era, most jazz styles relinquished popular-music status, although many jazz musicians were to achieve popular success from time to time.

cool

After the early 1950s, it became impossible to specify which style was in the forefront of the overall development of jazz—instead, many styles and substyles coexisted, competing for popularity. The next period of development, during the early 1950s, is called the **cool** era. Its roots may be traced to the elegant, linear style of saxophonist Lester Young, a featured soloist with the Count Basie orchestra. Whereas Charlie Parker, an innovator of bop, had pursued Lester Young's linear swing style in one direction, by heating it up, cool jazz pursued it in the opposite direction by reinforcing Young's sense of detachment and emphasizing his long, wistful melodic lines.

The cool musicians tended to avoid the frenzy of bop, its hectic tempos and its difficult soloistic melodies. Instead, they exchanged these features for stark, architectural tunes supported by an easier rhythmic feel and harmonized from time to time with techniques borrowed from the Impressionist composers (e.g., Debussy and Ravel) of the late nineteenth and early twentieth centuries. Between 1949 and 1950, an especially influential series of recordings was made by trumpeter Miles Davis, arranger Gil Evans, saxophonist-arranger Gerry Mulligan, and others which are now known as the "Birth of the Cool" sessions. In them, the more relaxed and approachable style attained maturity.

On the whole, cool was pensive and comfortable rather than daring and aggressive. Yet, despite the popularity of cool, bop was supported by many jazz fans and, as a style, it still exhibited potential for expansion.

concert jazz and third stream

The late 1950s witnessed an intensified effort to combine jazz with fine-art music (Chapter 12). Such experiments in **concert jazz** had been occurring since the 1920s, but the idea grew widely popular in the late 1950s and resulted in a fascinating mixture of twentieth-century contemporary music with modern jazz. Composer Gunther Schuller, in a lecture delivered in 1957, coined the expression "third stream" to refer to this repertory. **Third stream** musicians, from both the fine-art and jazz worlds, included Schuller, pianist-composer John Lewis (b. 1920), composer-arranger Gil Evans, and others. Their works were composed for various kinds of jazz groups, fine-art ensembles, or hybrid combinations. Meanwhile, jazz musicians continued to incorporate aspects of twentieth-century fine-art music into their pieces and, to the extent that it was possible, into their solos.

The jazz styles developed during the 1940s and 1950s differed considerably from the jazz of the 1920s and swing in that they could no longer be classified as popular music. This change of status, however, never enabled jazz to shake its reputation of being slightly unrespectable. Only the most clean-cut musicians such as Benny Goodman, Duke Ellington, members of the Modern Jazz Quartet, or third stream artists, have been able to avoid this unfortunate stigma. Despite its new connection with the arts, jazz, for the general public, was still associated with the underworld and criminal activities, and hence was commonly heard as background music for gangster films and television detective shows (e.g., composer Benny Carter's (b. 1907) *A Man Called Adam*), and composer Henry Mancini's (b. 1924) scores for the *Peter Gunn* series.

hard bop/gospel

As jazz upgraded its image by associating with fine-art music, some musicians, mostly black artists, countered by creating jazz at a gutsier, more basic level. For them, this meant returning to the roots of jazz and seeking a style more akin to gospel music and the blues. The result, called **funky jazz, hard**

bop, or **gospel jazz,** was still later combined with the **soul music** of the 1960s (for example, the music of Horace Silver). Closer to the popular-music side of the jazz spectrum, it was characterized by a blusier harmonic style with simpler, funkier melodies and improvisations. Top musicians who continued to play in the bop and hard bop traditions included trumpeter Clifford Brown and drummer Art Blakey (b. 1919).

free jazz

In addition to the hard bop, cool, and third stream styles, the late 1950s experienced the genesis of **free jazz,** which was at first associated with saxophonist Ornette Coleman. This style, notable for its avoidance of traditional harmony and melody, relied on spontaneity for all aspects of the performance. When compared to previous styles, free jazz was indeed "free," although the avoidance of traditional harmony and melody created aesthetic difficulties for both the musicians and listeners.

eclecticism

Most of the styles inaugurated in the 1950s continued to unfold through the 1960s with various mixtures and cross-fertilizations. Cool jazz metamorphosed into **modal jazz,** which, while more active rhythmically, emphasized linear playing through long harmonic areas. Interest in other cultures, particularly those of Africa and Asia, inspired combinations of jazz with world music. Free jazz continued to grow in popularity and was sometimes combined with political rhetoric urging, at first, integration and then black separatism. Gospel jazz and hard bop offered listeners a simpler alternative to the demands of free jazz and the other esoteric styles. Experiments in third stream music peaked, then began to decline.

jazz-rock

Toward the end of the 1960s pop music was again plundered for thematic material, a development that recalled the swing and dixieland eras. Moreover, the result was as revolutionary as the New Orleans style in its day: **jazz-rock.** It changed jazz by legitimizing rock-style rhythms and by incorporating the use of electric and electronic instruments such as electric pianos, rock-style electric guitars and bass guitars, and synthesizers. Important artists included Herbie Hancock, Chick Corea, Miles Davis, and John McLaughlin, and the bands Blood, Sweat & Tears and Weather Report.

further developments

Since the 1960s, various nonprofit organizations and collectives have been formed to support free jazz and explore the possibilities of integrating free jazz with musics of other cultures. These groups were successful in creating a favorable environment for musicians who wished to establish a noncommercial basis for their art form. Among the more prominent organizations were the Association for the Advancement of Creative Musicians (AACM) founded 1965 in Chicago, the Black Artists Group (BAG) founded 1968 in St. Louis, and the Jazz Composers Orchestra Association (JCOA) founded 1966 in New York. These organizations soon became associated with many of the most promising avant-garde players of the day such as trumpeters Leo Smith (b. 1941) and Lester Bowie (b. 1941), saxophonists Roscoe Mitchell (b. 1940) and Anthony Braxton (b. 1945), pianists Muhal Richard Abrams (b. 1930) and Carla Bley (b. 1938), and percussionist Don Moye (b. 1946).

plan of this book

Since the 1970s, a new interest in jazz history has arisen in which all previous jazz styles, including dixieland and swing, are performed widely, much as concert artists perform pieces written in all the previous periods of fine-art music. As laudable as this seems, I will argue in Part Three that such stylistic egalitarianism suggests a loss of creative vitality, since when the attention of the artists and the public refocuses on the greatness of the past, the current development of the art form probably interests them less.

I shall conclude this brief history of jazz by posing three hypotheses that will be examined in more detail in Part Three. You should not assume that these hypotheses are entirely true, but instead, during the presentation of the music in Part Two, you should think about them critically. Once the music is more familiar to you, it will be easier in Part Three to return to these ideas and assess their value.

1. *The large-scale features of jazz were established by 1930. (To decide whether this is true or not, it will be necessary to agree on just what "large-scale" refers to. Once we have done so, we will decide if jazz is a fully developed musical style that undergoes no* **essential** *changes after 1930.)*

2. *Jazz developed as a folk music, rapidly became a popular music in the 1920s, then finally established itself as a fine art by around 1950. By the late 1970s and early 1980s, jazz, despite its apparent popularity, was to undergo no further significant stylistic evolution because it lacked the necessary vitality.*

At that time all of its previous styles became recognized as artistic vehicles for performance. Indications are, therefore, that jazz will not undergo any further significant evolution.

3. *Jazz is the most easily identifiable, most widely influential American contribution to the world's music culture. The conditions for producing jazz were only available in America and America has not produced another art music with the same degree of cultural influence and wide recognizability as jazz.*

jazz aesthetics

An aesthetic attitude is a frame of mind, an intellectual posture that is assumed for the purposes of experiencing a work of art as genuinely and appropriately as possible. For example, if you listen to art music as a background to other activities such as eating or reading, then you are not assuming an aesthetic attitude. If, however, you listen carefully and critically without conversing, then you are assuming an aesthetic attitude.

Aesthetic attitudes differ for various kinds of artworks. At a movie or concert, most people are bothered by talking because it interrupts or inhibits their concentration. Others with a more casual attitude may feel that talking enhances their enjoyment. The expected behavior of people at fine-art concerts and movies has been informally codified and is generally practiced by everyone, but the proper aesthetic attitude for jazz remains controversial because of its unclear status as art or popular music.

In general, as the art form ranges from the fine-art to the popular and folk levels, greater shows of enthusiasm and participation are permissible. Hence, for jazz oriented to popular appreciation (e.g., swing-era jazz), dancing and singing along are tolerated and even encouraged. This response may be less appropriate for concert hall or third stream music. Others feel that dancing and singing along are inappropriate for any style of jazz performed at a concert hall because of its fine-art associations. On the other hand, it can be argued that because jazz was developed through the good-time participation of folk and popular music, a concert is simply the wrong forum for presenting jazz. Others with more fine-art inclinations contend that jazz should not be presented at nightclubs, where it competes with clinking glasses, smoke, and conversation.

For the most part, an aesthetic attitude consists of a set of expectations for optimally experiencing the artwork at hand. For example, your expectations at the beginning of a Marx Brothers movie necessarily differ from those at the outset of an Ingmar Bergman film. Similarly, one does not approach an Ornette Coleman recording with the same expectations one might bring to Elvis Presley, on the one hand, or to Beethoven on the other. Significantly, the set of expectations for listening to jazz is determined by the fact that almost all jazz, aside from some big band music, depends heavily on improvisation.

Because an improvising musician has not fully worked out his performance in advance, as is customary for popular and fine-art musicians, he is at a disadvantage. Although the finest jazz features improvisations as complex, subtle, and carefully wrought as the great compositions of fine-art music, most jazz is not at this level, necessarily, so we must have a more appropriate aesthetic attitude when listening to it. In experiencing jazz, you should "ride along," trying to feel what the musicians are getting at, taking in the improvisations as an adventure where anything is likely to happen.

A positive aesthetic attitude, though, does not mean an uncritical one. As a jazz recording becomes familiar to you, consider your changing attitude toward it and, especially, check to see that the repeated listenings enrich your understanding and enjoyment. Does the record deepen your appreciation of jazz in general by yielding a new experience? Since our goal in this book is to help you experience jazz as meaningfully as possible, you should assume a highly critical, fine-art attitude toward the recordings analyzed in Part Two.

chapter
two

the
european
and
african
legacies

contributions of the european musical tradition

The European musical tradition provided early jazz and prejazz black music with its formal and harmonic bases and most of the large-scale features of its rhythm. I shall deal first with rhythm and form before discussing harmony.

large-scale rhythm and form

Rhythm can be loosely defined as the durational organization of music. When you dance, or tap your feet, or clap to a song, you are responding to the song's rhythm and reinforcing its beat. The regular beats experienced in a piece of music are grouped into a pattern, usually of 2, 3, or 4 beats, known as **meter.** In most music, the beat itself usually remains steady, whereas much of the sound moves faster or slower than the beat. Almost all the music of the world is metrically organized.

To clarify what I mean, sing "Over the Rainbow" to yourself, clapping steadily, twice on each of the beginning syllables "Some" and "where." Then continue to sing and clap regularly. The clapping pattern, which signifies the beat, is shown in the lower staff of Example 2.1.

Note that some of the words and notes move faster than the beat while others move slower. Moreover, because each beat is either stressed or unstressed, the melody and lyric are arranged so that the musical and poetic accents or stresses are aligned. In the example above, the syllables "O" and "rain" are accented slightly stronger than "ver" and "bow." Because the accents occur every other beat the piece is in **duple meter.** Each set of 4 beats is called a **measure** or **bar,** and is enclosed by long vertical lines, called **barlines,** through the **staff** or staves. (**Measure** and **measures** will be abbreviated **m.** and **mm.,** respectively.)

Earlier I noted that the larger-scale rhythmic features of jazz derive from the European tradition, whereas the smaller-scale features are more typical of African music. Units of time of one beat or less will be considered smaller-scale, and events longer than a beat larger-scale. For example, in "Over the Rainbow" the duple meter is itself a large-scale rhythmic feature; the pitches used to set

the word "Somewhere" are each 2 beats long, that is, larger-scale rhythmic events; the pitches on the syllables "ver" and "the" in bar two, are each one-half beat long, that is, smaller-scale rhythmic events.

Conceptually, the first beat of each bar in music is thought to be stressed, although a composer can often generate musical interest and complexity by avoiding or underplaying the first beat stress. In a simple song such as "Over the Rainbow," the first beat of each bar is stressed throughout.

The most common meter in jazz is duple, with a stress every 2 beats and a greater stress on the **downbeat** (first beat) of each 4-beat bar. Although 4-beat measures dominate jazz throughout its history, a 2-beat measure is common in early jazz because of its association with nineteenth-century marching band music. In marches, the 2-beat measure corresponds to a left-right stepping pattern with the left foot usually on the first beat of each measure.

A simple duple or triple meter is part of the legacy of the European tradition. Although much African rhythm, which will be described in the next section, is frequently too complex to be thought of in terms of a simple meter, the meter of most jazz is easily heard as duple or triple.

Again sing the first two lines of "Over the Rainbow," clapping slowly and steadily. Chances are that you paused after "high" to catch your breath. Each line before and after the breath is called a **phrase.** In general, phrases are large-scale units of structure that are delimited by events of harmonic and melodic closure. The most common phrase length is 4 measures, although it can vary widely, depending on the speed and style of the music under consideration. Metaphorically, the phrase has been called a "musical sentence" since it encompasses a unit of musical thought that ties the basic building blocks of the sound together.

Simple duple and triple meters and 4-bar phrases are derived from European music and are examples of large-scale rhythm. A great many songs in jazz and popular music can be analyzed as a string of 4-bar phrases—"Over the Rainbow," for example. Occasional deviations from the 4-bar phrase length, usually consisting of 1- or 2-bar extensions, are customarily thought of in terms of the 4-bar norm. Further, "Over the Rainbow" is composed of 2 sections, one of which, labeled "A," comprises 8 bars and is performed 3 times. The "B" section, also 8 bars, follows the first repeat of the A section. Each section consists of two 4-bar phrases.

Somewhere | over the rainbow | way up | high, |
There's a | land that I heard of | once in a lulla | by. |

(. . . Section A)

Somewhere | over the rainbow | skies are | blue. |
And the | dreams that you dare to | dream really do come | true. |

(. . . Section A)

Some | day I'll wish upon a star
And | wake up where the clouds are far be | hind me. |
Where | troubles melt like lemon drops, |
A | way, above the chimney tops, |
That's | where you'll | find me. |

(. . . Section B)

Somewhere | over the rainbow | bluebirds | fly. |
Birds fly | over the rainbow, | why then, oh why can't | I? |

(. . . Section A)

An analysis of this kind reveals the overall **form** of the piece—the form of "Over the Rainbow," for example, is AABA. Because the term "form" is used rather ambiguously in writings on music, sometimes referring indeterminately to a variety of structural levels, I will use "form" only to denote the large-scale design of the piece. I will return to "Over the Rainbow" in the next chapter to discuss its form more specifically.

Besides being composed of 4-bar phrases, the songs heard in almost all jazz and popular music are normally divisible into 8-bar and 16-bar sections. Songs so composed are said to be in **standard song form** or just *song form*. (Blues songs, also performed widely in jazz, are most commonly in a one-section, 12-bar form.) A legacy of the European tradition, song form can be observed in European and American music, in both the popular and fine-art genres, throughout the eighteenth and nineteenth centuries. The form of a piece exemplifies a very large-scale rhythmic feature.

Very often, a jazz performance can be heard as a theme with variations. Particularly common in music by Classic era composers such as Haydn, Beethoven, and Mozart, the **theme and variation** is a repetitive form in which a theme, or tune, is stated and then varied afterward. The theme usually consists of a melody, harmonized simply and organized into regular phrases and sections. After the presentation of the theme, the variations usually elaborate it by recycling its sectional form, but with increasingly complex melody and harmony. Each variation is called a **strophe.** As you will see, this idea has been adopted by the jazz improviser, who will usually explore the harmonic and melodic properties of a song through improvisation.

harmony

Western tonal **harmony,** which can be traced back at least to the eleventh century, has undergone a complex evolution that has culminated, at least partly, in twentieth-century jazz harmony. Somewhat more difficult to conceptualize than rhythm and meter, harmony structures music vertically and horizontally by projecting certain sets of notes, called **chords,** through musical spans or lengths of time. These chords often accompany the melody and impart a sense of direction to the music. Music organized harmonically is generally called **tonal.**

The basic harmonic unit is a **triad,** a 3-note chord whose pitches are separated by intervals of a third. The chord F-A-C, for example, is an F **major triad.** The other most important triadic type is the **minor triad.** F-Ab-C is an F minor triad. (Note the difference of only one note—A and Ab—between the two triads.)

If "Over the Rainbow," in Example 2.1, were accompanied by a guitar, the player would strum an Eb major chord for the first 2 beats, a C minor chord for the next 2 beats, then a G minor chord for the next 3 beats, and so on. Normally only one harmonic center functions through a given musical span, unless the music is unusually complex.

The harmony occurring in a given bar of music divides the 12 chromatic pitches into either **chord tones,** which are members of the chord, or **nonchord tones,** which are the other pitches. The chord tones are defined as **consonant,** and the nonchord tones **dissonant.** The interaction between consonance and dissonance on a variety of structural levels provides direction, tension, and repose in tonal music.

Music structured by a given **scale** of notes together with appropriate harmonies is said to be in a **key,** the key being named by the first note in the scale. For example, a piece written with the pitches and harmonies of the C major scale (C, D, E, F, G, A, B) is in the key of C major. "Over the Rainbow," in Example 2.1, is written in the key of Eb major.

Roman numerals designate the harmonies relative to the key, so that a C major triad is a I chord (**tonic**) and a G major triad is a V chord (**dominant**) in the key of C major (Ex. 2.2a). In the key of G major, shown in Example 2.2b, a G major chord is a I chord (tonic) and a C major chord is a IV chord (**subdominant**).

a)   I   II   III   IV   V   VI   VII

b)   I   II   III   IV   V   VI   VII

The harmonic system in Western music is highly distinctive—it is one of the principal reasons that Western music does not sound like Peking opera or Javanese gamelan music, for example. In jazz the harmonies and chords are often called **changes,** because the chords change through the course of the piece. Because jazz chords normally contain or imply four or more pitches, jazz harmony differs significantly from the triadic harmony that characterizes, for example, the music of Mozart. Still, although jazz harmony can clearly be distinguished from the harmony of Beethoven, Debussy, Gershwin, or the Beatles, the use of harmony to accompany the melody and provide a large-scale aspect of structure is a legacy of the European tradition.

Other important theoretical musical terms, such as the various kinds of chords or the different scale types, are defined in the Glossary at the end of this book.

other contributions

Although jazz is basically an improvisational discipline, an **arranger** usually plans the music for a larger ensemble, since it is difficult for more than about seven or eight performers to improvise coherently at once. The arranger, who composes the parts for each member of the band, may write for small groups too, although his contribution is somewhat less critical to the sound of the band. In all instances, the musicians play the arrangements as written except for sections left open for improvisation. In a **head arrangement** the band members collectively work out the parts they wish to play.

The arranger artfully tries to mix improvisational strophes with arranged ensemble strophes. Hence, strophic form is usually employed in a big band arrangement, although the written music usually presents more textural variety than the continuous improvisation heard in a smaller group. Indeed, to maximize variety in arranging a familiar song, it may become necessary for the arranger to reorder its sectional form. Because arrangements are critical to the success of a larger group, during the swing era the numerous big bands competed for the best arrangers as intensely as they did for star soloists.

With the exception of the banjo, which is generally found only in dixieland groups, most of the instruments heard in jazz have been derived from the European tradition. Of course, modern instruments such as the electric guitar or synthesizer were developed from the instruments and technology of the Western tradition. However, the drum set could be seen as being based either on the snare drum, bass drum, and cymbals found in nineteenth-century bands, or on the ensemble (or "family") of drums played together in African drum groups. (Modern additions to the basic drum set are taken from all over the world— gongs, wind chimes, hand drums, etc.) The drum sets of the first jazz bands were concocted by arranging the marching band percussion instruments so that they could all be played at once by a single player.

contributions of the african musical tradition

In this section, I will identify some of the features of African music that have influenced jazz. It is necessary to point out, however, that African music is not fully homogeneous; significant stylistic differences exist among the numerous countries, states, and peoples. In particular, the music of the rain-forest peoples differs considerably from the music heard in the savannah areas and the northern deserts. Further, musical styles can vary considerably even among peoples of the same region. The features described in this section pertain in a most general fashion to the coastal peoples of West Africa, whose populations comprise the majority of slaves brought to the United States.

group participation

Perhaps the most important large-scale influence of the African tradition on jazz and other Afro-American music is its spirit of group participation. This spirit embodies an approach to music that is primarily non-Western, but still akin to our use of music for cultural events. A birthday party is a good example: everyone joins in the singing of a rousing chorus of "Happy Birthday," possibly the most often performed song in America. Rarely is anyone embarrassed about having a "bad" singing voice. The participants simply get into the spirit of it and enjoy singing.

If all of our music were performed with such mutual involvement and abandon, the result would be more similar to African music: all members of society participate in its creation. The concept of participational music as a part of life, as an essential element of daily experience, pervades much African music. Such spirit is especially characteristic of early jazz.

Africans devise songs for all aspects of living: for playing games, inducing rain, cooking, and celebrating puberty, marriage, childbirth, and death. While many societies employ professionals to provide music for the more important events, the nonmusicians would be encouraged to join in, too. Hence, the Western concert format, in which the artists perform while the audience sits quietly in judgment, is somewhat atypical of the African experience.

African dancing, with its sense of group participation, is highly integrated into the African musical experience. In traditional Western ballroom dancing, couples linked arm in arm jointly synchronize their steps; but African dances are often performed by larger groups. From time to time, an especially skilled dancer will separate from the group to execute a virtuosic solo routine (just as a jazz musician will perform a solo improvisation within the context of the larger ensemble). African dance eventually led to the development of such Afro-American dances as tap, the Charleston, and the numerous dances associated with rock music since the 1950s.

sound ideal

Another important influence on jazz has been the African sound ideal, or concept of tone production. In listening to African music, bent pitches, embellishments, the use of falsetto, nasal pitch production, and other imaginative sounds and cries can be discerned that dramatically contrast the Western concept of "pure" tone production. African singing, when heard by white European musicians in the eighteenth and nineteenth centuries, provoked amazement and often ridicule because it was so foreign to their experience. In the instrumental tone qualities of jazz, as well as in its singing styles, one may be able to detect traces of original African vocal techniques that were here an anathema to musicians with a bias for the European sound ideal.

The African sound ideal, a concern with the individual, emotional expression through music, has been retained in the jazz aesthetic. The greater freedom, the unexpected delays, the gentle lifting of the musical line away from the metered beat, and the slides between the notes are all derived from a performance practice common in African music. "Freely" interpreting melody is an important part of playing jazz and leads directly to improvisation, a concept I shall discuss shortly.

melody and rhythm

In addition to the sound ideal of African music, certain features of small-scale melodic rhythm, durations of a beat or less, also derive from the African tradition. In the music of the African drum ensembles, a clearly defined background beat can be discerned, but many of the drum rhythms seem to ride above and beyond that beat. The relationship of the various drum rhythms to the background beat is often so complex that the drums seem to effect independent and sometimes asynchronous meters.

Early New Orleans jazz, while rhythmically far less complex than the music of the African drum ensemble, reflects its rhythmic independence by the use of freely interacting trumpet, trombone, and clarinet melodies. More importantly, as jazz developed in the 1920s, the small-scale rhythms of the solo instruments gradually freed themselves from the gravity of the basic beat. This freer connection of the melody to the background helped in the development of **swing,** which, as a distinct Afro-American innovation, is discussed in the next section.

In addition to its freely interacting rhythms, the African drum ensembles exemplify the concept of **additive rhythm,** which has influenced jazz, jazz melody, and American popular music as a whole. Basically, short rhythmic figures, such as a pattern of two or three eighth-notes, are strung together to create longer rhythmic patterns. The longer patterns, continually repeated, form a web of background pulsations to accompany the main body of the melody and harmony. Many Latin rhythms, such as the **bossa nova,** effectively illustrate this procedure. In Example 2.3 the recurring pattern of three or four eighth-notes is shown in the top (clave) part.

In many African ensembles, the various rhythms, usually constructed additively and played on different instruments (or different drums within a drum ensemble), are often organized into a complex rhythmic texture that may accompany more prominent "lead" instruments or voices. In jazz and its derivative forms, this concept is reflected in the use of various distinct and usually contrasting rhythms, often added to the fundamental beat. Once an additional rhythmic pattern has been determined, the player tends to retain its relationship to the other rhythms. A simple example would be a tambourine player whose part has faster notes than the basic drum beat.

Another small-scale rhythmic technique heard in jazz, especially in jazz melody, and derived from African music is *syncopation*. In syncopating a rhythm, a pitch on a part of the beat that is normally unaccented is instead accented, while the normally accented parts of the beat are left unstressed, as shown in Example 2.4.

Line (a) shows a mundane rhythm with normal accents relative to the beat. (">" is the musical symbol for an accent.) Line (b) shows a succession of notes that first occur on the beat, then in a syncopated pattern where beat 3½ is accented while beat 4 is left unaccented and not even articulated.

Syncopation enlivens the rhythm because the alignment between the accents of the meter and the accents of the melody is skewed. Although syncopation is heard frequently in European music, it pervades African and Afro-American music and contributes to them a distinctive rhythmic edge. The specific syncopation shown in Example 2.4, eighth-note/quarter-note/eighth-note, is often heard in African music and has become the most important pattern of syncopation found in jazz.

improvisation

Improvisation, though essential to much African music, was not necessarily first practiced by Africans; it occurs commonly in most of the world's music cultures, though somewhat rarely in Western fine-art music since the late nineteenth century. Yet, improvisation as it is practiced in jazz, in both spirit and genesis, derives from Africa and has become an essential part of almost every jazz performance. Whereas in the West a piece of music is conceptualized as a composed entity, "pieces" of African music are sometimes only improvisational frameworks intended for elaboration in performance. As such, the frameworks are rarely notated, although the "compositions" may be passed on through **oral**

tradition. The performance with its attendant improvisations constitutes the piece.

As we have seen, many of the most colorful, most characteristic, and most well known aspects of jazz are a product of the African legacy. These features, not surprisingly, provoked ridicule from music educators in the early 1920s. According to Dr. Frank Damrosch, director of the Institute of Musical Art,

> Jazz is to real music what the caricature is to the portrait. The caricature may be clever, but it aims at distortion of line and feature in order to make its point; similarly, jazz may be clever but its effects are made by exaggeration, distortion, and vulgarisms. . . . We can only hope that sanity and the love of the beautiful will help to set the world right again and that music will resume its proper mission of beautifying life instead of burlesquing it.[1]

Henry F. Gilbert, an American composer, stated the following:

> It is true that for several years the rhythmic element in popular music has been growing more insistent and nervous, and it may have reached its culmination in jazz. I rather think it has. So, as far as simple rhythmic forcefulness and iteration are concerned, jazz can claim the proud distinction of being the "worst yet."[1]

According to Will Earhart, a director of music,

> I do not approve of "jazz" because it represents, in its convulsive, twitching, hiccoughing rhythms, the abdication of control by the central nervous system— the brain. This "letting ourselves go" is always a more or less enticing act. Formerly we indulged it in going on an alcoholic spree; but now we indulge it by going (through "jazz") on a neural spree.[1]

In fairness to the musicians of the day, it should be pointed out that many were far more receptive to jazz, including John Philip Sousa, who was also a contributor to this colloquy in *The Etude*. Still, in their naïveté these critics overlooked the most enjoyable and distinctive features of jazz: a unique blend of European-derived form, melody, and harmony and its African-derived rhythm, tone production, and, more importantly, spirit.

contributions of the afro-american musical tradition

In the previous two sections I noted some of the features of European and African music that significantly affected the development of jazz. In this section, I shall point out how these specific attributes were adopted and modified by the Afro-American innovators of early jazz into a style indigenously American.

[1]*The Etude,* August 1924, pp. 518, 520. The late Morroe Berger showed these quotations.

blues inflections

As we have seen, traditional European music bases many of its melodies and harmonies on the major scale, but much jazz is based on the **blues scale.** To construct the C blues scale from the C major scale, for example, an E♭ would be added, while the B would be lowered to B♭. Sometimes a G♭ is included as well. When these additional pitches are inflected, bent, and otherwise expressively emphasized, they are called **blue notes.** The concept of a blue note can even be applied to an entire chord and, moreover, the three cited pitches are not the only possible blue notes in the key of C major. Further, although the harmonic basis of jazz is European, features of the blues style and its scale have affected jazz harmony as well as melody.

The origin of the blues scale is unknown; however, locating a similar scale in African music would by no means be decisive proof of its origin because many African cultures with highly diverse musical styles contributed to the formation of Afro-American music.

Most likely, however, the blues scale came about as a result of the "Americanizing" of the African musician. As the slaves learned European instruments and entertained themselves and their masters, they would have had to perform songs based on the major or minor scales. In all probability, the slaves, accustomed to their own scales and the African sound ideal, would naturally begin to vary the European performance practices. Over long periods of time, the African sound ideal would produce a blending of the European system with their own; the blues scale was one result.

Other jazz scales, including types of blues scales, are derived from the European minor scale. Among the several types of minor scales, a common one, the harmonic minor, can be formed from the major scale by lowering the third and sixth tones (called **degrees**) of the scale a half step. An important variant of the minor scale, known as the **dorian mode,** occurs often in modern jazz. It can be constructed from the major scale by lowering the third and seventh degrees of the scale a half step (Ex. 2.5).

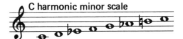
C harmonic minor scale

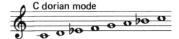
C dorian mode

swing

Rhythmic syncopation, described in the previous section, in no way exhausts the various subtleties and expressive nuances of jazz rhythm. Another rhythmic characteristic of jazz, heard especially in swing style music, is the subdivision of the beat into thirds. Because the pervasive use of this subdivision in jazz and in jazz-inspired music is not typical of either the European or African traditions, it is usually thought to be a specific contribution of the Afro-American innovators of early jazz. When the drummer executes the following rhythm on the ride or hi-hat cymbals, he is said to be playing a **swing beat** (Ex. 2.6), since articulating the third fraction of the beat seems to swing the rhythm ahead to the following beat.

The swing era featured much uptempo jazz played with a swing beat. Swing can occur in a jazz performance even in the absence of a swing beat; whenever jazz rhythm tumbles forward, driving along relentlessly, the piece or its rhythm is said to swing. Jazz musicians, especially drummers and bassists, must learn how to swing without overtly rushing or pushing the tempo faster.

Swing eludes precise definition, but it is often produced by playing a little ahead or behind the beat. For example, a bassist playing one note per beat, a **walking bass** line, might articulate each beat just before the drummer does. The drummer then seems to be holding the bass player back and the tension between them produces the feeling of swing. A horn player can effect the same feeling of interaction with the background rhythm. When the space between the beat and the player's early articulation of it remains extremely small, the effect is called "being on top of the beat," whereas a wider space is called "early," which connotes unskillful performance.

Not all swing is produced by playing on top of the beat. Many other kinds of effects, such as **accents, ghost notes** (implied with the breath and almost not played at all), **slides, dynamics** (playing with a full range of intensity from very loud to very soft), and unexpected changes in the melody line direction, can produce a swinging rhythm. The modern concept of swing was gradually developed by jazz musicians during the 1920s into an expected, almost essential feature of the music by the mid 1930s.

the rhythm section

Some of the responsibility for producing swing in a jazz group falls on the **rhythm section,** which usually consists of a drummer, a bass player (playing string bass, electric bass guitar, tuba, or occasionally bass saxophone), a pianist (or electric keyboard player), and/or a guitarist (acoustic or electric) or banjoist. Sometimes extra percussion players are added as well. Although the use of a rhythm section had occurred prior to its use in jazz groups, for example, in the marching band and in many dance orchestras, it reached a mature stage of development in the jazz band. It also epitomized the division of a jazz group into "sections." Each section of a band comprises instruments of similar function:

typically, the reed section of saxophones, clarinets, and other "woodwinds"; the brass section of trumpets, trombones, and sometimes tuba and french horns, and the rhythm section. The different instrumental sections often interact in a complex manner that may be reminiscent of the rhythmic texture within the African drum ensemble.

The rhythm section is anchored by the drummer who provides a time-keeping function by playing clean, regular patterns. The drums and cymbals found in a typical drum set roughly cover the full frequency range of the sound spectrum: bass drum (low), snare drum (middle), cymbals (high), and tom-toms (midrange). The drummer occasionally interrupts the timekeeping for **fills,** short sololike **licks** that enliven the regular beat, add interest to spaces at the ends of phrases, and articulate the sections of the piece being performed. The drummer also will deviate from the beat to provide special accents, **kicks,** which, when played together with the rest of the band, can generate much excitement.

The other rhythm instruments generally double and reinforce the function of specific drums, especially in dixieland and swing. For example, the bassist often plays the same rhythm as the bass drum, while the rhythm guitarist, in certain styles, doubles the **back beats** (beats 2 and 4) of the snare drum. Since the bass, guitar, and piano produce pitched sounds, they add a tonal factor to the rhythm of the drums and provide the rest of the band with a strong harmonic foundation.

The rhythm section is the nucleus of a good jazz group: no band plays well together without a good rhythm section. If the rhythm section swings, the band will tend to swing along with it. The rest of the ensemble cannot compensate the weakness of a poor rhythm section, despite the brilliance of the soloists, for good jazz usually requires swinging rhythm. Even a great improvisation may sound uninspired if the rhythm section is not supportive.

strophic form

The division of a jazz group into sections most likely was encouraged by the use of the call-and-response format in the blues and other Afro-American musical styles. The call-and-response format, inspired by the group participational spirit of African music in general, probably led to the repetitions of **choruses.** Previously, I pointed out the existence of a strophic form in European music, the theme and variations concept, which provides a very useful way to listen to jazz. Yet, strophic jazz forms seem more akin to the spirit of the long, multi-chorus compositions heard in African music.

Often, the strophic form is generated through improvisation, since, for each chorus, the soloist repeats the formal and harmonic structure of the original material while overlaying it with new melodic variations. For example, a song may be 32 bars long, but in a live jazz performance those 32 bars may be repeated from 4 to 50 times with each repetition defining one strophe. In other words, a band or soloist may play or improvise 50 choruses in a row of "Over the Rainbow," which constitutes that particular performance. Strophic structure, conveyed in almost all jazz performances (except free jazz) since the mid-1920s, has become one of the most important formal features of the music.

Many features of African music, especially participational performance, exhilarating and independent rhythms, syncopation, improvisation, and imaginative methods of tone production, were adopted and shaped by the Afro-American innovators of jazz and prejazz black music. The results, in turn, influenced many of the most prominent characteristics of early jazz, including features of blues and ragtime, the sense of swing, and the use of call-and-response. At the same time, the instruments, large-scale rhythm, and the overall formal shape and harmonic plan of European music were adopted by the Afro-Americans to provide jazz with its structural foundation. In all likelihood, the ingredients for this fascinating mixture existed nowhere else in the world.

chapter
three

thematic
material
and
improvisation

types of songs found in jazz

As noted previously, strophic improvisation on songs characterizes most jazz styles. The songs most often performed can be separated into three main types—popular songs, blues, and jazz tunes—though, of course, the categories overlap. For example, blues, though originally a black folk form that retained many features of its African legacy, has splintered into several substyles that are more appropriately categorized as popular than as folk. Each of the different song types will be examined to determine their use in jazz.

popular songs

For a particular song to be popular, it must be simple enough to be enjoyed by most members of a specified culture. Hence, a popular song is usually unpretentious and easy to sing, with a steady beat, a colloquial lyric, and clear, uncomplicated harmony. Jazz tunes, on the other hand, are generally more complex melodically and harmonically; their pulse and meter may vary as well.

A **standard** is a popular song that is well known, frequently performed, and remains in the popular repertoire for at least several years. Many songs that are today considered standards were written during the *Tin Pan Alley* era, which extended from the late nineteenth century to the beginnings of rock music in the mid-1950s. Tin Pan Alley, a collection of large, well-established music publishing companies located in Manhattan, provided America with most of its popular music for more than half a century.

The best songs of Tin Pan Alley, still well known to this day, are among the great treasures of American culture. They were written by such outstanding composers as Irving Berlin, George Gershwin, Fats Waller, Hoagy Carmichael, Harold Arlen, Cole Porter, Duke Ellington, Johnny Mercer, Richard Rodgers, Vernon Duke, and Jerome Kern. Some of their many songs, now standards, still enjoyed and performed by jazz musicians, include "Autumn Leaves" (Mercer), "I Got Rhythm" (Gershwin), "Embraceable You" (Gershwin), "Mood Indigo," (Ellington), "I Can't Get Started" (Vernon Duke), "It Might as Well Be Spring" (Rodgers), "My Funny Valentine" (Rodgers), "Stardust" (Carmichael), "I Get a Kick Out of You" (Porter), "Ain't Misbehavin'" (Waller), and "All the Things You Are" (Kern).

More recent tunes popular among some jazz musicians, written since the rock era, include "Michelle" and "Yesterday" (Lennon-McCartney), "Just the Way You Are" (Joel), "You Are the Sunshine of My Life" (Wonder), "Girl from Ipanema" (Jobim). These songs are examples of modern standards.

With the increasing popularity of rock in the 1950s and 1960s, the song business was gradually decentralized and sheet music publishers yielded much of their financial power to the rapidly expanding recording industry. At the same time, popular singers began to seek reputations as songwriters who performed their own material. This practice limited the role of the professional, nonperforming songwriters and their publishing companies. Although today Tin Pan Alley no longer dominates the popular song business, the large publishing houses still wield considerable influence.

In Chapter 2, Harold Arlen's "Over the Rainbow," a very popular standard, was analyzed and shown to have an AABA, 32-bar form. The A section is often called the **chorus,** while the B section is called the **bridge, channel,** or **release.**

In most good songs, such as "Over the Rainbow," the chorus is designed to highlight a principal phrase that is melodically strong and whose lyric summarizes the song's theme and provides the title. This phrase is called the **hook** and most often occurs at the beginning, at the end, or both, of the chorus. Most great songs, from the Tin Pan Alley days to the present, have great hooks. They also seem to be the songs most popular with jazz musicians.

The hook in "Over the Rainbow" occurs during the first two bars of the chorus. Notice how Arlen places it in a high register for emphasis (Ex. 3.1).

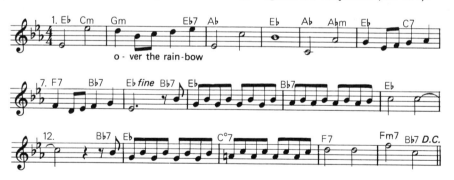

To provide a sense of cohesion and unity, composers often fashion their melodies from one or more **motives,** which are sets of two to perhaps eight notes linked by a characteristic rhythm. "Over the Rainbow" is constructed of three simple motives, the first beginning in the first bar. This type of motive is consequently transformed or "developed." Though development in music can take place on numerous levels, it usually involves a transformation or series of transformations of original ideas. Most fine composers and jazz improvisers are masters of the technique of development.

The other motive of the A section is first stated in m.2, the motive associated with the song's title. Note that the pattern of this motive is repeated in mm.6 and 7, but with different pitches. When the shape of a pattern is retained but placed onto different pitches, the pattern is said to be **transposed.** Transposition is one of many techniques associated with developing a motive or idea.

The third motive is heard at the beginning of the bridge. In m.10 the motive is transformed, but returns in m.13 and then is transposed in m.14.

Although "Over the Rainbow" is motivically structured by three different ideas, the motives are combined into a finely controlled overall shape. For example, the leap in m.1 unfolds a large intervallic space, the octave. During the remainder of the A section, the octave is filled in by a descending scale. The static character at the beginning of the bridge contrasts the dramatic opening octave of the A section and its descending scale. The alternating eighth-notes capture the sense of wonder and bewilderment expressed by the lyric, as if the singer were really dreaming.

"Over the Rainbow," an ingenious combination of the simple and sophisticated, has endured as a jazz standard for many years. As you will see in the next section of this chapter, the jazz improviser can be inspired by a tune to improvise a commentary on its internal structure.

In addition to the chorus and its bridge, many Tin Pan Alley songs include an introduction that sets the scene for the main body of the song. This introductory section is called the **verse.** However, repeated renditions of the chorus with its bridge are sometimes called verses, also. To avoid any confusion, in this book each run-through of the main body of the song will be called a "strophe" or "chorus," and the use of "verse" will be restricted to the introductory section of a song.

Contemporary songwriters still use AABA form frequently, but they vary the number of bars in each section more often than the Tin Pan Alley composers. For example, the form of the Beatles' "Yesterday" is 7-7-8-9 bars, Billy Joel's "Just the Way You Are" is 16-16-16-16, and Bacharach-David's "Raindrops Keep Falling on My Head" is 9-9-10-12. The great 32-bar standards most performed by jazz musicians, however, consist of four 8-bar phrases, 8-8-8-8. Jazz soloists find the symmetrical forms easier to internalize: because the symmetry frees them from concentrating on the song, they can concentrate on the improvisation.

The other traditional song form from the Tin Pan Alley days is the AA' form with two 8- or 16-bar sections called, respectively, the **first half** and the **second half.** (In the A' section the A section is somewhat varied.) Again, if the main body of the song is preceded by an introductory section, that section is called the verse, while the main body of the song is the chorus. This form, almost as popular as AABA form in the 1930s and 1940s, is rarely heard in modern songs. Many important standards still played by jazz musicians, however, were written in this form, or slight modifications of it; for example, "Laura" (Raksin), "There Will Never Be Another You" (Warren), "How Deep Is the Ocean" (Berlin), and "Sweet Georgia Brown" (Bernie-Pinkard-Casey).

Although many songs have been written in AA' form, the number of bars often varies from the 16- or 32-bar norm. Despite the variance in length, however, certain features are common. For example, the beginnings of the first and second halves are almost always identical, but the latter portions of each half usually differ: the end of the first half prepares the beginning of the second half, while the end of the second half brings the song to a close. Hence the AA' form can often be described more specifically as an AB-AB' form.

In view of our observations on AABA form, it is not surprising to learn that jazz musicians have traditionally favored the most symmetrical songs. "Sweet Georgia Brown," an old song still played by jazz musicians and otherwise well known as the Harlem Globetrotters' theme, is in typical AB-AB' form. This tune, seemingly always in style, can be heard in both dixieland and modern big band recordings.

| No gal made has | got a shade on | Sweet Georgia | Brown.
| Two left feet, but | oh so neat has | Sweet Georgia | Brown.
| They all sigh and | wanna die for | Sweet Georgia | Brown.
I'll tell you just | why, |
You know I don't | lie. Not | much! |

(. . .first half, 16 bars)

| It's been said she | knocks 'em dead when | she lands in | town.
| Since she came, why | it's a shame how | she cools 'em | down. |
Fellers she can't | get
Are | fellers she ain't | met.
| Georgia claimed her, |
| Georgia named her |
| Sweet Georgia | Brown. |

(. . .second half, 16 bars)

Because the musicians usually adhere to a song's harmony during an improvisation, its form and phrase structure are retained as a result. Jazz based on AABA or ABAB' songs projects an essential "fourness," based on duple meters, 4-bar phrases, 8- and 16-bar sections, and 32-bar tunes. Many modern jazz players have tried to circumvent these constraints with a variety of techniques, but the standard song forms with their 4-bar units have been and continue to be the most popular among musicians.

Nowadays the two-part song form has evolved into a sleeker format with a nonintroductory verse followed by a chorus. The archetype arrangement seems to be an 8- or 16-bar verse followed by an 8- or 16-bar chorus, though in many modern songs the number of bars varies quite widely. Usually the verse has two sets of lyrics, whereas the chorus has one set that is continually repeated. An example of a strict 8 + 8 verse-chorus form is the Beatles' "With a Little Help from My Friends." In this song, as in many other modern tunes with this form, two presentations of the verse-chorus pair are followed by a bridge that leads back to the main body of the song.

The songs of the Tin Pan Alley composers are often symmetrical, whereas many modern composers often will experiment from time to time with greater irregularity in form and harmony. Still, jazz musicians often prefer the older, more predictable songs because of their intrinsic quality, even if the lyrics are occasionally dated. As has been pointed out, the formal clarity and predictability of the older songs facilitate improvisation. Jazz musicians prefer elegant simplicity in a song.

blues

In general, a style of folk music within a given community tends to be uniform with respect to syntax, form, and performance practices. Because blues originated as a folk music, its traditional pieces tend to be more similar to one another than the works of the popular mainstream. Folk musicians often perform their music very informally, simplifying the harmony, embellishing the melody, and freely interpolating extra bars.

The classic blues was a musical style that exhibited elements of both folk and popular music. It generated other blues styles, such as urban blues, that are more properly categorized as popular music. The form of the classic blues can be represented as a single 12-bar chorus with a strict basic harmonic progression. Within this framework of basic chord changes (Ex. 3.2a), many variants can be constructed (Ex. 3.2b). All blues forms can occur in the minor mode as well.

Sometimes a verse introduces the chorus, much like the verse in a Tin Pan Alley song. The lyric, too, follows a sharply defined format: a phrase is stated,

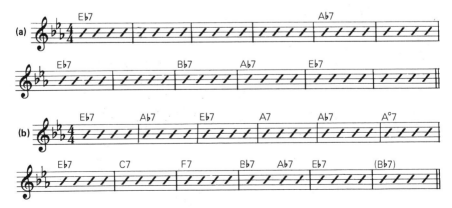

a second phrase repeats the first, then a third phrase, whose lyric typically clarifies the meaning of the first two phrases, concludes the strophe. This form is ideal for improvisational singing since the singer can invent the often rhyming third phrase during the repetition of the first (Ex. 3.3).

Note how the lyric in Example 3.3 fits into the first 3 bars of each 4-bar phrase. The chord change in bar 5, the IV or subdominant chord, reflects the harmonic poignancy of the blues and is found in almost every 12-bar blues.

Blues lyrics are often personal and anecdotal, telling tales of hardship, love, sex, and travel. Because many classic blues songs have retained their folk status, a jazz musician can employ them to explore the roots of jazz.

Despite the connection of classic blues to folk music, many popular songs have been written in the 12-bar blues style. For example, during the swing era a driving style of piano playing called **boogie-woogie** was developed by the blues pianists of the south and southwest and became extremely popular throughout the country. Such important songs as "In the Mood" (Garland) and "One O'Clock Jump" (Basie) were in fact blues tunes whose riffs were based on the licks of the boogie-woogie pianists. Later, in the early days of rock music, such songs as "Rock Around the Clock" (Freedman–DeKnight) and "Blue Suede Shoes" (Perkins) were written with blues harmony, form, and phrasing. These features of early rock offer evidence of its evolution from the blues and r & b (**rhythm and blues**).

In addition to the classic 12-bar blues form, by far the most common in jazz, 8- and 16-bar forms exist too, whose harmonic structures are somewhat more irregular. Although modern blues tunes have been written with highly irregular structures, much classic blues retains the simpler 12-bar, rhyming lyric structure.

jazz tunes

Jazz musicians tiring of mainstream popular songs often write their own material. These works, frequently without lyrics, tend to be more esoteric than songs of the popular mainstream repertoire. Still, from time to time an especially catchy jazz tune ascends the top-40 charts, such as Paul Desmond's "Take Five," or Joseph Zawinul's "Birdland."

Despite their occasional melodic and harmonic unpredictability, jazz tunes are often composed in the standard AABA form—like Desmond's "Take Five" and Thelonious Monk's "'Round Midnight"—or in a modern blues format—like Miles Davis's "Eighty-One." Frequently, irregular and experimental forms are found too, for example, in the work of such composers as Charles Mingus and Chick Corea.

Sometimes jazz melodies are composed to the chord changes of older popular songs. Listeners then enjoy trying to guess the original tune from the harmony alone. In writing these new songs, the composers usually avoid the commercial simplicity of the pop mainstream and intentionally write melodies that sound like improvisations themselves. Especially common in the bop era, examples of such songs include Charlie Parker's "Donna Lee" (using the changes of "Indiana") and Sonny Rollins's "Valse Hot" (based on the changes of "Over the Rainbow").

In this section I have presented the basic ideas underlying the three types of songs that constitute the bulk of most jazz players' repertoires. The remainder of the chapter will be devoted to a discussion of improvisation, the method with which jazz musicians develop the thematic material in performance.

improvisation

In most jazz styles, a song is stated first as a **head.** It is followed by the solos, or improvisations on the head, after which the head is repeated as the last chorus. Jazz musicians think of the head as thematic material, a musical point of departure that provides them with a beat, harmony, form, melody, and inspiration. As we have seen, jazz musicians usually select popular songs, blues, or jazz tunes for thematic material, but they also experiment with either larger compositions or smaller musical fragments such as phrases, chords, sets of notes, and even rhythms. Once a band or soloist decides on the basic thematic material, the essence of the jazz performances emerges: the improvisations.

the range of improvisation

During the improvisational choruses, the form and harmony of the original piece are usually recycled. A soloist, who must play an appropriate melody that readily conforms to the form and harmony of the head, might choose simply to repeat the head. Singers, for example, generally adhere quite closely to the original song, altering a few notes from time to time, but rarely straying too far from the tune.

Repetition is in fact an important musical technique: repeating patterns, from a note to a motive to an entire section, helps unify the composition. Noting the

44

extent and level of repetition provides a means of determining style. Early jazz, for example, contained much repetition.

Since literal repetition, however, is not especially adventurous, in repeating the tune most jazz soloists **embellish** it by adding extra notes here and there, a technique often called "melodic paraphrase." Jazz singers are sometimes distinguished from pop singers on the basis of their ability to embellish songs rather than perform them literally. Example 3.4 shows how "Over the Rainbow" might be embellished by a jazz soloist. Note the addition of syncopation and other small deviations from the song's rhythm.

In interpreting a tune, a player often adds notes to the original melody. An operation that complements embellishment is *simplification,* subtracting notes from the tune. Though somewhat less common, it is still heard from time to time.

Sometimes a jazz musician improvises as many as 40 or 50 choruses of a tune during an inspired performance. When a player is compelled to improvise at such extravagant length, he or she could never merely repeat or paraphrase the tune and expect to hold the audience's attention. Instead, the soloist engages in the real-time composition of an entirely new melody, though based on the form and harmony of the head. The melody of the head can figure prominently in the improvisation as well if the soloist chooses to repeat fragments of the original melody as points of reference within the solo. As I noted previously in the analysis of "Over the Rainbow," all good songs have strong potential motivic referents, which, in the hands of a good soloist, can serve as the basis for an improvisation.

The soloist may also treat some freely composed set of notes as a motive even if that set is not contained in the original song. Thus, the soloist, restricted by only the form and harmony of the head, is free to vary his or her choruses from literal repetition to extemporaneous playing on freely composed motives. Jazz, from its inception to the late 1950s, generally featured this range of improvisational freedom.

Free jazz players of the late 1950s often abandoned harmony and form altogether, retaining no features at all from the original song. Soon this practice led to dispensing with the head itself as extraneous, no longer an integral part of the jazz performance. In place of the head with its form, melody, and harmony, the free jazz players substituted spontaneity and emotional projection, which, in the best performances, prompts an almost magical interaction: each player seems to sense what the others will play next. Free jazz improvisers may choose a previously played strand of improvisation as a starting point for their own statement; then someone else might use the second musician's statement as their jumping off point; and so forth. Or, everyone may play at once—a type of collective improvisation. Whatever happens, the music should attempt to inspire an emotional response in a discriminating listener.

improvisational skills

A musician interested in acquiring the skill to improvise must begin to learn the jazz repertoire. For the most part, this process consists of memorizing the standards, blues, and jazz tunes that constitute the bulk of the literature. Because there are thousands of these tunes, however, the neophyte jazz improviser begins with the most important ones, then throughout his career gradually adds to his repertoire.

In order to improvise on a song, the soloist needs a thorough knowledge of its harmony as well as its melody. Pianists, playing both melody and harmony, perhaps have an advantage over other musicians in their ability to "see" and play the changes at once. As a result, most jazz musicians feel compelled to learn to play the piano.

The various deployments and arrangements of the notes in a given chord are called its **voicings.** A beginning jazz improviser must learn to spell and play the most important chords and learn at least a few of their voicings as well (Ex. 3.5).

$E\flat9(\sharp11)$

These sample voicings of the $E\flat(9)(\sharp11)$ chord do not at all exhaust the potential realizations of this chord, but these voicings occur most frequently. Keyboard players, guitarists, and arrangers study voicings in greater detail than most single-note instrumentalists, but all good jazz players work to acquire a thorough knowledge of the harmonic potential of any chord.

Chords do not proceed randomly from one to the next, but are grouped into patterns that tend to recur from tune to tune. The song repertoire of the dixieland, swing, and bop styles contains many works based on an especially important chord progression known as the **circle of fifths.** In this progression, the chords proceed by the interval of a *fifth* downward as in, for example, the root progression D-G-C in the key of C. Constructing chords on these roots yields a typical jazz progression, ii(7)-V(7)-I (Ex. 3.6). (Lowercase roman numerals indicate minor or diminished chords, while uppercase are used for major and dominant chords.)

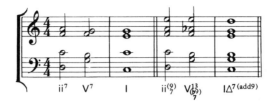

As the jazz improviser gradually acquires a greater knowledge of harmony, he must learn how to match his melodies to the chords. A common jazz theory, derived from practice, states that the different chords are associated with various scales. No precise, one-to-one match exists, however, because the same scale can be associated with different chords and one chord can be associated with various scales.

Several very important scale-chord matches, however, must be learned by all jazz musicians. For example, the major seventh chord is associated with the major scale, the dominant seventh chord with the mixolydian scale, and the minor seventh chord with the dorian mode. Because these three seventh chords are the most important jazz harmonies, their associated scales, among the numerous possibilities, are usually the first to be learned by jazz musicians. Some of these chord-scale associations are shown in Example 3.7.

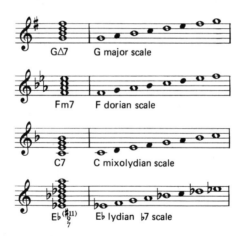

Note in the above example that while the chord itself is contained in the scale, the remaining notes are often chosen from the key of the piece. The more complex E♭(9)(♯11) requires an unusual scale in which the extended chord tones, the ninth and sharp eleventh, can be located. The jazz improviser must learn and practice the associated scales for the most important types of jazz chords constructed on all 12 pitches.

When the soloist adheres to the customary associated scales of the various chords and emphasizes the chord tones of the harmony, he or she is said to be playing **inside.** When playing *outside,* the soloist does not match the melody with the chord quite so exactly.

The improviser generally will not play the associated scales as such; that is, scales in ascending and descending order, because they are not particularly expressive or melodic. Instead, using the notes from the scale, the improviser must fashion new melodic lines.

In addition to keeping this complex set of chord-scale associations in mind, the improviser will often relate his or her solo to the original tune by referring obliquely to its motives, which can then become motives in the jazz improvisation. In the previous section, my analysis of "Over the Rainbow" revealed that it was constructed with three motives. A jazz soloist might, for example, select one of these motives and from it improvise a new melody, as in Example 3.8.

hook melody

When a pattern of notes is transposed several times at the same intervallic level, it is called a **sequence** (Ex. 3.8). Transposing the hook motive (Eb-C-D-Eb-F) twice, each time lowering it a step, enables the soloist to construct a tune from the shorter motive. Motives are frequently developed sequentially in this manner, both in songs and in improvisations. Slight alterations of the motive provide composers and improvisers with another method of development, as was seen in the "Over the Rainbow" analysis.

Many soloists will also mingle motives from the head with a special set of motives, generally having nothing to do with the head, called **licks.** That is, although each improvisation is substantially new, most jazz soloists memorize appealing patterns of notes to insert, whenever necessary, into their solos. When the licks are long, say two bars or more, their continual recurrence in different solos constitutes a mannerism or stylistic trait that often serves as a trademark for individual soloists.

Most beginning improvisers enjoy learning the licks of their favorite soloists. In fact, beginning jazz musicians often brag of having learned by heart the licks and even complete solos of their idols. This practice represents the first important step in learning to improvise: imitation. However, if overdone, it may lead to a loss of identity. In the 1950s, for example, many alto sax players copied Charlie Parker so attentively that they failed to develop their own styles. But cautious musicians can improve their own improvising by learning other players' licks: it helps develop fluency and may suggest melodic paths that otherwise might never arise on their own.

Example 3.9 shows a sample improvisation on the first four bars of "Over the Rainbow" in which song motives are identified as well as other motives, or licks, not contained in the song. In the example, each chord and its associated scale are also labeled.

The control of the pitch–rhythmic (melodic) fabric of the solo is by far the most engrossing aspect of improvisation. Nevertheless, the improviser must learn other techniques and special devices that can be inserted into solos for dramatic effect. Squawks, multiphonics (the production of more than one pitch at a time on a wind instrument), and slides, for example, can be highly effective, especially when used to support an effective choice of pitch and rhythm. These effects differ for various instruments, as will be pointed out as they arise in Part Two.

Although the evaluation of a jazz soloist depends on the particular instrument played and the style of the performance, certain general concepts should be kept in mind when listening to any improvisation.

1. *Variety and unity:* Does the soloist restrict the thematic ideas sufficiently to provide a coherent statement, but vary them sufficiently to maintain interest and excitement?

2. *Technique:* Does the soloist have an adequate knowledge of music theory to play correctly without too many technical errors? Can the soloist play quickly without losing control?

3. *Emotional projection:* Does the soloist excite or move the audience and the other musicians?

4. *Range:* Does the soloist balance use of the low, middle, and high registers of the instrument adequately?

5. *Pace:* Does the soloist insist on showing off his or her technique by an untasteful reliance on rapid scales and arpeggios, or is there a satisfying balance between thick and sparse textures?

While improvising, the soloist may be conscious of none of these technical points. To improvise fluently, in fact, most of these technical considerations need to be internalized. A great and sensitive jazz solo may be played while the improviser is consciously thinking about how his shirt collar is too tight.

Still, the improviser often engages in an internal dialogue, rarely verbalized, involving lightning-fast deliberations of "What next?" "Will this sound good?" "Too low, I need a high note." Although we can never know what the soloist is thinking, by listening intently and studying the structure of the improvisation, we can gradually deepen our understanding and appreciation of the music.

In this chapter I introduced some of the basic ideas behind jazz improvisation. For the most part, a musician who wishes to play jazz must devote a great deal of time to learning a complex theory of melodic-harmonic relations. In the solo itself, these theories are applied to developing improvisations that are often related thematically to the musical idea first stated as a head.

There are many ways to improvise, however; numerous styles have developed since the first jazz records were produced in the 1920s. In Part Two, I will examine the styles of some of the great jazz musicians, first concentrating on the ensembles, then on the soloists themselves.

part two

into the music

chapter four

small group jazz

During a jazz performance we can focus our attention either on the ensemble as a whole or on the players as individuals. Despite our usual preoccupation with the great improvisers, first concentrating on the entire ensemble will introduce us to the nuances and styles of jazz as well as its overall sound. With this overview, the achievements of the soloists will be made clearer in the context furnished by the ensembles.

Jazz bands are found primarily in two different sizes, a small group of seven or fewer players and a larger group of ten or more players. In particular, most bands have either three to six members, or twelve to nineteen members. The larger is often called the **big band, stage band,** or **jazz orchestra.** The smaller, with which this chapter is concerned, has no standardized name but has been referred to as a **jazz group, combo, band,** or **jazz band.** The small jazz group has been the primary expressive vehicle for jazz soloists throughout most of jazz history with the exception of 1935 to 1942, the **big band era.** Most of the advances in improvisational style have come from the smaller group and its members.

The small band has evolved in terms of instrumentation, with no fixed number of members for any stylistic period. However, it usually comprises a rhythm section, one or two brass (usually trumpet/cornet or trombone) and/or one or two reeds (usually alto or tenor saxophone and clarinet), or a combination of brass and reed instruments. As noted earlier in Chapter 2, the rhythm section includes drums, bass, keyboard, and/or guitar (or banjo), with guitar and piano providing either chords or lead lines.

More specifically, the typical dixieland ensemble of the 1920s included trumpet, trombone, clarinet, piano, banjo, drums, and bass or tuba. During the swing era, a small group might feature a trumpet, alto or tenor sax, clarinet, perhaps a trombone, piano, guitar, drums, and bass. The small band of the bop era established a very common instrumentation that is still heard frequently today: a quintet comprising trumpet, alto or tenor sax, piano, bass, and drums. Often this group is shrunk to a quartet by dropping one of the horns.

Aside from the quartet and quintet, the jazz trio and duo have become quite common small group jazz vehicles. The trio usually includes keyboard, bass, and drums or sometimes guitar, bass, and drums. Duos of piano and bass or guitar and bass are heard, too, especially in hotel lounges and restaurants, where drums would make the band too obtrusive.

Solo piano, since the ragtime era, has always been an important medium, except perhaps during the 1950s and 1960s, when pianists preferred one or two accompanying instruments. Although solo guitar in a bop or swing style is heard from time to time, other solo instrumentalists appear rather infrequently except in free jazz.

While these small group combinations are most popular, contemporary mixed instrumentation ensembles have included saxophone quartets, mixed wind ensembles, string ensembles, even an all-bass ensemble. Still, most small groups usually divide into rhythm and lead-instrument functions.

Possibly for financial and logistical considerations, less jazz has been produced by groups of eight to ten players, although during the past 25 years groups of this size have been used by Tadd Dameron (1917-1965), Charles Mingus, and Oliver Nelson (1932-1975), as well as more recently by David Murray, Dollar Brand (Abdullah Ibrahim), and Anthony Davis. Smaller groups are more often hired by jazz clubs, while the big bands are generally supported by a wealthier market: large hotels, concert auditoriums, and dance halls. Also, small groups are easier to manage, requiring less attention to accommodations, transportation, and other travel arrangements.

In this chapter and the next I will examine several jazz masterpieces for large-scale features such as the instruments, overall form, improvisational sections, arranged sections, and thematic material. Many of these pieces, as well as others, will be discussed again in later chapters with more emphasis on the solos, solo styles, and subtler structural and emotive details.

The following listening format is recommended to the reader. First, listen to the piece once or twice as you would normally listen to any piece of music. Second, read the commentary provided and try to remember from the first hearings the kinds of features described. Finally, listen again—many times if necessary—until you thoroughly understand the commentary. At no time, however, should you lose sight of what impressed you most on your first hearing. Listening for structural features should never override your emotional response to the music—instead, your technical understanding should add another layer of appreciation and enjoyment.

The examples of small group jazz will be presented in reverse chronological order, a method that will introduce the more familiar recent styles first. Afterward, for the remainder of Part Two, the examples will be presented chronologically.

herbie hancock: "chameleon"

Herbie Hancock: "Chameleon" from *Headhunters,* Columbia KC 3273, 1973. Herbie Hancock, electric piano and synthesizers; Bennie Maupin, tenor saxophone and other woodwinds; Paul Jackson, electric bass; Harvey Mason, drums; Bill Summers, percussion.

In the early 1970s jazz-rock emerged as a new style that combined features of late-1960s jazz with elements of 1960s rock. This style was crystallized in Miles Davis's album *In a Silent Way* (1969), though earlier recordings, such as "Stuff" from *Miles in the Sky* (1968), featured prominent jazz-rock characteristics. On *In a Silent Way,* Davis gathered many musicians who were to become the leaders of prominent jazz-rock bands in the 1970s, among them Herbie Hancock, Chick Corea, Tony Williams, and John McLaughlin.

The rock elements heard in jazz-rock include heavier, rock style drum rhythms with evenly played eighth-notes, the use of electronic instruments not traditionally associated with jazz, and the high-volume, high-energy presence of the entire band. The jazz contribution lies mainly in two areas: improvisation and the use of modal harmony derived from the modal jazz style of the 1960s. "Chameleon's" rock elements are more characteristic of black *funk* music than white rock music because of its harmonic and melodic debt to the blues and because of the repetitive, syncopated rhythms.

Not all the sounds heard in "Chameleon" were recorded at the same time. Instead, the piece was produced by *multitracking,* a popular recording method in which the recording tape is divided into tracks—24 in most production studios—which allows the instruments to be recorded at different times. The first parts to be recorded are called the "basic tracks" and usually include the drums, bass, and perhaps one or two lead or chording instruments. A player who records a new part, called an "overdub," listens to the previously recorded tracks on headphones and plays along with them. This practice allows a tape to be assembled like a canvas, the artist adding, subtracting, and changing the colors depending on how the work is turning out. Much jazz-rock, or *fusion,* as it is also called, recorded since the 1970s uses the techniques of overdubbing.

"Chameleon" is highly repetitive, a feature of funk that imparts a hypnotic quality to the style. As you listen to "Chameleon," try to feel the intensity increase until the tenor sax solo at the end. This solo and its fadeout release the growing tension that had culminated in the piece's climax, the section where our attention is riveted by the rapid shifts among instrumental textures and tempos (the piece's most "chameleonic" section). Throughout this section, the rhythm "cooks," that is, it projects a dizzying combination of tension and drive that supports the climax of Hancock's solo.

The piece begins with a funk bass line, probably played on an electric bass guitar and altered electronically to impart a processed, almost unreal character to its tone. The 2-bar bass line, repeated over and over, is called an *ostinato,* a typical feature of funk and jazz-rock funk styles. You should feel the beat emphasized on the second and fourth notes of the bass line (Example 4.1a). Note that the fifth and sixth notes of the line are not on the beat: these notes, occurring just before the beat, are syncopated.

In the second staff (b), the syncopated rhythm is written in a nonsyncopated manner to show how dramatically its funk character can change. The stylistic link between funk and the blues is evident from the important pitches of the bass line (Bb, Db, Eb, and Ab), which, when supported harmonically by a Bb7

chord (Bb–D–F–Ab), suggest the Bb blues scale. The melody of the head is also derived from the pitches of the blues scale.

Drums and percussion gradually join the bass line, followed soon by various synthesizer and electronic keyboard tracks. The different rhythms of these various parts combined recall the sound of African drum ensembles, with their complex, multilayered textures produced by the resultant combination of the simpler rhythms.

At last the melody enters, played by tenor sax with some electronic coloring added to the sound. The melody, like the rhythm, is very repetitive, but in a rhythm distinct from that of the bass ostinato. The bass line and melody together are in **counterpoint,** a technique of combining two or more individual melodies that sound good together.

The first tenor sax melody is followed by a new one, also repetitive, but characterized by a descending phrase down to the bottom of the tenor sax's range. Soon the bass player abandons the ostinato and the whole band plays together in **unison,** which signals the end of the section and releases its accumulating tension. This concluding passage returns throughout the piece, always to affirm the end of a section.

After a short drum solo, the ostinato bass line returns. Over it, Hancock plays his first improvisation, a synthesizer solo. This solo is improvised and makes use of fleet runs and melodic flourishes that would be too elaborate for a composed song. The synthesizer tone is recognizable here by its unrelenting organlike sound. The concluding passage, with the band playing accents together, returns to end section II.

In the third section the bass ostinato changes to a simpler, more diffuse vamp (on Bb and Db). The drums, reentering with the beat altered from the earlier one, join the bass in articulating a new background texture punctured by various synthesizer sounds. From time to time synthesizer sounds that simulate orchestral strings are added to this elaborate background texture to form a backdrop for Hancock's electric piano solo.

Hancock, during section III, plays a Fender Rhodes electric piano, a very popular electric keyboard instrument. A feature of most electric pianos, unlike most synthesizers of that era, is that they are "touch sensitive," like acoustic pianos, so that striking the key more sharply produces a louder sound. Compare this solo to the preceding synthesizer solo where the volume of the notes within a phrase rarely changes. The concluding passage enters again to complete section III.

In section IV a call-and-response format is employed, characterized by alternations of the electric piano with the rest of the band. As mentioned above, section IV culminates in an intense climax, a whirlwind of changing textures and tempos. After the concluding passage winds up section IV, the first bass ostinato returns to back up a new tenor sax improvisation, which, fading out, finishes the piece.

"Chameleon" can be analyzed as a large-scale ABA form divided into five smaller sections:

I	II	III	IV	V
A		B		A

The A sections, I, II, and V, are characterized by the opening bass ostinato while the B sections, III and IV, feature contrasting material. Section I presents the head, II presents Hancock's synthesizer solo, III features Hancock's electric piano solo, IV is a call-and-response between Hancock and the rest of the band, and V highlights Maupin's tenor sax improvisation.

The uninhibited improvisations contrast the tightness of the bass ostinato and the head, a dichotomy that renders the distinct jazz and rock elements more recognizable. The rock elements include the drum beat, the use of synthesizers and electronic instruments, the ostinato bass line, and the even eighth-note subdivision of the beat. The jazz elements include the improvisations, the use of extra percussion (though this occurs in rock contexts too), and the static, modal Bb7 harmony that dominates the entire tune. Moreover, the band pays homage to the African roots of jazz by including complex, overlaid rhythmic textures and many African percussion instruments.

chick corea: "light as a feather"

Chick Corea and Return to Forever: "Light as a Feather" from *Light as a Feather,* Polydor PD 5525, 1972. Chick Corea, electric piano; Stanley Clarke, bass; Flora Purim, vocal; Joe Farrell, tenor sax and flute; Airto Moreira, drums and percussion.

"Light as a Feather" is a Latin oriented example of early 1970s jazz-rock. Recorded in the traditional manner without overdubbing, except perhaps for a few percussion instruments, the selections on the album could be performed live without much change in the sound or its impact. As in "Chameleon," the piece is divided into clearly defined sections.

The instruments in the band have such dissimilar timbres that identifying them should be quite easy: drums, electric bass guitar, Fender Rhodes electric piano, voice, and tenor sax. Whereas "Chameleon" combined jazz with funk rhythms, "Light as a Feather" is characterized by a Latin drum rhythm, very similar to a **bossa nova.**

The lack of an introduction at the beginning of the tune imparts urgency and directness to the performance. The first part of the song itself, beginning with the words "Clear days," is stated twice, followed by a freer vocal **melisma** on the syllable "ah." After this, the keyboard settles down into a calm, almost static passage with alternating pairs of chords. This passage introduces the second part of the song beginning with the lyric "There's a place." Note that this song is not structured like the AABA or ABAB' tunes discussed in Chapter 3. Instead, it is a freer composition, more in the spirit of a jazz tune than a popular song. Section I presents the song as a head. It can be broken down into smaller sections, s1-s1-piano interlude-s2, where s1 and s2 are the first and second parts of the song itself.

The song climaxes on the word "free," the exact moment that Corea adds a "wah-wah" pedal for intensity. The sax and electric piano solos each build to climaxes that can be identified by the use of a wah-wah pedal. This device, most common in rock styles, is a pitch frequency filter operated by the foot. When the pedal is depressed, a note or chord held on the keyboard makes a "wah" sound. Since the 1960s, there has been a growing number of electronic devices available, like the wah-wah pedal, that alter the tone of electric and electronic instruments.

Section II features the keyboard solo. The drummer continues with the bossa nova beat heard in the head, but soon changes to a new pattern with a fast walking bass. The solo climaxes with the wah-wah pedal, then subsides into section III, the alternating-chords interlude that introduces the sax solo.

During the sax solo the rhythm does not change to a walking bass, as in the keyboard solo, but the wah-wah pedal is nevertheless added at the climax. The bass solo, section IV, starts immediately after section III. The conclusion of the bass solo is articulated by just one wah-wah chord before the alternating-chords interlude introduces section s2 of the song. After s2, s1 is restated to end the performance.

The large-scale form of "Light as a Feather" is ABA': head-solos-altered head. In more detail, the form can be represented by the following schema:

s1 s2 interlude s2 II1 II2 interlude III IV interlude s2 s1

I   II   III   IV   V

A   B   A

The title "Light as a Feather" characterizes this performance and even the album as a whole. The lightness is achieved by the relative lack of bass drum in the rhythm section sonority. Instead, the bass, never too heavy, dominates the lower frequencies. Unlike the bass heard in "Chameleon," the bass here has a more delicate sound, more akin to the acoustic bass.

The prominent Latin rhythms and the lively character of the performances imbue the work with a feeling of joy and exhilaration throughout. All in all, the contrast between the breeziness of "Light as a Feather" and the surging power of "Chameleon" dramatically demonstrates the emotional range of jazz-rock.

john coltrane: "acknowledgement"

John Coltrane: "Acknowledgement" from *A Love Supreme*, Impulse A-77, 1964. John Coltrane, tenor sax; McCoy Tyner, piano; Jimmy Garrison, bass; Elvin Jones, drums.

The John Coltrane Quartet was one of the most important small jazz groups of the 1960s. Coltrane himself had played with Miles Davis during much of the 1950s and established himself as one of the top saxophonists in jazz. Leaving Davis in the late 1950s, Coltrane founded a series of groups that eventually coalesced into this great quartet. *A Love Supreme* is one of their many fine albums.

The Coltrane quartet was especially well known for its contributions to the development of modal jazz, a loose, malleable style that was quite popular during the 1960s. In modal playing, a certain scale, called a **mode,** provides wide ranging melodic and harmonic material that extends over long timespans of music. Instead of dealing with the fast-changing harmonies of bop or swing, modal jazz players pile up chords, often in intervals of a fourth, freely chosen from the notes of the scale. The relationship of their melodies to the chords remains quite free also, often extending beyond the modal scale.

"Acknowledgement" begins with a sparsely accompanied, out-of-tempo passage called a **cadenza.** Cadenzas are often virtuosic and usually occur at the end of a work. The cadenza in this work, however, comes at the beginning and serves as an introduction.

Once the introduction fades out, the bass begins a 4-note ostinato pattern that establishes the tempo and the beat. Garrison, however, does not maintain the ostinato during Coltrane's solo, a feature that distinguishes this use of ostinato from the long **vamp** heard in "Chameleon." Soon the drummer joins the bass at first playing a relatively simple beat that grows more complex and insistent as the piece intensifies, followed by the piano, which completes the rhythmic backdrop for Coltrane's solo. The modal center is loosely established as F dorian.

The layered rhythmic complex, similar to what we heard in "Chameleon," is built up by the gradual entry of the rhythm section in forming the background texture of "Acknowledgement." The chief difference, however, is that in "Chameleon" each instrument maintained its rhythm and function more exactly. Here, although certain rhythms are clearly stated when the instruments first enter, they are quickly abandoned once the performers begin to play more freely. However, each instrument maintains the same overall "function" throughout.

Coltrane begins by improvising immediately rather than stating a head. His solo starts simply, but gradually becomes more elaborate and intense. At first Coltrane centers on a few notes, varying and exploring the numerous rhythms and patterns he can make with them. Because of the complexity and intensity of these explorations, a departure from a previously established pattern often suggests a new idea rather than logical development.

Coltrane soon strays from opening modal scale. Tyner follows him with chords that are not always contained in the F dorian scale. This work is an example of rather mature modal jazz: as the musicians became accustomed to improvising with modal scales, their employment of them gradually became freer.

After the solo achieves its greatest intensity, Coltrane winds down to a section in which the opening bass ostinato is repeated and transposed to a few different pitch levels, as illustrated in Example 4.2.

original motive

Once this transposing-motive section has been completed, an accented piano chord introduces the rather unexpected vocals. At once we hear the 4-note motive from the beginning of the piece as the melody for the lyric "A Love Supreme." Thinking back to the bass ostinato that introduced Coltrane's solo, we realize that the ostinato itself had provided the thematic material for the improvisation. As was pointed out in Chapter 3, sometimes jazz musicians prefer to improvise on fragments rather than songs or more elaborate compositions. The transposing-motives section followed by the vocal provides a recapitulation of this minimal, but cogent, thematic material.

"A Love Supreme" exemplifies Coltrane's deeply felt spiritual commitment at the time of the recording. As the poem in the liner note of the album reveals, the entire work is conceived as a confirmation of Coltrane's religious faith. As such, the vocal can be understood as a form of chanting, Coltrane's musical evocation of God.

In the midst of the vocal section, the motive is transposed down to E♭, a whole step lower than the original modal center of F. Then, one by one, the vocals, the piano, and then the drums drop out, disassembling the background texture erected at the beginning of the piece, to leave the bass to finish alone. As "Resolution," the next movement of the suite, begins, the bass continues to solo in E♭ dorian, the new modal center. Thus, the shift to E♭ dorian provides a connecting link between the two pieces. This connection underscores Coltrane's conception of the album as a complete work in four movements rather than as a collection of separate pieces.

The following schema illustrates the sections of "Acknowledgement":

Intro	I	II	III	IV	V
cadenza	+ bass + drums + piano	sax solo	transposed motives	vocal	− piano − drums bass solo

The texture of "Acknowledgement" differs considerably from the texture of the two jazz-rock pieces studied earlier in the following ways:

1. Electronic instruments are not used. The only keyboard used is an acoustic piano rather than the multikeyboard "stack" heard in much jazz-rock.
2. The rhythms played by the musicians are much less hard-edged or tight. The musicians accent patterns together far less frequently.
3. The drum pulse is freer.
4. The bass tone is lighter. The tone of the acoustic bass dies away more quickly and is far more unobtrusive.
5. The sections are less clearly defined. Instead of strong accents announcing the beginning and end of sections, a more continuous web of sound gradually unfolds through the piece.

Coltrane's sense of sound and the flow of his ideas are hypnotic. In part, this effect derives from Coltrane's deep interest in the music of Asia and the Near East. Uniting non-Western musical models and modal jazz with his original training and mastery of bop, Coltrane created some of the most personal, powerful, and exciting jazz of the 1960s.

miles davis: "so what"

Miles Davis: "So What" from *Kind of Blue*, Columbia PC 8163, 1959. Miles Davis, trumpet; John Coltrane, tenor sax; Cannonball Adderley, alto sax; Bill Evans, piano; Paul Chambers, bass; Jimmy Cobb, drums.

In the early 1950s, Miles Davis established a reputation as an innovator in modern jazz, and he has remained in the limelight since then, except perhaps for a short time in the middle and late 1970s. He has been prominently involved in more varied jazz styles than any other major player in jazz history. In the late 1940s, he played on bop recordings with Charlie Parker, then during the 1950s he became the leading figure in the cool jazz movement. In the 1960s, the cool style was transformed into a kind of postcool movement, dominated by the modal jazz sound developed during the cool era. Then finally in the late 1960s and early 1970s, he became the founding father of jazz-rock.

Arguably, Davis reached the apex of his improvisational ability in the 1950s and 1960s with a stream of brilliant albums and solos. Among his many fine small groups, a classic sextet was established in the 1950s with John Coltrane, alto sax player Julian "Cannonball" Adderley (1928-1975), and pianist Bill Evans (1929-1980). *Kind of Blue,* which contains the classic recording of "So

What," is one of this sextet's finest albums. "So What" can also be heard on the *Smithsonian Collection of Classic Jazz* (SCCJ).

"So What" can be compared to "Acknowledgement" as a showcase for modal improvising, though in this case the musicians adhere far more closely to the pitches of the modal scales. Because *Kind of Blue* was one of the first important albums devoted entirely to modal improvisation, it is not surprising that its application of the theory was somewhat stricter. I will discuss Davis's solo in more detail in Chapter 6.

"So What" begins out of tempo, the bass and piano laying down a moody, simple introduction. Afterwards the bass plays an ascending figure that announces the beginning of the head and establishes the beat. The piano, answering with a repeated two-chord figure that suggests a shoulder shrug and the expression "So What," links up with the bass as the first chorus of the song begins.

After 8 bars, the alto and tenor saxes and the trumpet join the piano on the two-chord answering figure. They continue for 8 more bars before the same tune is played a half step higher. The mode, which during the first 16 bars was D dorian, is now shifted to Eb dorian. After 8 bars of Eb dorian, the mode shifts back to D dorian for the last 8 bars. Hence the song is in 32-bar AABA form, with B exactly the same as A a half step higher.

The soloists use this 32-bar form for their improvisations. The formal similarity between "So What," a jazz tune, and the AABA popular song demonstrates the historical link between the earlier jazz styles and the new directions taken in the 1950s. The musicians in Davis's group had all been trained in swing and bop style jazz. Although they decided to overturn the older tonal style in favor of the modal sound, they retained the formal plan of the popular song.

Once the formal plan of the head becomes clear to you, try to follow it during the improvisations, counting the bars if you can. You can be sure to know where you are in the form if you can predict the beat on which the changes of mode occur.

After the head, a cymbal crash announces the change to a walking bass and the two-chorus trumpet solo. The tenor and alto sax solos follow, each also two choruses long. The intensity of Coltrane's solo here foreshadows his more mature style in "Acknowledgement." Because the tenor and alto sax solos follow one another, the differences in their timbres can easily be compared. The range of the alto is slightly higher and the tone is somewhat lighter than that of the tenor sax.

A one-chorus piano solo follows the alto sax with horns accompanying on the "So What" figure. Something of a walking bass solo, also accompanied by "So What" chords on the piano, refocuses attention on the bass line before it recapitulates the ascending figure of the head. After one chorus of the tune, the rhythm section quickly fades out.

The clarity of the 32-bar AABA melody on which the piece is based facilitates the formal analysis shown in the following schema:

intro	A	A B A	2 choruses	2 choruses	2 choruses
piano	piano	tutti	trumpet	tenor sax	alto sax
bass	bass				
	drums				
	(head)				

1 chorus	A	A A B A	fade
piano	bass	tutti	piano
		(head)	bass
			drums

Although the rhythm section is no different in instrumentation from Coltrane's rhythm section on "Acknowledgement," the playing here is far more sparse and understated. The use of the walking bass pattern complements the swing style rhythm of the drums. Evans, on piano, adds chords here and there but does not try to keep a beat. This style of rhythm section piano playing became common during the bop era: the piano "feeds" chords to the lead instruments, while stricter timekeeping is left to the bass and drums.

The first three pieces studied in this chapter represent various methods of planning the large-scale structure of the jazz performance. The forms of those performances occur somewhat less often than the usual "head-solos-head" format with the solos strictly patterned after the form of the head. "So What" and the pieces presented in the remainder of this chapter all follow strict strophic form.

dave brubeck: "blue rondo à la turk"

The Dave Brubeck Quartet: "Blue Rondo à la Turk" from *Time Out*, Columbia CL 1397, ca. 1960. Dave Brubeck, piano; Paul Desmond, alto sax; Eugene Wright, bass; Joe Morello, drums.

Whereas Miles Davis was perhaps the major creative force in cool jazz, no jazz artist had a greater public impact at the time than pianist Dave Brubeck. Extremely popular in the late 1950s and early 1960s, Brubeck embraced a composing and improvising style that drew upon the European heritage of jazz and its sense of architectural planning, dispassionate coolness, and studied thought. These qualities could at times degenerate into a rather stern, bloodless formality, yet at its best Brubeck's music was fresh and inventive. As his reputation grew, he would occasionally incorporate elements of European art music into his jazz pieces.

"Blue Rondo à la Turk," one of Brubeck's finest efforts, elegantly unites features of European music and cool jazz. The title of the piece immediately suggests Western art music, particularly in its reference to the rondo, a form employed by Classic-era composers Haydn, Mozart, and Beethoven. This form was often placed at the end of the Classical sonata to provide the audience with an upbeat finale. The rondo has a very specific formal design; most common

Dave Brubeck Quartet (left to right): Joe Morello, Eugene Wright, Paul Desmond, Dave Brubeck (seated) (Courtesy Institute of Jazz Studies, Rutgers University).

in ABACABA. The noteworthy feature of rondo form is the alternation of a main theme, A, with other tunes or sections that either contrast A or develop its motivic structure. After each of these other sections, A returns.

Brubeck's piece is also a "Turkish" rondo. In the late eighteenth century, Turkish music enjoyed a vogue in Vienna, with many composers writing rondos and other pieces that incorporated some of the more adaptable aspects of Turkish music. Brubeck's piece has a tinge of the Turkish spirit (not unlike the finale of Mozart's Piano Sonata K. 331, a famous Turkish rondo).

Finally, Brubeck calls the piece a "blue" rondo; you'll hear how blues enters into its structure. The improvisatory section of the piece consists of 12-bar blues choruses, although the section has no motivic or formal links to the other rondolike themes that surround it.

The piece begins directly with the A theme played on the piano and accompanied by bass and drums. Its rhythm, quite unusual for jazz, suggests the European basis of the composition. The 9/8 rhythm found in European fine-art music is customarily subdivided 3 + 3 + 3; that is, three groups of three eighth-notes. "Blue Rondo à la Turk," however, features the irregular subdivision 2 + 2 + 2 + 3, occasionally interspersed with the more normal 3 + 3

+ 3. Alternating between the two kinds of subdivisions effects still another layer of rhythmic complexity.

In the B section, a rendering of the F major theme in A minor, Desmond's alto sax is added to the ensemble, after which the A section returns with solo piano. The piano also takes the C section, which is a new tune composed in the same 9/8 rhythm.

At the next return of A, the alto sax harmonizes the original tune which is still played by the piano. The piano alone has the D theme, followed again by A. The E theme is also stated entirely on the piano with the sax joining in from time to time.

The piano alone begins the ingenious transitional section, F. During the F section, the sax alternates two bars of normal 4/4 time with two bars of the piano playing the A theme in 9/8, as seen in Example 4.3.

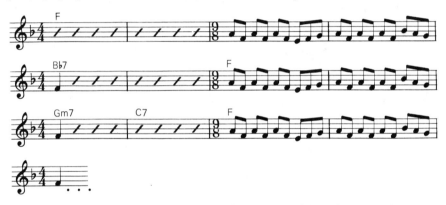

The clever aspect of this transition is that, as in a 12-bar blues in F, the return of the A theme in F major corresponds precisely to the point at which the F chord would naturally occur as part of the 12-bar blues progression. Hence, although the blues improvisations have nothing to do with the rondo themes, section F merges the disparate parts of the piece into a single unit.

Once the F transition section is completed, the improvisatory portion of the performance begins. The improvisations comprise eight choruses of blues in F, four each for the piano and alto sax. Desmond gracefully weaves four choruses of lyrical, beautiful lines to a climax at the beginning of the fourth chorus.

Since Desmond's solo is accompanied by only bass and drums, Brubeck avoids all left-hand chords in his first chorus and instead develops a compelling, single-note line to establish a smooth transition between the solos. Beginning in his second chorus, Brubeck builds to full chords by bar 5 and maintains the intensity through the third chorus. The fourth chorus returns to a single-note line that prepares the entry of the sax for a repeat of F, the transitional section.

The transitional chorus glides into the A theme, played in its entirety with the sax harmonizing the last half. Because repeating the entire rondo would be tedious, the band moves directly to the E theme, the final section that earlier had led to the transition section. This time, however, a finale ends the performance in a climactic manner, though in the key of A rather than F. The following schema summarizes "Blue Rondo à la Turk":

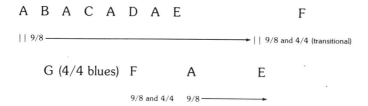

"Blue Rondo à la Turk" deftly combines cool jazz and European styles into a **third stream** mixture. Among the cool-jazz elements: (1) an overall cool ambience and fairly unemotional playing; (2) a light, airy sax tone that contrasts the full-bodied sound of Coltrane or Adderley; (3) a simple, clear swing beat with a walking bass; (4) few flashy displays of technical prowess; and (5) little use of the slides, blue notes, and other expressive effects of blues playing (although a blues form is used). The fine-art aspects of the performance include a detailed formal plan inspired by the Classical rondo form and clever use of a compound meter.

Whereas many of the formal experiments of third stream music sound contrived and dated, "Blue Rondo à la Turk" sparkles, largely because of its rhythmic drive and its beautifully contrasting blues improvisations. The piece is an admirable mixture of the experimental and the conventional, both of which are carefully planned and impeccably performed.

charlie parker–dizzy gillespie: "koko"

Charlie Parker's Re-boppers: "Koko," Savoy M9-12079, November 26, 1945. Charlie Parker, alto sax; Dizzy Gillespie, trumpet and piano; Curly Russell, bass; Max Roach, drums.

The unhurried, deliberate pace of cool jazz was in part a reaction against the high-energy virtuosity of bop. As we have seen, however, musicians seeking to advance or revolutionize a style always proceed to replace some of its elements while, perhaps inadvertently, retaining others. However fervently the newer artists dedicate themselves to radical change, historical perspective reveals that the older style remains the structural basis of the newer. Bop, although radical in tempo, harmony, and improvisational line, retained much of the structural basis of swing.

Three of the bop period's paramount performers and innovators were sax-

ophonist Charlie Parker, pianist Thelonious Monk, and trumpeter Dizzy Gillespie, who together helped shape the style in the early 1940s. "Koko" (SCCJ),
recorded during the period when Parker and Gillespie were playing together
often, presents one of Parker's greatest solos.

"Koko" is unusual in that the piece contains no specific head. Also unusual
is the fact that Gillespie, when not playing trumpet, doubles on piano during
Parker's solo, so that no piano is heard in the introduction or the coda.

In place of a head, "Koko" substitutes an elaborate introduction, with rapid
shifts among several textures at an extremely bright tempo. The trumpet and
alto, for example, play solo, in unison, in octaves, and in harmony. When they
play alone, their parts are improvised, as can be determined by comparing the
repeated "introduction" at the end of the recording to its first presentation.

During the introduction, Max Roach (b. 1925) plays with brushes rather
than sticks. The swishing sound of the brushes contrasts the sound of the sticks
during Parker's solo and the following drum solo. Furthermore, because the bass
plays little during the introduction, the drums provide the entire rhythmic foundation for the lead horns.

Parker's improvisation, two AABA choruses, consists of a vast series of motives and licks from Parker's own personal repertoire. Indeed, with no tune presented as a head, only the changes serve to identify the preexisting harmonic
model as (Ray Noble's) "Cherokee." Apparently, Parker was trying to infuse
new life into this song, which admittedly he was tired of, and had been working
out various ideas with its harmonies, experimentations that eventually led him
to a more pervasive use of extended chord tones. This famous improvisation
may have been partly worked out in advance, but Parker's new preoccupation
with complex harmony and irregular, jagged melodic lines ushered in a new
concept of improvisation.

After Parker's two choruses, Max Roach follows with a drum solo, almost
entirely played on the snare and bass drums. The denseness of his playing evokes
the fiery runs heard in Parker's solo, thus texturally unifying all the solo choruses.

The introduction returns as a *coda*, or tag, to round out the performance.
Its inconclusive ending reveals the emphasis on improvisation that characterizes
bop. During the swing era, the public expected the flashy arrangements and
grandiose effects of the big bands. The bop musicians reacted by underplaying
the concept of the arrangement, at least in small group jazz, to the point where
even the endings of pieces were occasionally haphazard.

We can summarize the important bop characteristics heard in "Koko" as
follows: (1) an extremely bright tempo, unsuitable for most dancing; (2) the use
of a preexisting song as a harmonic model; (3) AABA improvisational structure;
(4) timekeeping on the drummer's ride cymbal supported by a walking bass; (5)
occasional bass drum accents or *bombs;* (6) sparse piano chords suggesting the
harmonies but not articulating each chord change; (7) brilliant, dense, and an-

gular improvisational lines; (8) melodic material based on the soloist's repertoire of licks rather than on the tune being played; and (9) the use of an original rather than popular-song head.

"Koko" is the first recording mentioned in this chapter old enough to have been recorded on a ten-inch 78-rpm record rather than on a twelve-inch 33⅓-rpm LP. Before the long-playing record was popularized in the 1950s, jazz, like other music, was recorded on 78s, which limited the length of each selection to about three minutes. (Very infrequently, a twelve-inch 78 was issued with a longer performance.) Later, the LP enabled the soloists to stretch out with longer statements more akin to their concert performances.

benny goodman: "i found a new baby"

> Benny Goodman Sextet: "I Found a New Baby," Columbia 36039, January 15, 1941. Benny Goodman, clarinet; Cootie Williams, trumpet; George Auld, tenor sax; Count Basie, piano; Charlie Christian, electric guitar; Artie Bernstein, bass; Jo Jones, drums.

Early on, in the 1920s, producers realized the advantage of bringing good musicians together to play, regardless of their other professional associations. The record produced at this sort of studio session most likely featured a soloist—often a singer—while the supporting musicians often remained anonymous or were only mentioned in passing. Early examples of great jazz studio sessions include many of the classic Louis Armstrong Hot Five and Hot Seven recordings of the late 1920s. In the 1930s, at the height of the swing era, small group sessions were regularly produced with players drawn from the best big bands. "I Found a New Baby" (SCCJ) demonstrates what brilliant jazz studio bands could play.

The recording begins with 2 bars of swing beat, played by Jones on the hi-hat cymbal, followed by the main motive of the melody stated by solo clarinet. Goodman's clarinet is accompanied by the bass and guitar players who together articulate a walking rhythm.

From the introduction Goodman glides into the clarinet improvisation. Omitting the head provides more time for the solos that dominate the recording and, furthermore, the introduction itself had effectively announced the song title by stating its main melodic motive. Goodman's low-key, well-crafted solo, lasting 32 bars, reveals an AABA harmonic structure derived from the original tune.

During the A sections, a muted trumpet and tenor sax repeat the melodic motive as a background for Goodman. The repetition of such a figure for the duration of a tune or section of a tune is called a *riff*. Riffs, derived from the blues and developed by local Kansas City bands in the late 1920s and early 1930s, became standard devices in the big band arrangements of the 1930s.

Riffs were often played in unison by the entire section of a big band to back up a soloist. Throughout "I Found a New Baby," the soloists are accompanied by riffs, as shown in Ex. 4.4.

Charlie Christian's electric guitar solo follows. The angularity of some of his melodic figures anticipates the lines soon to revolutionize jazz in the bop era. Christian demonstrates the great versatility of the electric guitar by changing his tone, depending on whether he plays background chords or lead lines. Although he cuts through incisively during his solo, his rhythm sound remains unobtrusive, merely a gear in the rhythm section machine.

Count Basie's spare piano solo typifies his extremely economical style: only a few pitches, but pitches that are phrased perfectly. As a background, the A-section riff is played by muted trumpet, guitar, and tenor sax. In the B section, Basie alternates licks with Goodman.

Cootie Williams's 16-bar trumpet solo is played with the trumpet tightly muted. *Mutes,* devices that fit on or into the bells of brass instruments, usually reduce the low frequencies and emphasize the higher overtones of the pitch. Brass players equip themselves with a wide variety of mutes to change the color, or **timbre,** of their sound. Williams's impassioned statement effectively contrasts the cooler ruminations of the previous solos. Because Williams only plays for 16 bars, the final 16 bars of the AABA chorus are completed by George Auld's tenor sax solo.

Jo Jones's tasteful drum solo, which follows, remains in tempo for 8 bars. When playing an in-tempo solo, the drummer, like the other soloists, improvises for a specific number of bars, usually 8, 16, or some other complete section of a chorus. When playing out of tempo, the drummer is free to change the tempo at will or just play virtuosically without referring to any particular beat.

Drums solos most often occur as the final improvisation of the performance, probably for these reasons: they are visually flashy, providing a climax to the improvisations; they excite the audience with a climactic ending; and they contrast the earlier melodic improvisations and thus lead effectively into the restatement of the theme.

The drum solo in "I Found a New Baby" leads to a short statement of the song, the only place in the performance where the lead instruments all play together as voices in the ensemble. Their exuberance contrasts the coolness of the individual solos and drives the performance to a stimulating and satisfying conclusion.

To summarize the swing era characteristics present in "I Found a New Baby," I should point out the use of: (1) a swing beat supported by a walking bass; (2) an AABA harmonic structure for the improvisations; (3) a popular song for thematic material; (4) piano and guitar to provide harmony and rhythm; (5) riffs to back up the soloists; (6) smooth melodic contours for the improvisational lines; and (7) an easily danceable swing tempo.

louis armstrong: "west end blues"

Louis Armstrong and His Hot Five: "West End Blues," OKeh 8597, June 28, 1928. Louis Armstrong, trumpet and vocal; Fred Robinson, trombone; Jimmy Strong, clarinet; Earl Hines, piano and vocal; Mancy Cara, banjo and vocal; Zutty Singleton, drums.

Among Louis Armstrong's many great recordings from the late 1920s, "West End Blues" (SCCJ) stands out for its opening cadenza and its final trumpet chorus which bears a surprisingly close thematic relationship to the cadenza. As a blues, the performance can be divided into regular 12-bar choruses, each featuring a different soloist and background accompaniment. The instrumentation heard on this recording is that of the classic dixieland ensemble.

The opening cadenza, ebullient, forceful, and eloquent, winds down to a long chord held by the whole band. The first chorus, the head, is played by Armstrong with answering and accompanying parts in the clarinet and trombone. Because the drums and banjo are inaudible throughout much of the recording, the piano's regular on-the-beat chords often seem to be the sole rhythm accompaniment. At the end of the first chorus, Armstrong's triplet ascent echoes the conclusion of this introductory cadenza.

The second chorus features Robinson's trombone solo, during which the drums are finally heard in a kind of clip-clopping rhythm. Conflicting accounts are told of the perils of recording in the 1920s. According to some it was necessary to place the drums far from the microphone because their dynamic range upset the acoustic recording devices. Electrical recordings, perfected around 1925, were able to reproduce drums more credibly, but, as can be heard in "West End Blues," were still quite unsophisticated. Other writers claim that drums were intentionally underrecorded, that their occasional clarity demonstrates the technical feasibility of obtaining a good drum sound. In any event, drums are rarely recorded adequately before the 1930s.

Robinson's trombone solo is followed by a one-chorus duet between clarinetist Strong and Armstrong improvising a vocal response. This use of nonsense syllables for vocal jazz improvisation is called **scat** singing. Armstrong's "Heebie Jeebies" was the first scat recording of major consequence. The use of call-and-response is demonstrated by Armstrong's answering the clarinet with similar phrases.

Next follows a piano solo, totally unaccompanied, in which Earl Hines demonstrates Armstrong-like fluidity and reveals a strong musical personality. Although the clarinet and trombone playing help maintain the somber, bluesy mood of the recording, the technical levels of these players scarcely compare to Hines and Armstrong. Hines was later to become one of the greatest piano players in jazz.

The band joins in for the final chorus, featuring Armstrong's soaring lead. The long high B♭ with which Armstrong begins this chorus is the same pitch that ended the first chorus. This helps establish large-scale continuity between the trumpet statements at the beginning and end of the piece. The final chorus also features a series of wistful, pensive piano runs that introduce a short coda with Armstrong again playing the lead. Zutty Singleton gets in the last word with his clip-clop tag.

In 1928, the rhythm section as the nucleus of the jazz band had not been standardized as a three- or four-man unit. In many recordings there were neither drums, to speak of, nor bass. If a bass player were unavailable, a tuba or sometimes bass saxophone player was often substituted. Banjos foreshadowed the later use of unamplified rhythm guitar.

We can summarize the **Chicago style** features of "West End Blues" as follows: (1) typical instrumentation of trumpet, clarinet, trombone, banjo, piano, and drums; (2) group improvisation in which the trumpet carries the lead accompanied by trombone and clarinet countermelodies; (3) horn solos accompanied by the rhythm section; (4) use of call-and-response; and (5) frequent use of expressive blues elements—slurs, slides, blue notes, etc.

In addition to Armstrong's fine solos, which will be discussed in more detail in Chapter 6, the contrast of the piano and trumpet virtuosity with the less "polished" performances of Strong and Robinson heightens the emotional impact of the record as a whole.

king oliver: "dippermouth blues"

> King Oliver's Creole Jazz Band: "Dippermouth Blues," Okeh 4918, June 23, 1923. King Oliver and Louis Armstrong, cornets; Johnny Dodds, clarinet; Honore Dutrey, trombone; Lil Hardin, piano; Bud Scott, banjo and vocal break; Baby Dodds, drums.

"Dippermouth Blues" (SCCJ), an example of New Orleans dixieland, is certainly King Oliver's finest recording and probably his most influential cornet solo, a solo in fact copied by many cornet and trumpet players throughout the 1920s. Even today, it remains a prime example of a highly effective improvisation structured with an extreme economy of motivic material.

The **New Orleans style** is apt to sound cluttered, even a little chaotic at first, because of the thickness of the sound and the exuberance of its hot style. After several listenings, however, the three or four lead instrumental parts of the ensemble grow clearer and their distinct functions within the dense texture begin to separate.

When the entire New Orleans ensemble plays, the cornet carries the main melody. In Oliver's band, Armstrong (playing second cornet) either harmonized the lead or added a countermelody. The trombone played a countermelody below the cornets, much like a melodic bass line, while the clarinet played what is sometimes called an **obbligato** above the cornets. The obbligato, usually containing more notes than the cornet parts, was often quite virtuosic. The rhythm section in Oliver's band consisted of piano, drums, and banjo.

"Dippermouth Blues" begins with a 4-bar introduction before the rhythm section initiates a driving, on-the-beat pattern at the beginning of the head. The lead instruments all play an introductory figure, a descending diminished-seventh chord that eventually slides into a dominant chord.

After a short pause, the main body of the piece begins. Like "West End Blues," it is structured as a series of 12-bar blues choruses that are arranged for various combinations of instruments. The horns play their figures together in the introduction. However, at the first chorus they separate into their different functions.

Both the first and second choruses are played in classic dixieland fashion, the horns' functions separated as described above. **Polyphony** is the term describing distinct, simultaneous melodies in counterpoint. Polyphony, as applied to the New Orleans ensemble, however, is slightly inaccurate. Normally the term refers to equally important melodies, but in New Orleans playing the lead cornet predominates in the ensemble texture while the other parts are more accompanimental.

After the opening **tutti,** a clarinet solo follows in what is called **stoptime:** the rhythm instruments stop on a downbeat and the accompanying horns, together with the rhythm section, play a simple figure to accompany the soloist. The stoptime figure heard in "Dippermouth Blues" consists of three chords, one on each beat, with a pause on the fourth beat. The clarinet solo, two choruses long like the opening tutti section (the entire ensemble together) leads to another tutti, this time only a single chorus long.

Oliver's three-chorus solo follows, accompanied by the other instruments in rhythm, not stoptime as was heard during the clarinet solo. Oliver builds his solo very slowly through the three choruses, which, despite their simplicity, are a fascinating combination of passion and logic. The inclusion of the other horns during Oliver's improvisation typifies early New Orleans style where, at times, all the instruments continue playing through the entire performance, even the solos. In later small group jazz, the horns lay out during each other's solo, except for occasional accompanimental riffs.

A final tutti section follows the cornet solo. The drummer plays more heavily in this one-chorus finale (often called the **out-chorus** or **sock-chorus**) so as to increase the feeling of drive. Such a device, which we also heard in "I Found a New Baby," was to become popular in both jazz and popular music.

To round out the whole performance, a final two bars, called a **tag,** are appended to the out-chorus. Proceeding directly into the tag without interrupt-ing the rhythm maintains the momentum of the whole performance and pro-vides it with an exhilarating conclusion.

Reviewing "Dippermouth Blues," we find that the following New Orleans characteristics are evident: (1) typical instrumentation of two cornets, clarinet, trombone, piano, banjo, and drums; (2) improvised tutti sections with the first cornet on the lead melody and the other instruments providing countermelo-dies; (3) hot style with exuberant performances by all the musicians; (4) a driving 4/4 meter, with emphasis on the beat, but not yet a swing rhythm; and (5) simple rhythm-section parts with all the rhythm instruments articulating the beat.

In the preceding examples I have examined a few small group recordings, from 1970s jazz-rock back to Chicago and New Orleans dixieland. In all cases the small group comprised one or more lead instruments, usually horns, and a rhythm section in which the piano or guitar could perform both lead and rhythm functions. In tracing the chronology backward, the following jazz styles were examined: jazz-rock, 1960s modern jazz (modal), cool jazz, bop, swing, Chi-cago dixieland, and New Orleans dixieland.

In Chapter 5 I will discuss the development of the big band in chronological order. After the various styles have been presented, you should be able to sum-marize more succinctly the features of each period in jazz history.

chapter
five

the
big
band

The big band evolved, for the most part, from the early twentieth-century dance orchestra, gradually transformed by the hot rhythm and improvisation of the dixieland jazz players during the 1920s. The dance orchestra and large jazz ensemble became all but synonymous during the swing era (ca. 1930-1945). Their popularity was extended by the Lindy hop, or jitterbug, a rather frenetic and virtuosic dance that required an uptempo, hot jazz sound. Because the larger jazz ensembles were so numerous then, the swing era is often called the big band era.

Depending on whether a band emphasized jazz or smooth music, it was called either **hot** or **sweet,** though most bands performed some of both. The large black ensembles, which were primarily jazz oriented, included the bands of Count Basie and Duke Ellington. Most white orchestras, like Benny Goodman's, tended to balance jazz and sweet music quite evenly. Other white bands, such as those of Guy Lombardo or Lawrence Welk, played relatively little jazz. The distinction between hot and sweet also applied to the bands of the 1920s.

In this chapter I will focus on the arrangement, or **chart,** as the primary means of differentiating bands and their styles. For a smaller band the arrangement is less critical and may consist of not much more than a **lead sheet** (the melody with chord symbols) and perhaps a harmony part or two. The form of the arrangement is often improvised during a small band performance. In a big band chart, however, the amount of detail is quite extensive, and significant alterations of melody, harmony, or form must either be laboriously undertaken by the whole band in rehearsal or else rewritten by the arranger. With so much at stake, good arrangers have always been in demand. More than any single musician, the arranger establishes the overall sound of the work being performed.

The demands on the musicians playing in a big band significantly differ from those of the small group jazz player. The extensive "library" or "book" of arrangements that all big bands develop requires that each musician be skilled in reading his own separate part. The musicians playing by ear in the dixieland ensembles we listened to in Chapter 4 would have had to learn how to read music in order to play in the big band. Even Louis Armstrong, hired in the early 1920s by Fletcher Henderson for his New York big band, at first experienced difficulties with the arrangements. Of course, Armstrong quickly sharpened his reading skills and performed quite brilliantly with Henderson.

Playing with a big band requires orientation toward musical priorities other than just reading. Instead of aiming for individuality of sound and line, as we heard, say, in dixieland music, big band musicians must be able to blend with a section of similar instruments, playing together precisely and with excellent intonation. Given the demands placed on big band musicians, few have been both excellent improvisers and ensemble musicians: usually one or two players in each section are hired for their first-rate improvisational ability. These musicians are sometimes called the "jazz players" of each section. Armstrong, for example, was hired to be the jazz trumpet player in Henderson's orchestra.

As has been mentioned earlier, members of big bands occasionally devise head arrangements by themselves. In fashioning head arrangements by ear, each band member works out his or her own part or suggests parts to the others. Therefore, much rehearsal time is required. Also, the outcome of a head arrangement is likely to be simple and riff oriented, since this type of structure arises most naturally. Thus, head arrangements often did not display the variety of textures heard in written arrangements.

The big band is usually divided into four sections of instruments: trumpets, trombones, woodwinds, usually called "reeds" (saxophones and related instruments), and rhythm. The trumpets and trombones are often grouped together as the brass section. Throughout the evolution of the big band, the arranger's tendency has been to write for each section as a separate textural unit. Experiments with irregular unit groupings are far less common. However, the following grouping suggests one of many possibilities:

Unit 1:	cup mute trumpet	*Unit 3:*	bass
	trombone		trumpet
	tenor sax		baritone sax
Unit 2:	2 trumpets	*Unit 4:*	2 trombones
	straight mute trombone		drums
	3 clarinets		guitar
	piano		

Such textural combinations as these suggest that the arranger need not, for example, always write for the trumpets grouped together, all playing the same kind of part. Instead the trumpet players can be divided—some muted, some open, or some grouped with other instruments in the band. Experimental big bands in the 1960s, such as the bands of Don Ellis, tried arrangements with such unusual textural groupings.

The arranger normally writes arrangements falling between two theoretical extremes: the entirely improvised or the entirely composed. That is, the arranger must decide upon the degree of improvisation vs. writing in each chart, proportions that can affect the overall style of the band as well. Count Basie's group, for example, always featured much improvisation, possibly because head arrangements, in which improvisation arises quite naturally, dominated the band's early book. Other groups, such as Stan Kenton's in the late 1940s, were thought of more as arrangers' bands; the solos in these seemed almost to interrupt the continual emphasis on dramatic big band textures.

Throughout its history, big band instrumentation has been extended or enlarged in several ways. String sections consisting of violins and perhaps violas and cellos are sometimes added. The big band then begins to approximate the symphony orchestra, except that the arrangements tend to emphasize the wind instruments over the strings. The Paul Whiteman orchestra of the 1920s exemplified such an ensemble. A similar group has become the basis for most large studio ensembles used in recordings.

The big band is sometimes enlarged by the addition of a French horn section, though this practice is somewhat more rare. French horns, with their velvety tone, blend well with either the trumpets and trombones or with the reeds. Composer-arrangers Gil Evans and Frank Foster have written effectively for French horns. Stan Kenton has experimented with them as well.

Assuming the band leader to be sympathetic, the arranger can also extend the number of instruments found in each section. For example, the brass may be increased to as many as six trumpets (with some doubling on flugelhorn), five trombones, and tuba (used as a bass for the brass rather than as a rhythm instrument as in dixieland style). Moreover, the rhythm section may be extended with extra percussionists who might play hand drums, like bongos or conga drums; small rhythm instruments, like tambourines, maracas, bells, or chimes; or melodic instruments, like vibes or marimba. The pianist may also play electric piano and/or synthesizer. The usual battery of instruments in the reed section includes soprano, alto, tenor, and baritone saxophones, but may also include flutes (concert, alto, and piccolo), clarinets (Bb concert and bass clarinet), and even oboe and English horn.

The big band is an incredibly flexible ensemble, whose size and instrumentation can be adapted to the needs of the arranger. The big band can play just about any style of music, as you will hear in the following recordings.

fletcher henderson: "the stampede"

Fletcher Henderson and His Orchestra: "The Stampede," Columbia 654-D, May 14, 1926. Fletcher Henderson: piano; Don Redman: arrangement; Russell Smith, Rex Stewart, Joe Smith: trumpet and cornets; Don Redman, Buster Bailey, Coleman Hawkins: saxophones and clarinets; Benny Morton: trombone; Charlie Dixon: banjo; Ralph Escudiro: tuba; Kaiser Marshall: drums.

During the 1920s, many established dance orchestras began to hire hot jazz soloists with the hope of enlivening their more staid, traditional ensembles. I have already mentioned an example of this trend, Louis Armstrong's moving from Chicago to New York to become the jazz soloist in Fletcher Henderson's orchestra. In addition to helping the Henderson band, Armstrong himself gained exposure in New York, thus increasing his popularity and self-confidence to the point where he would soon consider leading his own band.

Largely because of the presence of Armstrong and the hot, trend-setting arrangements of Don Redman, Fletcher Henderson's orchestra became one of the first great jazz big bands. Henderson's writing was also first rate and later in the 1930s, after Henderson had dissolved his own group, Benny Goodman hired him as an arranger and bought some of his old charts. Many of Fletcher Henderson's arrangements formed the basis for Goodman's hot style—a prime example of a white band popularizing the musical innovations of a black ensemble.

"The Stampede" (SCCJ) begins with the kind of writing that is characteristic of almost all big band arrangements, the repetition of a lick or motive tossed back and forth among the instrumental sections. In this case the piano begins with a short lick, which is imitated first by the saxes, then by the brass. A trumpet solo follows, as if answering the entire band, and then the whole procedure is repeated. This rather complicated ordering of call-and-response sections, played twice, constitutes the first section of the piece.

Section two is more subdued, with all the instrumental choirs in the band contributing parts to the general texture. The end of this section is marked by the alternation of piano solo breaks with the whole ensemble. In a **solo break** the rhythm section stops to allow for a short solo improvisation, often one or two bars in length. This very common arranging technique can also be applied to an entire section of instruments. Throughout "The Stampede," the solo breaks tend to descend. Their identical shapes suggest that Redman conceived of them as motivically unifying the arrangement.

Section three features Coleman Hawkins's tenor sax solo. Hawkins, who went on to become one of the greatest tenor sax players in jazz, had not yet fully developed his style at the time of this recording. On "The Stampede" he plays rather stiffly, with a reedy quality somewhat typical of saxophone playing of the 1920s. However, his mature sound was magnificent: smooth and loose, yet projecting a big, full-throated tone.

During Hawkins's solo the rest of the band plays background chords, softly accented. This use of the band on simple background parts to frame the busier, more active soloist is another common big band technique, an instance of the arranger assigning certain functions of the rhythm section to other groups of instruments. Toward the end of the sax solo the band takes up the first theme again, which includes the solo breaks at the end of the section.

Following section three, Redman inserts an **interlude,** a short passage usually two to four bars in length that is not part of the song itself. Its usual functions are to relieve the continual recycling of the basic song strophes, to set up the following chorus as being of special significance, and often to modulate to another key. In this case the interlude, played by the sax section, prepares Rex Stewart's trumpet solo.

To recapitulate the arrangement thus far, section I was largely introductory, section two was the head (the presentation of thematic material), and section III was an improvisation on that material. Stewart's trumpet solo, section four, presents new thematic material. For this solo, Redman, or perhaps Henderson in the original composition, varies the work's harmonic structure by modulating to the minor mode. The melodic character of Stewart's solo, especially with its almost classical, exerciselike conclusion, suggests that little if any of the solo is improvised. During the solo, the sax section accompanies with soft, lower-register chords.

To introduce the fifth section, the interlude preceding section four is repeated, but now played by the piano. The use of solo piano, a pleasing contrast to the full band, provides the sax section with the opportunity to switch to clarinets.

Section five features a clarinet trio, a combination of instruments that was popular in the 1920s. The chord structure of section four is repeated as well as the exerciselike fragment at the end of the chorus. Since the clarinet trio begins with long notes, the banjo player decides to speed up his part with a more aggressive strum. Stewart jumps in with a solo break that introduces another short trumpet solo, section six, which is the first part of the end of the piece. Here the looser quality of the solo suggests improvisation and leads quite effectively to the ensemble passage that winds up the arrangement.

The heavy oom-pah feel of the tuba on the first and third beats followed by the banjo on the back beats (two and four) anchors the performance throughout. Tubas or bass saxophones are found more frequently in big bands than in the small groups of the 1920s, because in a small band, tuba or bass sax might overwhelm the other instruments.

"The Stampede" presents an interesting case of styles in transition, combining elements of both dixieland jazz and the newer elements of swing. Most like dixieland are: (1) the use of the clarinet trio, popularized by Jelly Roll Morton in the early 1920s; (2) the oom-pah tuba part that recalls the marching band legacy of jazz; (3) the squarer feeling of the rhythm; and (4) the syncopated hot rhythms.

Characteristics of the developing swing style include: (1) fully developed sectional writing; (2) solo and section breaks; (3) soloists to contrast the full orchestra; (4) the saxophone section; and (5) interludes used to introduce new sections and to modulate to different keys. "The Stampede" is also clearly strophic, a feature of both swing and dixieland styles.

duke ellington: "east st. louis toodle-oo"

Duke Ellington and His Orchestra: "East St. Louis Toodle-Oo," Victor 21703, December 19, 1927. Duke Ellington: piano and arrangement; Bubber Miley, Louis Metcalf: trumpets; Joe Nanton: trombone; Otto Hardwick, Harry Carney, Rudy Jackson: saxes and clarinets; Fred Guy: banjo; Wellman Braud: bass; Sonny Greer: drums.

Duke Ellington (Courtesy Institute of Jazz Studies, Rutgers University).

By the late 1920s, Edward Kennedy "Duke" Ellington (1899–1974) had established himself as a major force in the two intersecting worlds of jazz and popular music; he remained prominent in both for his entire life. Although Ellington's work was to remain consistently fine throughout his career, he produced particularly brilliant recordings in the late 1920s and in the years surrounding 1940. Ellington should be included with Louis Armstrong and Charlie Parker as the greatest of all jazz artists because of his superb compositions and arrangements, his influence on other jazz players, his excellent piano playing, and the consistently fine quality of his band. Interestingly enough, he is the only truly great jazz artist who was not primarily an improvising musician,

81

for although Ellington played piano quite well, leading the band from behind the keyboard, he is remembered more for his arranging and composing.

Ellington's big band, an expression of his artistic vision, was a credit to both his managerial ability and his musical understanding. He successfully carried out his personal artistic intentions without sacrificing the creativity of his musicians. They were always able to satisfy their personal needs for artistic freedom without betraying Ellington's sense of musical expression. Throughout his multidecade career Ellington's diplomatic skill and his continuing artistic growth assured the tenure of the band's personnel, enabling him to mold his sound around the individual players.

"East St. Louis Toodle-Oo" (SCCJ) is a fine example of the band's style in the late 1920s. The somewhat mournful quality of the piece can be attributed in part to the string bass which, when bowed, imparts an eerie somberness to the dark chord voicings of the band. Given the underrecorded presence of the drums, the beat is often audible only in the banjo strumming the back beats and in the occasional chords of the piano flavoring the more lightly scored sections.

The piece begins with an 8-bar introduction consisting of richly voiced chords in the saxes, piano, and bass, an Ellington trademark. These chords, a continuous string of half-notes, form the background for Bubber Miley's following trumpet solo. The baritone sax, the lowest sax part, is played somewhat louder than the other saxes and imparts an earthiness to the chords. The baritone sax is given a solo later in the arrangement.

The trumpet solo by Bubber Miley captures the "jungle" sounds for which he and the band as a whole were famous. This particular style, probably suggested by the expressive blues playing of the New Orleans musicians, was developed by Ellington and the band during their long residence at Harlem's Cotton Club in the late 1920s. Many of the floor shows there, which were accompanied by the Ellington band, featured "exotic" dancing with jungle scenery and costumes.

Miley's growling and his ability to bend notes and blend his sound into the dark saxophone chords are especially memorable features of the piece. The solo itself is in 32-bar AABA form with the sax chords accompanying the A sections. In the B section a muted trombone takes over the accompaniment.

"East St. Louis Toodle-Oo" has been up to this point entirely in the minor mode. In the next section, Harry Carney contrasts the somber mood with an almost jaunty baritone sax solo in the major mode. His sound, not unlike that of Hawkins's tenor sax, which we heard in "The Stampede," recalls the somewhat harsh and reedy quality of saxophone playing of the 1920s.

Carney's solo divides into two parts, an 8-bar section with a break in mm. 7–8, followed by a 10-bar section. The two sections are equivalent in form, but for a 2-bar extension toward the end of the second section. "Tricky" Sam Nanton's trombone solo, although identical in form to Carney's baritone sax solo, features the muted growling sounds first heard with Miley.

A reprise of the thick, opening chords forms the background for the clarinet solo, which begins with growling in the lower register. Later in the solo the upper register is explored as well, without a loss of intensity or mood. The B section, which had formed a bridge for the A sections in the head, is omitted here, leaving a 16-bar AA solo.

After the clarinet solo, the first tutti passage of the arrangement follows, structured by the harmony and form of the baritone sax solo. As in that solo, the tutti section is in two parts, first 8 bars, then 10 bars, with a break in mm.7-8. Rounding off the arrangement, Miley returns with an 8-bar reprise of A, accompanied in half notes by the saxes and trombones.

In contrast to Redman's arranging in "The Stampede," Ellington is more inclined to employ mixed instrumental groupings. For this reason, his scoring is often harder to identify on first hearing and his textures differ from those of most other ensembles. Moreover, "East St. Louis Toodle-Oo" is conceived as a jazz composition, not an arrangement of a popular tune.

Ellington continually strived for distinctive timbres and a unique overall sound to his band. A tone we might call "brooding," as heard in "East St. Louis Toodle-Oo," is created by: (1) atypical use of bowed string bass; (2) solos that feature growling, "jungle" sounds; (3) dark, muted timbres; (4) thick chord voicings; and (5) interplay of the major and minor modes.

Our study of jazz so far has revealed the ubiquity of the "head-solos-head" format. Ellington, however, insisted on a refreshingly different approach. In arranging an AABA song for a band it is often difficult to vary the basic "head-solos-head" pattern creatively and still fashion a workable, uncontrived arrangement. Ellington circumvented this problem by both composing *and* arranging the material. In so doing, Ellington not only composed great popular songs such as "In My Solitude," "Sophisticated Lady," and "Mood Indigo," but also penned more extended works such as "East St. Louis Toodle-Oo," and later very lengthy works such as "Black, Brown and Beige," "Liberian Suite," and the "Sacred Concerts." Particularly in the extended works, the arrangement was conceived as an intrinsic part of the composition. Given the brilliance and originality of his work, there is little doubt that Ellington was one of the foremost arranger-composers in twentieth century American music.

duke ellington: "ko-ko"

Duke Ellington and His Orchestra: "Ko-ko," Victor 26577, March 6, 1940. Duke Ellington: piano and arrangement; Wallace Jones, Cootie Williams, Rex Stewart: trumpets and cornet; Joe Nanton, Lawrence Brown: trombones; Juan Tizol: valve trombone; Barney Bigard, Johnny Hodges, Otto Hardwick, Ben Webster, Harry Carney: saxophones and clarinets; Fred Guy: guitar; Jimmy Blanton: bass; Sonny Greer: drums.

"Ko-ko" (SCCJ), from the productive Ellington years around 1940, is another example of a big band jazz composition. Although rather simple in its large-scale from, the piece provides great structural interest through the complex interaction of its clearly laid out sections. At the same time, the work draws its emotive power from the dense stacking of the instrumental groupings in the climactic sections and their contrast to the passionate solo statements. Instead of using simple melodic material to be developed orchestrationally and improvised on by the soloists, "Ko-ko" generates its thematic content sequentially, each new instrumental section seeming to grow out of the previous one.

A short tom-tom figure leads to the introductory section, 8 bars of jabbing trombone chords over a *pedal tone* in the baritone sax. The drummer emphasizes the tom-toms throughout the piece, which adds considerably to the quality of its driving, persistent rhythms.

The harmonic structure of the second section is based on 12-bar blues changes in the minor mode. Blues changes are found in each of the remaining sections except for the coda, which recapitulates the introduction with an additional four bars at the end. The second section, one chorus long, presents the thematic material, never to be heard again in the piece: a pair of call-and-response riffs between the cup-muted solo valve trombone and the saxes.

The third section features Tricky Sam Nanton in a two-chorus muted trombone solo. The rest of the brass back him with punctuated chords whose off-the-beat phrasing helps maintain the tension. The "oo-ah-oo-ah" sound of these chords is produced by alternately covering and uncovering the bell of the horn.

Ellington provides himself with a one-chorus solo in the fourth section, but the activity of the instrumental writing purposefully covers these tense, taut *arpeggios*. The off-beat chords continue in the brass, but their pattern is changed from that of the previous chorus.

The first tutti passage of the piece follows Ellington's solo. Thematically related to the second section, this tutti passage nevertheless avoids any literal restatement of the riffs first heard there. This newer section builds through to the solo breaks played by the string bass.

The radical change of texture and volume heard in the bass solo chorus at last releases some of the tension, but Blanton's hard plucking and rhythmic intensity project a great deal of passion. The use of the bass for these solo breaks is a masterful orchestrational idea: our attention is transferred to an instrument rarely used then for such solos, but without the expected loss of energy.

After the solo bass breaks, the last tutti section climaxes the intensity that has so far been unrelenting. Here the instrumental sections join together to create blocks of sound that follow logically from the previous tutti sections. To end the piece at such a feverish level without any letup or release of energy would perhaps have sounded awkward and melodramatic. Ellington therefore repeats the introduction which, in contrast to the previous climactic passage, now seems quite cool. The repeat of the already static introduction guides the piece gently to a satisfying conclusion. This repeated introduction then yields to a quickly rising coda in which the intensity of the previous tutti returns for a final statement.

"Ko-ko" is certainly one of the most original jazz recordings ever produced. Ellington's new aesthetic is suggested by the emotional depth and forthrightness evident throughout the piece, in which the listener is compelled to accept the music on its own strikingly original terms. Though recorded at the height of the swing era, "Ko-ko's" intensity and uncompromising emotional directness suggest the innovations of the nascent bop era, whose exponents at this time were just beginning their experiments.

count basie: "doggin' around"

Count Basie and His Orchestra: "Doggin' Around," Decca 1965, June 6, 1938. Count Basie: piano; Herschel Evans: arrangement; Buck Clayton, Ed Lewis, Harry Edison: trumpets; Eddie Durham: trombone and

Count Basie (Courtesy Institute of Jazz Studies, Rutgers University).

85

guitar; Benny Morton, Dan Minor: trombones; Earl Warren, Jack Washington, Herschel Evans, Lester Young: saxophones; Freddie Green: guitar; Walter Page: bass; Jo Jones: drums.

The original group from which the Basie big band evolved was the Benny Moten band of Kansas City. William "Count" Basie (1904–1984) had been their piano player and became the band's leader after Moten's death. In the recordings of the Moten band we can hear something of the evolution of **Kansas City style** into swing.

In addition to running a great big band, Count Basie's solo piano style, first discussed in Chapter 4 ("I Found a New Baby"), was quite distinctive. In "I Found a New Baby," Basie played economically, generally avoiding the more typical, virtuosic swing styles of Earl Hines and Teddy Wilson. In fact, Basie's style was not widely copied most likely because doing so would be dismissed as too derivative. Solo and small group recordings of Basie's piano playing show that he was also an accomplished *stride* pianist.

"Doggin' Around" (SCCJ) begins with Basie playing one of his famous introductory vamps. Widely recognized as a trademark, this 8-bar vamp usually suffices to identify the Basie band. The easy-going but swinging arrangement, by tenor–saxophonist Herschel Evans, provides the soloists with a good deal of solo space. The head, in 32-bar AABA form, contains no specific melody for the bridge, which is instead improvised by alto saxophonist Earl Warren. The A-section melody is played by the sax section with brass answering figures. As in Ellington's "Ko-ko," brass section "oo-ahs," now considered something of a swing cliché, are heard throughout the arrangement. In the B section the brass figure switches to punctuated chords; the space between the chords allows the sax player more freedom to improvise.

The next chorus features a tenor sax solo by arranger Evans. The AABA form of his solo, with the chords derived from the head, is retained for improvisations throughout the arrangement. Note that the brass continue with "oo-ah" figures during the A sections of this tenor solo.

Then, for the first time in the arrangement, we hear the lead played by a brass instrument: Buck Clayton works his way through a swinging 16-bar trumpet solo that completes the first half of the AABA form. A baritone sax finishes with the bridge and last 8 bars of the chorus.

Next is Basie's piano solo, which on first hearing, might seem to consist of unrelated, delicate melodic figures. In fact, Basie succeeds admirably in what is an especially difficult improvisational or compositional technique: unifying a series of simple but disparate motives into an elegant, coherent whole. Effective in its simplicity, Basie's "Doggin' Around" solo is assembled in such a way that each part of the solo depends on the other, yet there is no obvious repetition or other motivic coherence.

The next chorus features one of the greatest improvisers in jazz: Lester Young. Young's original style, based on the easy looseness of Kansas City blues, influenced the future of both cool jazz and bop. He couples suave coolness with great melodic elegance and, from time to time, unexpected irregularity of rhythm and phrase shape. Young's style has also been called "horizontal" or "linear": rather than emphasizing or delineating each chord change as it occurs, he aggressively clings to his melodic idea and thereby "plays through" the changes, as if floating above them.

Like Basie, Young often seems to be disregarding motivic structure in favor of a more casual sense of coherence. However, this consummate solo projects intriguing and unexpected melodic shapes, while the coolness of his sound does not hide the warmth of his expression. Such an improvisational concept, though possibly not originated by Young, certainly became popular because of him.

The tendency of drum solos to occur before the final climactic tutti was pointed out in the previous chapter. Jo Jones's 8-bar solo gradually gains in complexity, leading dramatically to the final out-chorus. That final chorus, only 8 bars long instead of a full strophe, avoids repetition of the head and in contrast builds the arrangement to an exciting conclusion.

The Basie ensemble exemplifies the big band of the swing era. The arrangement of "Doggin' Around," which is in classic swing style, features: (1) an underlying swing beat in the drums, consisting of an even 4 beats to the bar played on the ride or hi-hat cymbals and bass drum; (2) walking bass with 4 notes to the bar; (3) rhythm guitar and piano emphasizing the meter and articulating all the chord changes; (4) four homogeneous instrumental sections consisting of trumpets, trombones, saxophones, and rhythm, with each section treated as a unit in terms of the arrangement; (5) *antiphonal* writing among the sections, suggesting call-and-response formats; (6) improvised solos that contrast the timbres of the sections and the full band; and (7) a strophic 32-bar AABA harmonic and thematic structure.

Basie's group also featured the following qualities that distinguished it from most other swing bands: (1) emphasis on uptempo jazz and improvisation over sweet dance music; (2) a fine balance between ensemble tightness and uninhibited, swinging solos; and (3) first-rate personnel, including some of the finest improvisers of the day.

Another distinctive quality of "Doggin' Around," and of Basie's performances in general, is the understated tone throughout. Unlike the driving, sometimes strained urgency found in the uptempo recordings of Benny Goodman and Glenn Miller, the Basie band manages to rivet our attention without frantically pushing themselves. The arrangements, almost underwritten, provide the soloists with the opportunity to develop ideas in a freer, more relaxed atmosphere. This philosophy contrasts, for example, the approach of the Ellington band, whose emphasis was on the composition and the arrangement, despite its array of great soloists. The Basie band epitomizes big band jazz as a collection of soloists working together, while the Ellington band was a "unit," a single instrument for Ellington's compositional inspiration.

woody herman: "four others"

Woody Herman and His Orchestra: "Four Others," Columbia JCL 592, September 11, 1953. Woody Herman: clarinet, alto sax; Jimmy Giuffre: arrangement; Stu Williamson, Ernie Royal, Bernie Glow, Harold Wegbreit, Bobby Styles: trumpets; Jerry Coker, Dick Hafer, Bill Trujillo, Sam Staff: saxophones; Kai Winding, Frank Rehak, Vernon Friley, Urbie Green: trombones; Nat Pierce: piano; Red Kelly: bass; Art Mardigan: drums.

After World War II the big bands declined in popularity. Swing itself had become rather old-fashioned and staid. The new trend in jazz was bop, a style more suitable to the small jazz group. For the most part, bop style big bands had great difficulty surviving, yet in addition to the various Woody Herman bands, or "herds," Dizzy Gillespie and Stan Kenton ran generally successful groups.

Perhaps only Dizzy Gillespie wholly succeeded in transferring bop style to a big band format, but even his venture had little chance of long-lived commercial success since the style of bop was intrinsically nondanceable and nonsingable. For the most part, the big bands did not assume significant leadership in the stylistic evolution of jazz in the 1950s and 1960s. Instead, the small group took the lead. The large band, however, was put to work in the recording studio.

The band of Woody Herman (b. 1913) was significant because it managed to remain popular for many years while still playing excellent jazz, a mixture of bop and swing. Many of the top jazz musicians of the time played with Herman including Stan Getz, Zoot Sims, Kai Winding, and Urbie Green. While avoiding the sentimentality that dominated popular music in the late 1940s and early 1950s, they managed to cut several hit records, including "Woodchoppers' Ball," "Early Autumn," and "The Four Brothers."

"The Four Others," a followup chart to "The Four Brothers," was written by Jimmy Giuffre (b. 1921), a well-known arranger and clarinetist. This chart manages to capture an element of bop in the swinging and agile trombone melody, as well as a feeling of swing in its smooth, straightforward rhythm. The arrangement is clearly laid out and flexible enough to be extended in live performance.

The introduction, played by the whole band, seems slightly irregular because of its 6-bar length, but it leads naturally into the head, an AABA tune played in harmony by the trombone section. The tune also deviates quite refreshingly from the usual 32-bar AABA form because of its 12-bar A section. The B section retains the usual 8-bar length.

Throughout the head, the trombone choir surprises us with the unexpected agility of its playing. As accompaniment, the trumpets and saxes fill the spaces between the trombone phrases with sharp, accented chords.

After the head, the solo portion begins with each trombone player soloing on one section of the AABA form. (This alternating of short solos, "trading," is usually heard in small group jazz contexts: for example, the final solo choruses of a blues will often be spent *trading fours*.) In a live performance, this entire portion of the arrangement could be repeated as often as necessary, providing the soloists with greater opportunity to interact. The saxophones softly accompany the trombones with chords, while the trumpets are silent except for a brief figure at the end of the B section.

An abrupt key change from Ab to F begins the last section, a restatement of the tune, this time with the addition of the trumpets on the melody. The arrangement of the A section here includes a trumpet lead for 4 bars, unison trombones for 4 bars, then trumpets again for 2 bars (plus 1 beat), followed by a drum fill. This format is repeated for the second A section.

In the B section, the modified tune returns to the trombone choir. The final A section, again with the tune modified, features 4 bars of tutti, 4 bars of trumpets in unison, then a brief final appearance by the trombones for 2 bars before the whole band finishes out the chart.

In their solo section, the trombonists play melodic lines that are similar enough to maintain a strong sense of continuity from player to player. Closer listening reveals, however, that they each have their own style and that in lengthier solos these stylistic differences would become more acute.

While featuring the trombones, the arrangement tastefully blends and varies the big band's colors. Moreover, like "Doggin' Around," the performance features several prominent characteristics of big band swing: (1) smooth swing tempo with walking bass; (2) antiphonal use of instrumental sections; (3) AABA strophic forms; and (4) contrast of solo and ensemble sections. The angularity of the trombone lines and the bright tempo of the piece suggest the accretion of a few bop elements to the declining swing style. The rhythm section throughout is tight and mobile, confidently supporting the dense sound of the brass. Effective as this piece is, it makes no significant stylistic advance over the standard swing arrangement heard earlier in the chapter; however it serves as a transition between those and the following selections.

dizzy gillespie: "woody'n you"

> **Dizzy Gillespie Big Band: "Woody'n You," Victor LPV-530, December 22, 1947. Dizzy Gillespie: trumpet and arrangement; Dave Burns, Elmon Wright, Lammar Wright, Ernest Bailey: trumpets; Howard Johnson, John Brown, Joe Gayles, George "Big Nick" Nicholas, Cecil Payne: saxophones; William Shepherd, Ted Kelley: trombones; John Lewis: piano; Al McKibbon, bass; Kenny Clarke, drums; Chano Pozo: congas.**

Dizzy Gillespie was fortunate to operate the only big band that played bop almost exclusively. Gillespie was not, however, content merely to adapt bop style to the large group. He was among the first to experiment with incorporating

Latin melodies and rhythms into modern jazz. His band played with a great deal of spirit and verve, showing that genuine, uptempo bop could be performed successfully by a large group.

Gillespie embraced Latin music and its rhythms enthusiastically, allying them to the brilliant eighth-note lines of bop. The incorporation of Latin rhythms into jazz dates back at least to Jelly Roll Morton's "Spanish tinge," which is discussed in the section on Morton in Chapter 9. Throughout the swing era many of the big bands played rhumbas, congas, and other Latin-derived dance numbers which were then quite popular.

Among the excellent musicians in Gillespie's big band was Chano Pozo, whose outstanding contribution helped stimulate further interest in Latin percussion. Pozo played bongos or conga drums with an intensity that was quite new for Latin jazz at the time, and blended elegantly with the new bop concept of fast tempos. Many big bands now regularly augment their rhythm sections with at least one percussionist who usually plays congas and other Latin (and African) percussion instruments.

The Gillespie big band produced several excellent recordings, often featuring compositions and arrangements by Gillespie himself, who wrote not only for his own groups but for others too. "Woody'n You," for example, was originally written for the Woody Herman band. Gillespie's own recording of his composition and arrangement, however, seethes with energy and includes a dazzling Gillespie solo. The arrangement begins with a 10-bar introduction based on the melody and chord progression of the tune itself and features an intriguing counterpoint between the brass and sax sections. At the end of the introduction, the saxes settled into a short vamp.

For the head, a lyrical tune is played by solo trombone, accompanied by chords in the sax section. The tune itself consists of a melodic pattern that is repeated, gradually moving lower. The harmonic pattern of the accompaniment, a common one in bop, features the circle of fifths (discussed briefly in Chapter 3). At the end of the first 8 bars, the trumpets answer with a typical bop phrase. The A section is then repeated.

To contrast the A section, the 8-bar bridge features a fiery exchange between the brass and the saxes, whose counterpoint recalls the introduction. After the bridge the A section returns to complete a 32-bar AABA head.

An entire 32-bar chorus is devoted to the Gillespie trumpet solo that follows. The accompaniment is quite active, with sharply accented phrases, short enough so as not to cover the trumpet solo, in the brass and saxophones. Gillespie perfectly balances the phrases of his solo: fluent runs are often followed by more sustained passages in the higher register, for example, at the end of the bridge followed by the beginning of the last A section.

After Gillespie's solo, three short, punctuated chords glide from the uptempo rhumba-like rhythm into straight jazz time. The bass begins to walk and the ride cymbal of the drums overtakes Pozo's conga rhythms to form an accompaniment for John Brown's alto solo. The harmonic changes of the accompaniment are new. However, since the chords of this section are also based on the circle of fifths, they fit well into the overall structure of the piece.

An exuberant brass fanfare at the end of Brown's solo sets up a 2-bar break for the conga drums. After the conga break Gillespie presents a climactic section again based on the circle of fifths, derived from the changes heard earlier during the alto solo. Counterpoint between the brass and saxophones and intense brass writing characterize this section, which, like the alto solo, finishes with a 2-bar conga solo break. Toward the end of the section, Gillespie's trumpet screeches over the band while the saxophones begin a unison chromatic descent. The Latin rhythm returns, replacing the walking bass and straight jazz feel.

The conga break introduces a reprise of the head, scored as before but played only once this time. After the head, the saxophones alone replay the vamp first heard at the end of the introduction to usher in the coda. Gillespie develops the short phrases of the saxophone vamp into the material for the coda, rapidly bringing in the trumpets and trombones. This new, unexpected section features an exciting dialogue between the saxes and brass that rises quickly to the final chord. The coda is the only part of the piece whose harmonies are not derived from the circle of fifths.

Stylistically, "Woody'n You" differs from the swing-bop recording to Herman's "Four Others" in that (1) the writing is far more angular with the bop phrases, played by all the sections, often placed in counterpoint with one another; (2) the writing for each section is more virtuosic, with the trumpets often playing in the exciting high register; (3) Latin rhythms are alternated with a very fast 4/4 bop tempo; (4) a jazz-tune head is used in place of a popular song; (5) circle-of-fifths harmonies with extended chords can be heard throughout; and (6) the playing is exceedingly intense, with everyone pushing to full capacity.

Many of the traits of swing band arranging persist, however. Most noteworthy is the use of each section as a unit throughout the arrangement, though occasionally the sections may be divided to play in counterpoint within themselves. Further, the arrangement is strophic and features solo improvisations contrasting the timbre of the ensemble.

The Gillespie big band established the sound of the modern jazz big band. Few bop style big bands since then have altered the basic distribution of the instruments in their arrangements. Most occasionally use Latin tunes and rhythm. A big band revival took place in the late 1960s with various fine groups established, such as the Thad Jones–Mel Lewis band and the Don Ellis band. In the 1970s, the Toshiko Akioshi big band soon dominated the field. Stylistically, however, these groups offered little that had not been anticipated by the swing and bop big bands, except perhaps Ellis's experimentations with complex rhythms. The following two recordings examined in this chapter present two prominent composer–arrangers whose big band work differed significantly from the more popular Gillespie approach.

miles davis—gil evans: "summertime"

Miles Davis with Gil Evans's Orchestra: "Summertime," from *Porgy and Bess,* Columbia PC 8085, August 18, 1958. Miles Davis: trumpet; Gil Evans: arrangement; John Coles, Bernie Glow, Ernie Royal, Louis Mucci: trumpets; Joe Bennett, Frank Rehak, Jimmy Cleveland: trombones; Dick Hixon: bass trombone; Willie Ruff, Julius Watkins, Gunther Schuller: French horns; Bill Barber: tuba; Julian "Cannonball" Adderley, Phil Bodner, Romeo Penque, Danny Bank: woodwinds; Paul Chambers: bass; Philly Joe Jones: drums.

In the 1950s, the most successful big band studio jazz was produced by the collaborative efforts of Miles Davis and the imaginative composer–arranger Gil Evans (b. 1912). Rather than continuing to adapt bop styles to a big band format, Evans and Davis experimented with the newer approaches of cool jazz and third stream music. In "Summertime" (SCCJ), written by George Gershwin, a very simple structural framework is animated by an excellent Miles Davis trumpet solo. The orchestra, large enough to project an unusually rich palette of sumptuous colors, features Evans's characteristic use of French horns, less often heard woodwinds (flutes, oboes, clarinets, bassoons, etc.), and tuba. The tuba and clarinets are not deployed in the soloistic New Orleans manner, but as integral members of the brass and woodwind choirs respectively.

Avoiding an introduction, which might have sounded pretentious in an arrangement with such literal sectional repetition, Evans begins by stating the melody itself, played with the harmon-muted trumpet sound for which Davis is famous. The 16-bar tune is accompanied by a 2-bar riff in the French horns that pervades the entire arrangement. Although the riff undergoes orchestral development, its modifications are so subtle that our attention is never distracted from the trumpet solo. In contrasting it to those of the swing style big bands, we find that Evans's riff is not based on the blues and is not syncopated. In bar 13 the riff is briefly interrupted, a pattern that is maintained for the rest of the arrangement.

After the 16-bar head, the remainder of this formally simple arrangement consists of four choruses of improvisation followed by a short tag. This tag features the accompanimental riff again, and then gracefully slows down into the final chord.

In the first and second choruses, flutes take up the riff in a lower, then a higher, register. Beginning with the second chorus, a new detail is added by the brass in mm. 14–16, where the riff undergoes a rhythmic development that sounds at first as if 2 beats or so were subtracted from the 16-bar strophe. This does not actually occur and can be verified by counting the beats and measures in the chorus.

In the third chorus the flutes return to a lower register. The fourth chorus features a solo entrance by the tuba playing low Bb's in the spaces between repetitions of the riff. At the end of this chorus, Davis finishes his solo just before the final tag. The constant use of the accompanying riff creates a seamless texture, almost hypnotic in its effect. In typical swing style big band performances, the arranger most often tries to vary the texture of every chorus to maximize variety. However, Gil Evans seems more concerned with successfully creating a consistent mood throughout the arrangement.

The performance as a whole is a fine example of cool jazz, with its understated quality throughout. The predominating feeling is one of detachment, albeit one within a lush setting, but still lacking the warmth of expression typical of a pop ballad. This feeling of detachment is enhanced by the hollow sound of Davis's muted trumpet, which was to become practically a cliché of cool jazz trumpet style.

The third stream features of the performance include the use of: (1) an atypically large ensemble; (2) instruments not often previously associated with jazz; (3) a very tight, formal arrangement, with every note precisely determined and performed; and (4) a "cool" execution of the accompanying, rhythmically square riff. The performing ensemble could be viewed as consisting of a "jazz unit," Davis and the rhythm section, and a "classical unit," the rest of the ensemble.

charles mingus: "hora decubitus"

Charles Mingus and His Orchestra: "Hora Decubitus," Impulse AS-9234-2, September 20, 1963. Charles Mingus: bass, Bob Hammer: arrangement; Eddie Preston, Richard Williams: trumpets; Britt Woodman: trombone; Don Butterfield: tuba; Eric Dolphy, Dick Haffer, Booker Ervin, Jerome Richardson: woodwinds; Jaki Byard: piano; Walter Perkins: drums.

Charles Mingus (1922–1979) was a fascinating jazz personality. Originally from Arizona, he was raised in the Watts section of Los Angeles. After paying his dues as a bass player and sideman with swing bands and bop groups, he evolved his own modern style in the 1950s, which led him to direct and write for his own groups. He was one of the very few bassists in jazz to contribute directly to the formation of a jazz substyle and a new way of thinking about music.

Much of Mingus's unique position in jazz derived from the individuality of his music. Formally designed, his writing borrowed ideas from free jazz, but tended to remain tonal, imbued with great consciousness of bop and older jazz styles, as well as the blues and other roots of Afro-American music. This historical awareness set him apart from many other avant-garde players who often wished to jettison traditional concepts wherever possible.

Throughout Mingus's career as a leader, he worked with both large and small ensembles, but the unique manner in which he handled a large band effected a new sound in jazz. Very often he avoided the use of a piano in his

Charles Mingus (Courtesy Institute of Jazz Studies, Rutgers University).

rhythm sections, a practice that allowed his own very strong, melodic, often contrapuntal bass playing to shine through.

"Hora Decubitus" (SCCJ) is a hybrid work, straddling traditional and free jazz quite adroitly. Mingus's bass introduction is characterized by alternating octaves and reveals the strength and sense of forward momentum that typified his playing. Throughout the performance, Mingus manages never to recede too far into the background by playing forceful and interesting bass lines.

Mingus's 12-bar introduction sets the tempo, harmony, and mood for the blues choruses that follow. The statement of the head consists of five ensemble choruses. The first chorus is a rifflike blues tune played on the baritone sax.

Though the rhythmic and melodic character of the tune is traditional, it borders on *atonality*.

For the second chorus, the baritone continues to play the theme, joined now by the other saxophones sometimes playing in unison but occasionally splitting into different parts. For the third chorus, a trombone is added, playing a counter-riff that often seems to clash with the saxophones, who meanwhile repeat their second chorus.

In the fourth chorus, an alto sax separates from the full sax section to add still another part, while the trombone and remaining saxophones repeat what they had played in the preceding chorus. For the last chorus of the head, a trumpet player joins the others with still another riff in counterpoint with the ongoing parts. This set of contrasting and competing lines remains traditional in its blues-riff orientation as well as in the marvelously cacophonous effect of everyone playing together.

The finish of the head leads directly to a traditional blues solo by tenor saxophonist Booker Ervin. At first reminiscent of gospel jazz, Ervin's solo finishes with the fleet, atonal runs that are somewhat more typical of free jazz. As accompaniment, the orchestra enters from time to time with background figures derived from the opening riffs of the head. On Ervin's last chorus, Mingus pushes the beat so forcefully that he almost seems to be ahead of the pulse.

After Ervin's statement, Eric Dolphy (1928-1964) sneaks in unobtrusively with a short alto saxophone solo. A leading player of the free jazz "school," Dolphy, like Mingus, combined a respect for tradition with a modern jazz sensibility. In this solo, for example, after beginning with the more "outside" melodic lines of free jazz, Dolphy returns to a more typical blues line, though, admittedly, many of his pitches still purposely avoid the chord changes. Meanwhile, Mingus briefly quotes his opening introductory statement in the middle of Dolphy's solo as if trying to forge together the disparate sections of the work. The other instruments freely enter with riffs and sharp punctuations as if to comment on Dolphy's solo.

A blazing trumpet solo by Richard Williams follows. Like most modern trumpet players interested in free jazz, he tries to get away from the bebop concept of improvisation, but a few bop licks can still be heard from time to time. The passionate cries he injects into the solo are both expressive and appropriate.

For the recapitulation of the head, some of the opening riffs are exchanged, that is, played by different groups of instruments. This section comprises three choruses in which the alto saxes lay out during the second. During the third chorus of the recapitulation, the main riff tune is played in unison, which lends a feeling of finality to this climactic ending of the performance.

The tag at the end of the piece consists of two chords that may be heard as echoing the IV-I "Amen" cadence heard in church music. On the first of these chords, the instruments freely interpolate runs and fills in the manner of a cadenza. The second chord is not so heavily scored, and as it dies out Mingus plays the last few notes himself, thus recalling his solo introduction.

Mingus's big band sound is distinctive and truly established a new direction for the large ensemble. Bob Hammer is listed as the arranger of "Hora Decubitus," but it seems likely that Mingus himself arranged the elaborate counterpointing blues riffs. Other band leaders, such as Sun Ra (b. 1928), have also developed ensembles that incorporate the spirit of Mingus's approach, and bridge the old and new quite successfully. Today, the big band ensemble continues to provide composers and arrangers the opportunity to experiment with fascinating combinations of instruments.

summary of jazz styles

To summarize the broad survey of small group and big band jazz undertaken in Chapters 4 and 5, I offer these capsule definitions of the major jazz styles:

New Orleans and Chicago dixieland (ca. 1920-1930)

Instrumentation: Small groups featuring three or four wind instruments—one or two cornets, clarinet, and trombone—and a rhythm section of piano, banjo, string bass or tuba, and drums.

Texture: Cornets play the lead, with trombone countermelody and clarinet obbligato. Much ensemble improvisation with occasional solos. Strophic forms. Simple harmony. Expressive playing—use of the blue notes, glissandos, and other special effects.

Rhythm: Hot rhythms, that is, jagged, syncopated, and driving, with underlying 4/4 or 2/4 beat. Rhythm section heavily accents the beat.

Pre-Swing Big Bands (ca. 1925-1930)

Instrumentation: Ensemble grouped into sections: two to three trumpets or cornets, three to four saxophones doubling on clarinet, one to two trombones, string bass or tuba, piano, guitar or banjo, drums.

Texture: Arranger provides structural organization, though often the players themselves devise head arrangements. Antiphonal writing among instrumental sections. Solo improvisation to contrast ensemble textures. Strophic forms. Use of riffs.

Rhythm: Heavy beat with all the rhythm instruments clearly articulating a 4/4 or 2/4 meter. Dixieland rhythms molded to the underlying beat.

Swing (ca. 1930-1945)

Instrumentation: Big band: three to five trumpets, three to five saxophones/clarinets, two to four trombones, piano, guitar, bass, and drums. Small band: one to four wind instruments, piano, guitar, bass, and drums.

Texture: Strophic forms. Improvisation to contrast ensemble textures. Antiphonal writing among instrumental sections. Popular-song heads. Elaborate arrangements and head arrangements. Use of riffs.

Rhythm: Use of swing beat, smoother feeling of forward momentum, time-keeping on ride and hi-hat cymbals, walking bass. Guitar and piano often keep time as well.

Bop (ca. 1940-1950)

Instrumentation: Big bands less frequent, but maintain instrumentation of swing big band. Small band of one to three wind instruments, piano, bass, drums, guitar, and possibly vibes. Quintet of trumpet, sax, piano, bass, and drums established.

Texture: Irregular phrase lengths. Use of jazz-tune heads that sound improvisational. Contrast of solo improvisation with ensemble. Jagged, angular melodies. Extended chord harmonies. Strophic forms. Use of riffs.

Rhythm: Tempos often extremely fast or very slow, not intended to be danceable. Even 4/4 beat articulated on ride cymbal with walking bass. Accents or "bombs" on snare and bass drum. Hi-hat often on beats 2 and 4. Use of Latin rhythms. Pianist feeds chords, does not keep a regular beat. Walking bass. Occasional addition of extra percussionist in big bands.

Cool and West Coast Jazz (ca. 1950-1960)

Instrumentation: Little use of big band. Small group: one to four wind instruments, piano, bass, drums, guitar, perhaps vibes.

Texture: Smooth, light chord voicings. Experimental, complex forms, simple strophic forms sometimes avoided. Breathy, light wind instrument playing, often with little vibrato. Solo improvisation to contrast ensemble. Use of space to contrast thicker textures. Incorporation of European fine-art characteristics.

Rhythm: Easier swing beats, often danceable tempos. Rhythm section maintains roles adopted during bop.

Modern Modal Jazz (ca. 1960-1970)

Instrumentation: Same as cool jazz.

Texture: Broad application of modal scales and techniques. Improvisation to contrast ensemble textures. Improvisation often freeform and modal rather than strophic. Irregular phrasing.

Rhythm: Rhythm section functions as in cool jazz, but complexity and speed may increase. Complex rhythms on drums, though sometimes underlying swing feel maintained.

Jazz-Rock (ca. 1970)

Instrumentation: Electric guitars, electric pianos, synthesizers, and electric bass guitars combined with the instruments heard in modern modal jazz. Typical group might contain one or two guitars, one keyboard player, one to four horns, bass guitar, drums, and percussion.

Texture: Rock ambience with amplified, high-volume, high-energy playing. Improvised solos to contrast ensemble. Nonstrophic modal improvising.

Ostinato bass lines sometimes doubled by guitar or keyboard. Tight playing. Occasional collective improvising.

Rhythm: Use of even eighth-notes and rock drum rhythms. Ostinato bass patterns. Extra percussionists.

Free Jazz (ca. 1959-)

Since I have not discussed a free jazz piece yet, the description of this style is reserved for the summaries at the end of Chapter 8.

The styles summarized above do not, of course, include all the jazz styles, but they are some of the most important ones. In the remainder of Part Two I will outline the harmonic, melodic, and rhythmic characteristics of various jazz improvisational styles, looking more closely at the individual musicians grouped according to their instruments. The chronological ordering should enable you to trace the vast stylistic and technical developments made by some of the most notable performers in jazz.

chapter
six

trumpet
styles

Since the 1930s, trumpet and saxophone have been two of the most important wind instruments in jazz. In the 1920s, however, the saxophone was less important, as the clarinet predominated in the dixieland ensemble, and the cornet was heard as often as the trumpet. During the course of the decade, however, trumpets replaced cornets and saxophones became as common as clarinets. Interestingly enough, the major innovators of melodic line solos in jazz improvisation have tended to be sax (or clarinet) and trumpet players, probably because horns, playing one note at a time, are intrinsically melodic. Pianists, although able to play single-line melodies, have been responsible for much of the harmonic evolution of jazz.

In early New Orleans and Chicago jazz, the cornet or trumpet, trombone, and clarinet were the melodic instruments while the piano, banjo, bass, and drums, constituting the rhythm section, remained mostly accompanimental. Moreover, the legendary, trendsetting New Orleans musicians such as Buddy Bolden, King Oliver, Bunk Johnson, and Freddie Keppard were all cornet players. In the 1920s, Louis Armstrong was by far the most influential jazz musician of the time. Bix Beiderbecke, another cornet player, was highly respected and widely copied, his melodic style eventually becoming a source of inspiration for cool jazz. Even the revolutionary piano style of Earl Hines has been often described, quite accurately, as Armstrong's cornet style adapted to the piano.

Once the swing era began, it was Armstrong, Coleman Hawkins, Lester Young, and Benny Goodman, all wind players, whose melodic styles influenced most everyone else. In the 1940s Dizzy Gillespie and Charlie Parker were the most prominent exponents of bop style, although they usually worked out their harmonic ideas on the piano. The cool improvisational style was launched by Miles Davis, influenced by Lester Young. The trends toward free jazz, modal jazz, and other modern styles in the 1960s were paced by Davis, Ornette Coleman, John Coltrane, and Sonny Rollins, all wind players. Although the genesis of jazz-rock centered around Miles Davis, only in that style can the melodic trendsetters be identified as nonhorn players, for example, keyboardists Chick Corea and Herbie Hancock and perhaps guitarist John McLaughlin.

Prior to jazz-rock, it can be argued that only pianist Thelonious Monk defined new melodic areas where the ground was not first broken by trumpet and sax players. Of course, piano players have always had the most significant influence on each other's keyboard styles, but only with Monk did his improvisational ideas establish melodic directions for nonpianists as well.

For most instruments there has been a conspicuous stylistic continuity through the course of jazz history that can be followed in considerable detail for each instrument. By "stylistic continuity," I mean that each new major player has extended the concepts and improvisational ideas of the previous major players. Most solo improvisation in jazz seems to develop quite naturally from the previous style. In proceeding through the history of each major jazz instrument, I will follow the most important stylistic innovations for each major instrument.

transcriptions

Some of the solos discussed in the next few chapters have been transcribed (see Transcriptions, pp. 231–259). Readers with the ability to follow music may wish to refer to these transcriptions from time to time. Further notes on the music sometimes accompany these transcriptions. In a transcription the music precedes the notation, whereas a written score directs the performer to produce a particular sound that is intended by the composer. Therefore, a score is **prescriptive** notation and a transcription is **descriptive** notation. In a transcription it is the music that came first, including unnotatable sounds and inflections and even such mistakes as wrong notes and unsteady rhythm. No transcription reproduces all that can be heard in a jazz solo; therefore, for practical purposes these transcriptions will merely pinpoint the notes referred to in the musical analysis, providing masterful solos as examples for further study. Although there is no theoretical restriction on the amount of information that can be included in transcriptions, the transcriptions found at the back of this book use the level of detail necessary for underscoring the comments at hand.

Please keep in mind that these transcriptions are intended only to be supplemental to the actual music itself. The inability to read music should in no way lessen the enjoyment you derive from the experience of listening.

The following system will be used to identify the specific measures or sections being discussed in multichorus solos:

Blues	AABA
C = chorus	C = chorus
m = measure	m = measure
	A = first A section
	A' = second A section
	A" = third A section
	B = B section

Chorus (C) and measure (m) will be followed by the appropriate arabic numeral. Therefore, for the blues, C2m4 means chorus 2, measure 4. For an AABA form, C3A'm7 means chorus 3, second A section, measure 7. In this way you will be able to compare the same bar occurring in different choruses and sections.

king oliver

Joe "King" Oliver was the only major cornet player whose playing may have resembled the jazz marching band styles common in New Orleans in the late nineteenth and early twentieth centuries. Oliver's style—very solid, though not especially adventurous in either range or technique, and occasionally staid—could never generate the kind of excitement soon to be heard in Louis Armstrong, yet at his best he fashioned solos that were quite compelling within their narrow emotional and technical boundaries. In fact, though admittedly lacking flash and bravura, some of his playing is exquisite. Although King Oliver's mastery of the cornet never quite reached the level of Louis Armstrong's, most of the older New Orleans musicians spoke of him as one of the best players of the day.

Oliver (1885-1938), born and raised in New Orleans, was working with brass bands and other groups at least as early as 1907. Among the prominent musicians who left New Orleans after the closing down of Storyville in 1917, Oliver settled in Chicago and formed the Creole Jazz Band. The band was a great success there and Oliver eventually hired Louis Armstrong, in 1922, to become his second cornet player. Armstrong himself credits Oliver with coaching his development during the early 1920s. Their joint recordings generally feature solos by Oliver, but Armstrong can frequently be heard poking through

(Left to right) Baby Dodds, Honoré Dutrey, King Oliver (seated), Bill Johnson, Louis Armstrong, Johnny Dodds, Lil Hardin Armstrong (Courtesy Institute of Jazz Studies, Rutgers University).

the instrumental texture with countermelodies and harmonizations of Oliver's lead line.

After the Creole Jazz Band was broken up in 1924, Oliver formed the popular Dixie Syncopators group, which continued to work in Chicago until 1927. Thereafter, Oliver's life declined tragically; bad health, especially pyorrhea, affected his ability to play. He intended to make a comeback, but died in poverty in 1938, practically forgotten.

Oliver's solo on "Dippermouth Blues" (SCCJ) is one of the most famous jazz improvisations of the 1920s. It is highly effective as a simple and orderly development of a single motive through three choruses of blues. Stated at the very beginning of the solo, this motive (M) consists of the syncopated presentation of the notes Db and Bb, the flat third (a blue note) and tonic pitches. The syncopation of M is effected by the placement of the notes before the downbeats. As an unstable blue note, the pitch of the "Db" often wavers between D and Db—for example, its frequency changes through the presentations of M in the first 4 bars of the solo.

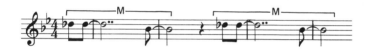

The simplicity of M as a motive is enhanced through the graceful logic with which Oliver retains it in various forms through the course of his solo. In fact, Oliver's three choruses develop progressively away from M, though M is always kept somewhere in view.

Oliver's solo builds masterfully in both register and intensity through its three choruses. The first chorus, rising no higher than Db, uses very little more than the three pitches, Db, C and Bb. In the second chorus the range is extended to a high F for the first 3 bars, but then returns to the Db-Bb range except for one high F toward the end of the chorus. The complex rhythm occurring at the beginning of the chorus is remarkable, anticipating the swing era emancipation of jazz rhythm from the heaviness of the beat.

Clarinetist Johnny Dodds takes over the melodic line momentarily, at the third chorus, and extends the high F to a G, a simple, but satisfying continuation. Oliver returns to end the solo with a renewed concentration on the opening pitches.

The pertinent factors characterizing Oliver's playing in "Dippermouth Blues" include: (1) predominant use of the cornet's middle range; (2) blues effects in which notes are bent and inflected; (3) a variety of note values and rhythms, so that one type of rhythm is not overemphasized; (4) simple, solid playing without technical flashiness; (5) concentration on playing pitches most closely related to chords in the head and the blues scale; (6) motivic structure with cumulative development; (7) fairly plain cornet tone; and (8) small but effective emotional range.

One mark of a great improvisation is that the careful listener does not lose his or her place in the solo in terms of its form. It is easier for an improviser to hold a listener's attention by always playing motivically. That many great popular songs consist of largely one motive (e.g., Gershwin's "I Got Rhythm" and "'S Wonderful") shows that such an approach can be lasting and effective, as long as the motive and its development are well executed. Oliver's solo on "Dippermouth Blues" is like such a song in its simplicity and melodic catchiness.

bix beiderbecke

> **Wolverine Orchestra: "Jazz Me Blues," Gennett 5408, February 18, 1924. Bix Beiderbecke, cornet; Al Grande, trombone; Jimmy Hartwell, clarinet and alto sax; George Johnson, tenor sax; Dick Voynow, piano; Bob Gillette, banjo; Min Leibrook, tuba; Vic Moore, drums.**

Whereas King Oliver's style foreshadows Louis Armstrong's, the style of Bix Beiderbecke, a most distinctive approach to the instrument, remains unique among the major trumpet/cornet players of the 1920s and 1930s. Derived from a more European concept of playing, Beiderbecke's methods were perhaps typical of white dance band trumpet players of the time; that is, a style with few blues inflections and little use of hot rhythm.

It is possible that Beiderbecke's lyrical elegance was developed more by saxophonists Lester Young and Johnny Hodges (1906-1970) than by the successive trumpet players who, dazzled by Armstrong's brilliance, tended to emulate the New Orleans style. In fact, the next major trumpet player whose playing can be clearly compared to Beiderbecke's is Bobby Hackett (1915-1976). Along with trombonist Jack Teagarden (1905-1964) and Armstrong himself, Hackett was a major figure in the dixieland revival of the late 1940s.

Beiderbecke had the misfortune of never playing with musicians of his own caliber. He performed with only three important bands during his short lifetime: the Wolverines and the groups of Frankie Trumbauer and Paul Whiteman. Beiderbecke's solos certainly are the focal point of the recordings by these ensembles.

Among solos remarkable for their elegance and simplicity, few rank higher than Beiderbecke's "Jazz Me Blues," from a 1924 recording of the Wolverines. Like Oliver's "Dippermouth Blues," no bar or even a single note could be changed without detracting from the lyrical quality of its melodic line. The technical performance is exquisite and confident, yet at the same time expresses a cool reticence captured by no other major trumpet player, except possibly Miles Davis some 30 years later.

Like "Dippermouth Blues," "Jazz Me Blues" opens with a motivic lick composed of two notes the interval of a minor third apart. No blue notes are involved in the first two bars, however, since the first blue note, an A♭ that is not heavily inflected, occurs during the break in mm.7-8. Moreover, unlike "Dippermouth

Bix Beiderbecke (Courtesy Institute of Jazz Studies, Rutgers University).

Blues," Beiderbecke does not concentrate on a single opening motive, but instead, without overtly repeating any single idea, opens new paths gradually from phrase to phrase.

While unfolding the melodic phrases, Beiderbecke discreetly refers to the original song in m.9. This reference fits the solo perfectly, is wholly contained within the logic of the phrase sequence, and does not interrupt the melodic development for the sake of a gratuitous quotation. In avoiding obvious motivic repetition, providing coherence by some other means becomes necessary. That is, the solo, to be truly convincing, must move from pitch to pitch, each new note and phrase progressing from the preceding ones in such a manner that the listener is not jolted by clumsy and unintentional continuations. An important technique for providing coherence, heard in almost all tonal music, is **voice leading,** whose basic principle is **step connection.**

In step connection, pitches are thought to proceed naturally to other pitches a half or whole step away in the associated scale of the harmony. This principle is derived from the natural tendency for sung melodies to proceed mostly, though not exclusively, by step. (The melodies in Gregorian chant, for example, one of the oldest European musical traditions, proceed largely by step.)

Pitches that have no stepwise connection to succeeding pitches are often considered to be left hanging. In a solo or melody that employs classical voice leading, few if any pitches are left hanging for long. In particular, chord tones, pitches that are included in the prevailing harmony, are often followed in the next chord change by stepwise related chord tones.

"Jazz Me Blues" exhibits ingenious use of voice leading to provide the listener with a sense of coherence in lieu of obvious motivic development. An impression of clear voice leading is often obtained from a work when its overall development is smooth and no pitches seem out of place. (For a transcription and further notes on "Jazz Me Blues," please see pages 232-233.)

Beiderbecke's performance is both a brilliant solo on its own terms as well as representative of certain aspects of his general style: (1) concentration on the middle register; (2) a lyrical, mellow tone; (3) rhythmic variety; (4) extreme subtlety of melodic continuation; (5) restrained use of blue notes; (6) small but compelling emotional compass; (7) little use of vibrato; and (8) "inside" playing.

Every aspect of Beiderbecke's performance contributes to the overall effect of the melodic line he improvises. His liquid tone rolls effortlessly and confidently from phrase to phrase: the high F in m. 7 is articulated perfectly with just the right amount of emphasis. The final F of the solo is so satisfying because it is prepared both by the syncopation of the preceding phrase and by the voice leading lines stretching through the entire solo. Beiderbecke's slight accent on this pitch and his continuation of it for seven full beats close out the solo without unnecessary or meretricious showiness. Combining perfect structural balance, thoughtfulness, and cool emotional projection, Beiderbecke's "Jazz Me Blues" is one of the greatest cornet solos of the 1920s.

louis armstrong

Surpassing both the simple assertiveness of Oliver and the cool elegance of Beiderbecke, Louis Armstrong's devil-may-care brilliance epitomizes the sound of jazz in the 1920s. His dominating presence can be heard in almost every jazz trumpet style since.

Armstrong, perhaps the most influential jazz musician ever, helped transform the emphasis in jazz from the group as a whole to the individual improvisations. His technical ability raised the level and sophistication of jazz performance dramatically, and, as an outstanding entertainer aside from his brilliant playing, he interested the whole world in jazz. While Armstrong's excellence as a trumpet and cornet player dominated instrumental jazz in the 1920s, his development of scat singing (the use of his voice as an instrument like the trumpet) influenced numerous important jazz vocalists.

Louis Armstrong (Courtesy Institute of Jazz Studies, Rutgers University).

Much of Armstrong's greatest playing can be heard on his recordings from the 1920s, when his youthful, impetuous virtuosity was tempered with the clear thought of a well-seasoned musician. During these years he was still playing in the classic New Orleans ensemble of his youth. Later, Armstrong would favor performing with big bands.

Although Armstrong's traditional birthdate has been given as July 4, 1900, he may have been born some years earlier. Raised in New Orleans by his mother, he was eventually arrested at the age of 13 and sent to the Colored Waifs Home where he was taught how to play the cornet. Armstrong was fortunate to meet King Oliver in 1918 and was encouraged by the older musician to continue developing his cornet playing. For several years Armstrong played in Kid Ory's Band, replacing Oliver, after which he left New Orleans for Chicago to join his mentor's Creole Jazz Band in 1922. Armstrong's reputation spread as a result of the Creole Jazz Band recordings in 1923.

Armstrong resigned from Oliver's band in 1924 and soon departed for New York to become the solo cornetist with Fletcher Henderson's orchestra. Shortly thereafter Armstrong returned to Chicago where he led the famous Hot Five and Hot Seven studio recordings that established him as a star.

In 1928 he recorded with the Carroll Dickerson band, a larger ensemble, and for the next two decades he appeared primarily as the soloist in his own big band. Capitalizing on the New Orleans (dixieland) revival in the late 1940s, he returned to the small ensemble format, making many fine records with trombonist Jack Teagarden and others. For the remainder of his life, Armstrong was honored as a great musician and entertainer throughout the world. He died on July 6, 1971.

Despite the many great performances throughout his lifetime, Armstrong rarely surpassed the superb playing heard on the Hot Five and Hot Seven recordings. Among them is the great 1928 recording of "West End Blues" (SCCJ). (See Chapter 4 for further discussion of this recording. Also, see pp. 234–235 for a transcription of Armstrong's solo.) The flashy exuberance of Armstrong's solos dramatically contrasts the playing of the rest of the group, but remains effective because of its structural and emotional affinity with the song itself.

The references to motive M (F♯-G-B♭), the association of the C and B♭ pitches, and the repetition of the triplets in the first chorus connect the solo sections together quite remarkably. By avoiding literal repetition Armstrong always seems to be moving forward; he finds new variations on previous figures, different ways of developing the material at hand.

Armstrong's general stylistic traits observable in "West End Blues" include: (1) exuberant, fiery tone; (2) use of the full range of the trumpet; (3) blues inflections; (4) impetuous, emotional projection; (5) perfectly balanced range of rhythmic values (long notes vs. short notes); (6) ingenious, subtly motivic melodic connections; (7) wide *vibrato*, especially at the end of held notes; and (8) "inside" playing with use of blues scale.

A perusal of the best improvisations of the great jazz soloists reveals relatively few licks repeated in a similar context from solo to solo. Armstrong had the ability to present a staggering variety of motivic material, even within a single solo. Yet, while careful listening may reveal several evolving patterns of coherence, the impression remains one of continually shifting ideas. For these reasons, Armstrong's brilliance and inventiveness, continually inspiring to all jazz trumpet players, single him out as one of the greatest improvisers of all time.

roy eldridge

Roy Eldridge and Benny Carter: "I Can't Believe that You're in Love with Me," Atlantic SD2-306, May 25, 1940. Roy Eldridge, trumpet; Benny Carter, alto sax; Coleman Hawkins, tenor sax; Bernard Addison, guitar; John Kirby, bass; Sidney Catlett, drums.

Roy Eldridge (b. 1911) is probably the greatest of the swing trumpet players. With both vigor and impulsiveness, his debt to Armstrong is clear, even if he tends to lack Armstrong's surprising motivic twists. In turn, Eldridge influenced such greats as Dizzy Gillespie, who adapted the elder's basic style to bop. (Interestingly enough, one of Gillespie's major breaks came when he was hired by the Teddy Hill band because he sounded so much like Eldridge.)

Eldridge, originally from Pittsburgh, worked with several local bands before establishing himself as a major trumpet player in the early 1930s. Although he has led his own groups, he performed with many other bands as well throughout his long career, perhaps most memorably with Fletcher Henderson and Gene Krupa. He has also worked with Artie Shaw and Benny Goodman, while playing on some of the Teddy Wilson small group sessions with Billie Holiday. He has continued to be active, appearing at jazz festivals and on recording sessions right into the 1980s.

As much as one can hear Eldridge in Dizzy Gillespie's playing, one can hear Armstrong in the tone and sound of Eldridge. Such was the domination of this trio of trumpeters throughout the 1930s and 1940s that few players deviated from the basic stylistic patterns they developed. Miles Davis, in the early 1950s, was perhaps the first major trumpet player to devise a totally different approach to the instrument.

Eldridge's two-chorus solo on "I Can't Believe that You're in Love with Me" (SCCJ), rivals Armstrong's playing in inventive melodic connections. Throughout the solo we hear Eldridge's use of ghosted pitches. The effect renders the surrounding notes more prominent, imparting to them a great deal of swing.

As is usual in the eighth-note melodic lines of swing and bop, continuity is based mostly on voice leading through the changes and large-scale balance among the melodic gestures. The latter quality is evident throughout Eldridge's solo: high register is juxtaposed with low, long phrases with short, and louder passages with softer. From time to time, motivic relationships will unite longer lines and shorter, more rhythmic passages. Eldridge often applies Armstrong's ending vibrato on longer notes, generally those lasting for 2 beats or so. Also like Armstrong, Eldridge will sometimes introduce a brassy, rasping sound into his tone to heighten the excitement.

Eldridge's style can be summarized as follows: (1) brilliant, full tone; (2) smaller range of rhythmic values than 1920s trumpeters, with more reliance on eighth-notes; (3) concentration on middle and upper range of instrument; (4) vibrato on ends of notes; (5) some blues inflections; (6) emotional playing, but greater reliance on technical display; (7) good melodic connections but not as varied motivically as Armstrong, and more reliance on voice leading; and (8) "inside" playing.

Great subtlety and control of voice leading can be followed throughout "I Can't Believe that You're in Love with Me." Such continuity, supported by a balance of melodic contour and gesture, is often responsible for the feeling of cohesion in a solo that otherwise might seem to lack clear motivic structure.

Eldridge plays with the confidence we heard in Beiderbecke and Armstrong, always seeming to know in advance where the solo is going. He likes to start many of his phrases around the third beat, with or without syncopation. Most of his phrases end on the first or third beats. Eldridge's note bending is reminiscent of Armstrong's, a technique that becomes less pronounced in uptempo bop style. Most importantly, Eldridge plays with a beautiful, flowing swing line, full of passion, but governed by thought.

dizzy gillespie

> Dizzy Gillespie's All Star Quintet: "Shaw 'Nuff," Prestige P-24030, May 11, 1945. Dizzy Gillespie, trumpet; Charlie Parker, alto sax; Al Haig, piano; Curley Russell, bass; Sidney Catlett, drums.

After several years of emulating Roy Eldridge's swing style, John Birks "Dizzy" Gillespie established a reputation as the first bop trumpet player. Both technically and emotionally, his playing epitomized the new approach to the instrument. Among the innovators of bop, Gillespie along with Charlie Parker founded a revolutionary improvisational style with greater emphasis on virtuosity, even rhythms, and a more angular melodic contour. As was pointed out in the last two chapters, bop style tended to avoid songlike melody and smooth dance rhythms, even in the performances of slower pieces.

Gillespie was born in 1917 in Cheraw, S.C. After playing with various swing bands throughout the 1930s and early 1940s, including groups led by Teddy Hill and Cab Calloway, Gillespie began experimenting with bop. He met Charlie Parker during the early 1940s. In 1944 both musicians joined the Billy Eckstine band, which soon began to stimulate interest in the new music.

Once Gillespie had established his reputation with Parker in a small group

Dizzy Gillespie (Courtesy Institute of Jazz Studies, Rutgers University).

setting, he formed his own big band in 1946, proving that bop could be performed by a large group in a dancehall environment. By this time, he had become one of the best known jazz musicians in America. For the rest of his career
he has continued to play throughout the world in clubs and concert halls and
at jazz festivals with both small and large jazz groups.

As I pointed out in Chapter 3, many bop tunes are composed on the changes
of popular songs. Among the most popular of these are the chord changes
based on Gershwin's "I Got Rhythm," hence their nickname *rhythm changes*. The
changes are so simple, logical, and adaptable that improvising musicians
have been using them since the song was first written. These accessible chords
can be modified without disrupting the overall thrust of the harmonic progression. "Shaw 'Nuff" (SCCJ) is a tune composed on rhythm changes.

This performance, one of the earliest bop recordings, features solos by both Gillespie and Parker, both of which typify the new style. (Gillespie's solo is presented at the end of this book under Transcriptions.) Gillespie begins characteristically and dramatically with a shrieking high note. This striking opening grabs the listener's attention away from the end of the previous Parker solo. Afterward, a long rest lets the listener, as well as the trumpet player, recover before a lengthy phrase is begun which completes the first A section of the tune with a string of eighth-notes broken up by one triplet figure. This phrase ends the A section with a figure, Bb–F, that is heard frequently in bop solos and helped give the new style the name bebop.

The A′ section also consists of a single phrase broken up from time to time by ghosted pitches. Ghosting provides an element of rhythmic variety in the lengthy bop and swing phrases dominated almost entirely by eighth-notes. The second A section, like the first, ends with the bebop figure. The bridge begins with the only simple melodic phrase of the solo. This phrase is placed in the high register and makes use of the extended-chord tones often heard in bop solos.

Gillespie's long phrases in "Shaw 'Nuff" relate to each other more in their shape than in their motivic content. Moreover, the phrases sound all the more spontaneous whenever they begin and end on unexpected parts of the measure. In this solo all of the phrases start very high, descend to the lower register, then ascend to the trumpet's upper range. The large-scale shape of descending long phrases can be heard often in bop improvisations, including many solos of both Gillespie and Parker.

Gillespie's style echoes much bop melodic playing in its use of the following elements: (1) angular melodic lines made up largely of eighth-notes; (2) less rhythmic variety because of the eighth-note emphasis; (3) phrases of irregular length; (4) long phrases that may complete a section or more of a chorus; (5) use of extended and chromatic extended chord tones; (6) lack of vibrato in uptempo playing; (7) emotional though virtuosic playing; (8) emphasis on middle and high range of instrument; (9) melodic continuity based on voice leading and large-scale phrasing; (10) deemphasis of motive structure, at least in uptempo playing; (11) few blues inflections in uptempo playing; and (12) more adventurous chord-scale associations.

clifford brown

> Clifford Brown-Max Roach Quintet: "I'll Remember April," from *At Basin Street*, Trip TLP-5511, 1956. Clifford Brown, trumpet; Sonny Rollins, tenor sax; Richie Powell, piano; George Morrow, bass; Max Roach, drums.

Clifford Brown (1930-1956) was a tremendously talented bop and *hard bop* (or "postbop") trumpet player. Although his tragic death in an automobile accident at the age of 26 cut short a very promising career, his recorded legacy establishes him as one of the great trumpet players in jazz. Brown, originally from Wilmington, Del., worked mostly in the Philadelphia and New York areas. In 1953 he toured Europe with Lionel Hampton's band and made several records there. Just prior to his death, he co-led a group with drummer Max Roach and was considered one of the most talented hard bop players.

Brown's technique was based on the running eighth-note style of bop, but with a very personal, intimate sound that is arguably warmer than Gillespie's. Brown's playing emphasizes clean technique, a wide variety of articulations, and a satisfying, logical progression of thought throughout his solos. Among his many strengths, most prominent is his nonreliance on previously composed licks; instead, each Brown solo seems to weave paths of eighth-notes that were never before played. Even Parker and Gillespie can be faulted more than Brown for overreliance on favorite patterns.

Brown's early death is all the more unfortunate because his stylistic development had not yet fully matured. As bop became gradually less fashionable in the late 1950s and early 1960s, had Brown lived, he may have struck off in new and fascinating directions, perhaps combining his brilliant bop technique with the earthier playing of the gospel jazz musicians or the modal styles of Coltrane and Davis.

Brown did his best work with the quintet co-led by him and the outstanding drummer Max Roach. Eventually the quintet included tenor saxophonist Sonny Rollins, who contributed some excellent solos. Among their finest recordings is "I'll Remember April," which features a great, stylistically typical solo by Brown in which his debt to Gillespie is clear. The tune itself is formally atypical, an ABA with 16 measures per section.

Long strings of eighth-notes are threaded throughout the solo, but they are interspersed with shorter but more compact passages. Also evident in Brown's solo is his use of the entire range of the trumpet, including even the lowest notes, a difficult technique because the **embouchure** (the positioning of the mouth and lips on the mouthpiece) preferred by many jazz trumpeters tends to favor the upper register. Brown's high range is very strong but in this solo, as in his style generally, he does not indulge in gratuitous high notes just to show off his range.

In general, the overall structure of the improvisation is largely projected by the voice leading and by the delicate gestural balance between the phrases. As in many uptempo bop solos, obvious motivic relationships are avoided. Another feature of most of Brown's solos, evident here, is the use of a conclusive *cadence* to the improvisation. The final measures of the solo provide a satisfying sense of resolution to the complex working out of the voice-leading patterns.

These items summarize the essentials of Brown's uptempo style as heard in "I'll Remember April": (1) angular melodic lines of eighth-notes; (2) irregular phrase lengths extending from short to extremely long; (3) full use of the trumpet range; (4) no gratuitous technical gestures; (5) emotionally involved playing; (6) little use of blues inflections on uptempo tunes; (7) rich, full tone; (8) little rhythmic variety; (9) melodic continuity based on good voice leading; (10) little reliance on previously worked out licks; and (11) "inside" playing, with chord-scale associations generally conservative.

Brown extends Gillespie's work by his exquisite balance of phrase, his choice of articulations, his full use of the trumpet range, and his always logical development based on voice leading, phrase balance, and variation in register. Brown avoids the mechanical feeling of some bop improvisers by allying much personal expression to his commanding technique.

miles davis

Bop trumpet styles reached the peak of virtuosity with such players as Dizzy Gillespie and Clifford Brown. Not surprisingly, new directions were sought by the trumpeters of the cool era whose leading player was Miles Davis. Other trumpet players who received wide acclaim, like Chet Baker, have been historically outdistanced by Davis who not only achieved reasonable bop fluidity in his best 1940s recordings with Charlie Parker, but also went on to develop other jazz styles.

Davis was born in 1926 in East St. Louis, Ill. In his early career he seemed blessed with the ability to meet the right people at the right time. For example, he met Charlie Parker by sitting in briefly with the Earl Hines band in 1944. After graduating from high school Davis left for New York to study at the Juilliard School of Music. Instead of pursuing fine-art trumpet playing, however, Davis began to frequent jazz clubs, eventually dropping out of Juilliard and befriending Parker and most of the important bop musicians. Though Davis could scarcely approximate Parker's technical proficiency, he was asked by Parker to join his quintet, evidence that the alto saxophonist heard potential in the younger musician. Davis went on to cut several records with Parker and other bop players.

In the late 1940s Davis joined arranger Gil Evans and saxophonist Gerry Mulligan in a large-scale recording project now known as the "Birth of the Cool." Davis has since become one of the most acclaimed jazz musicians in the world, and has led his own bands, generally quintets and sextets, playing cool and modal jazz in the 1950s and 1960s, then jazz-rock in the late 1960s and early 1970s.

The trumpet styles examined so far reveal an evolutionary trend toward greater density and rhythmic evenness, especially in the eighth-note oriented efforts of bop. Arguably, bop sacrifices the range of expression achievable with the use of more varied rhythms and, to be sure, the efforts of many less talented bop soloists tend to be monotonously mechanical.

Overt reaction against bop helped lead to the development of the cool style, which, though occasionally monotonous in its own way, imparts a feeling of sensitivity drawn from a fewer number of blues-inflected, sometimes hesitantly

Miles Davis (Courtesy Institute of Jazz Studies, Rutgers University).

played, notes. Miles Davis's solo on "So What" (SCCJ), a masterpiece featuring his style in transition, combines elements of cool with the emerging modal style that became popular in the 1960s. (For a transcription of Davis's solo on "So What," see pp. 237–238.)

In modal playing, the rapid chord changes heard in swing and bop are usually avoided. Instead, longer harmonic areas, based on modes are substituted. A mode is a scale that is used to define a harmonic area and provide a set of pitches for melodic construction. For example, as mentioned in Chapter 2, the dorian mode is a popular jazz scale.

As I pointed out in Chapter 3, the dorian scale is thought by jazz musicians to be associated with a minor-seventh chord constructed on the first degree of the scale. D dorian thus implies the harmony D–F–A–C, a Dm7 chord. By extending the chord with the ninth, eleventh, and thirteenth, a Dm13 chord results, D-F-A-C-E-G-B, that includes all the pitches of the mode. This chord and various arrangements of it, especially arrangements in fourths, provide the harmonic basis for melodic improvisations in D dorian.

In comparing this solo to the Brown or Gillespie examples from the previous sections, the greater use of space is quite evident. The frequent rests (measured silences) and the longer note values separate the phrases from one another. Much of the sense of hesitation and searching in the solo comes from beginning and ending the phrases on weak beats (**off-beats**). Two important exceptions to this tendency consist of the first and last phrases, both of which end with a squarely placed tonic D on the downbeat, as if to emphasize the formal boundaries of the solo. Throughout the solo, Davis fashions his melodies from the pitches of the appropriate D or Eb dorian scale, yet occasionally he changes the mode just in anticipation of the section boundary.

On many pitches a half-valve effect can be heard, a prominent feature of Davis's style. In producing a half-valve effect, one or more trumpet valves are depressed only halfway; this technique partially blocks the flow of the air stream and results in a peculiarly muffled, slightly flattened note. Davis features this device on many cool and modern solos in the 1950s and 1960s. Moreover, the slides between pitches, into pitches, and away from pitches help enhance the expressiveness that has always characterized Davis's slower playing.

Although Davis has undergone various style changes throughout his career, the following items summarize his cool/early modern playing: (1) sensitive melodic lines with frequent blues inflections; (2) irregular phrase length; (3) wide range of note values; (4) use of space between phrases; (5) concentration on mid-range of trumpet; (6) full but reticent tone (especially obvious in his playing with harmon mute); (7) melodic connections based on motives and large-scale gestures; (8) sensitive yet cool expression; (9) little reliance on previously composed licks; and (10) "inside" playing, using conservative chord-scale associations.

"So What" is effective because it so artfully combines tentativeness of phrase structure, use of long pitches, and frequent rests between phrases with a dynamic, large-scale plan of building to climactic eleventh chords in the final B and A sections. Davis's mastery of his material, his looseness, and his strong personal style are all responsible for his continued popularity for the past 30 years.

chapter
seven

woodwind
styles

The important improvisatory styles of the major jazz woodwinds, the alto and tenor saxophones and the clarinet, will be examined in this chapter. Because many woodwind players play both sax and clarinet to at least some extent, the improvisational styles on these instruments have mutually influenced each other.

coleman hawkins

Coleman Hawkins and His Orchestra: "Body and Soul," Victor 20-2539, October 11, 1939; Coleman Hawkins, tenor sax; Tommy Lindsay, Joe Guy, trumpets; Earl Hardy, trombone; Jackie Fields, Eustis Moore, alto saxes; Gene Rodgers, piano; William Oscar Smith, bass; Arthur Herbert, drums.

Although tenor saxophone, along with trumpet and alto sax, eventually became one of the three most important horns in jazz, it was used far less frequently as a jazz solo instrument during the 1920s, when the New Orleans and Chicago styles were in vogue. It seems likely that use of the saxophone in jazz probably evolved from prior use in the dance orchestras and marching bands of the early part of the century.

The first important tenor sax soloist was Coleman Hawkins. The history of his style reveals the crossover from the heavier, dance orchestra method of playing to the lighter, more understated method of sound production that was to gain favor in the 1930s and 1940s.

Hawkins (1904-1969) was born in St. Joseph, Mo., and rose to prominence as the acclaimed tenor sax soloist with the Fletcher Henderson orchestra in the 1920s. Throughout his early tenure with Henderson, he strove for the big booming sound we first heard on "The Stampede" (SCCJ). Hawkins's syncopations on that solo recall the dixieland style of Armstrong, who had recently been performing with Henderson's band, but at this point lacked the trumpeters ease and sure sense of swing.

After leaving Henderson in 1934, Hawkins played with many groups, several of them overseas. Just as Europe seemed likely to plunge into another world war, Hawkins returned to America in 1939 and recorded his great performance of "Body and Soul," the record that established his fame. Hawkins was to spend the remainder of his life playing recording sessions, participat-

Coleman Hawkins (Courtesy Institute of Jazz Studies, Rutgers University).

ing in Jazz at the Philharmonic Tours, and working with many different jazz artists.

The unified large-scale effect of Hawkins's solo on "The Stampede" is created by the various arpeggiated patterns, the syncopations, and the repeated notes and half-step figures, variations of which occur throughout the solo. By slapping the mouthpiece with his tongue, Hawkins produces particularly sharp single-note articulations. This technique, slap-tonguing, unsuitable for smooth, eighth-note lines, rapidly lost favor among saxophonists during the swing era. The stolid, syncopated patterns repeated throughout the solo, although fitting nicely into the heavy beat of the tuba-banjo rhythm section, were soon to be considered corny by other jazz musicians.

The mature style of Coleman Hawkins can be heard on "Body and Soul" (SCCJ). There, Hawkins achieves dramatic stylistic contrast by reducing the edginess of his sound and the insistence of his articulations while maintaining his full-bodied tone. The romantic, understated eloquence of "Body and Soul" remains unimpeded throughout, even by the forceful phrases in the last part of the second chorus. Indeed, much of the structural and emotive brilliance of this solo derives from the uninterrupted melodic surge to the climactic statement of the C2A" section.

The syncopated figures that pervade the solo are at once more complex and less heavy-handed than in "The Stampede." In part, these syncopations, floating above the beat, murmur rather than hammer the rhythm. Syncopations such as sixteenth-eighth-sixteenth, heard for example toward the end of the C1A section and in C1A' m3, are liquid rather than martial. Unaccented patterns, as in C2Bm7, hover freely above the beat, only tenuously connected to it.

The delicacy of Hawkins's interpretation is reinforced by the extremely uneven phrase lengths, which are frequently out of phase with the customary subdivisions of the standard song form. That is, Hawkins almost never phrases with the 2-bar groupings of the original tune, but instead constantly varies the phrase lengths as well as their starting and ending points relative to these groupings. This practice cuts against the grain of the form and meter, increasing the effect of a contemplative melodic line. And the effect is not overdone, since it remains counterbalanced both by the buildup to the climax toward the end of the second chorus and by the solo's recurring motives.

The following items summarize the important features of Hawkins's later style as heard in "Body and Soul": (1) sensitive, smoothly articulated melodies; (2) complex melodic connections based on motivic development and voice leading; (3) rich, sensuous tone; (4) loose, free phrasing over the beat, with irregular phrase lengths; (5) emotional expression; (6) large variety of note values; (7) use of entire range of the instrument; (8) "inside playing" with clear chord-scale associations.

The gradual freeing of rhythmic dependence on the beat was important in the evolution of both trumpet and saxophone styles, from 1920s Chicago style to swing. This transition is especially clear in Hawkins's ballad improvisation. Moreover, the actual concept of tone production on the saxophone had changed. No such evolution occurred on the trumpet, as Armstrong had far too great an influence on succeeding players for them to deviate much from his standard.

benny goodman

Benny Goodman Quartet: "Avalon," Victor 25644, July 30, 1937. Benny Goodman, clarinet; Lionel Hampton, vibes; Teddy Wilson, piano; Gene Krupa, drums.

Benny Goodman (Courtesy Institute of Jazz Studies, Rutgers University).

Of all jazz clarinet styles, none has ever achieved the popularity of Benny Goodman's easygoing, swinging melodiousness. Goodman's style features a suave, songlike sweetness, exquisite sense of timing, and underlying structure masked by melodic and rhythmic accessibility. In the 1930s, Goodman's clarinet playing, and swing improvisation in general, captured the mood of the public so accurately that no other clarinet style has been able to replace it. Goodman remains one of the premier swing musicians and clarinet stylists in jazz.

Goodman (b. 1909) began his jazz career with bands in the Chicago area. Soon he was performing as a sideman with Red Nichols, and Ben Pollack in the late 1920s and early 1930s. His own big band, organized in 1934, achieved stardom after a legendary performance at the Palomar Ballroom in Los Angeles, in August of 1935. Shortly thereafter, he became known as "the king of swing," leading perhaps the most successful big band of all time.

Goodman's popularity in the 1930s led to numerous big band recordings, many of them quite excellent, but much of his best playing can be heard in small group performances, including his trio, quartet, and sextet, and with pickup bands for record dates. Goodman was more likely to attempt an adventurous solo within the more flexible small band than in the 8- or 16-bar slot of a big band arrangement.

Goodman is credited with being the first important white musician to hire blacks, specifically pianist Teddy Wilson, then later vibraphonist Lionel Hampton and guitarist Charlie Christian. Before racially mixed bands could be seen publicly, however, blacks and whites often played together on studio recordings, such as the performance of "I Found a New Baby" (discussed in Chapter 4). Although Goodman featured Wilson, Hampton, and Christian as soloists within his larger big band in the late 1930s, racially mixed groups were rarely seen until the 1950s.

The swinging small group recording of "I Found a New Baby" presents a Goodman solo that is somewhat more restrained than usual. To re-create a jam session atmosphere and produce a coherent recording at the same time, all within three minutes, it was necessary to balance the expressive ranges of the competing solos. Accordingly, Goodman's contribution fits perfectly, sparking a slightly diabolical mood for the performance as a whole.

On the Goodman quartet recording of "Avalon," however, Goodman plays one of his greatest solos. Listening to this improvisation, one is struck by the simplicity of Goodman's ideas and his unhurried, sure sense of direction at every moment, a manner that recalls the styles of Beiderbecke and Eldridge. There are no long periods of silence during the "Avalon" solo, but the exquisitely timed spaces between the phrases insure that its cool overall tone will not be cluttered by excessive material. Throughout the solo, the lack of small-scale motivic coherence is counterbalanced by the interconnections of the voice leading on various levels. (For a transcription of "Avalon" and further notes on the voice leading, see pp. 239–240.)

Contributing to the Goodman elegance are the following features: (1) supple melody characterized by few large skips within a phrase, and frequent arpeggiation and use of scale fragments; (2) a basic eighth-note rhythm; (3) limited space between phrases; (4) lyrical tone; (5) use of the entire range of the instrument; (6) avoidance of blues effects; (7) melodic connections based on voice leading; (8) cool expression occasionally contrasted by fast vibrato; (9) slightly irregular phrase lengths; and (10) "inside" playing, with unambitious scale-chord relationships.

A quintessential swing stylist, Goodman displays most of the qualities associated with that era, particularly smoothness of melodic line. This important swing characteristic is perhaps more easily achieved by the avoidance of obvious motivic referents which, when not executed well, seem heavy-handed.

lester young

Lester Young inspired the new style of jazz saxophone playing heard in the early 1930s possibly more than any other single artist. Even his early recordings seem free of the heavy, beat oriented syncopation of 1920s hot jazz playing.

Previously, I pointed out the dramatic shift in Coleman Hawkins's tone and melodic rhythm that took place between the 1920s and the 1930s. Young's sound, already lighter and more fluid in the 1920s, probably influenced Hawkins to change his style. More generally, the new looser concept of improvisation, characterized by Young and the other Kansas City musicians, helped propel the evolution of jazz toward swing in the late 1920s.

From Woodville, Mo., Young (1909-1959) began his musical career as a drummer playing for his father's carnival shows before later switching to tenor sax for more serious work with other bands. After gaining experience in the Midwest, he eventually joined the Kansas City band of Bennie Moten (1894-1935) in 1933. Young performed with Moten and various other groups until joining Basie from 1936 until 1940. Many of the great sessions with Billie Holiday and others were recorded during this period.

Unsuccessful as a leader of his own bands, Young recorded with pianist and singer Nat King Cole in the early 1940s and was drafted in 1944. After returning to civilian life, Young was unable to recapture the consistency of his great swing playing, although several fine records of his later work can be heard.

Young received his greatest acclaim as a star soloist with the Count Basie band. Despite Young's unsuccessful efforts to make it on his own, his recorded legacy with Basie, Holiday, and others is extensive, containing many exceptional solos. Young devises a typically fine improvisation on Basie's "Doggin' Around" (SCCJ), a tune harmonically structured on a variant of rhythm changes. (For a transcription of Young's solo on "Doggin' Around," see p. 241.)

Young achieves a remarkably fragile balance among the contrasting motivic elements. Throughout we can hear unlikely transitions among swinging eighth-note lines, blues-inflected slower pitches suspended over the beat, repeated em-

Lester Young (Courtesy Institute of Jazz Studies, Rutgers University).

phasis on single pitches, and smooth runs up to accented pitches that form a descending line. Additionally, Young's melodic voice leading unites these elements so that even when a change of mood occurs the new pitches have been prepared by the preceding harmonies.

From Young's performance on "Doggin' Around," we can infer the following aspects of his style: (1) "bluesy" melodies with rhythmic variety in contrast to eighth-note swing lines; (2) light, airy tone; (3) use of space between phrases; (4) irregular phrase lengths; (5) melodic connections based on motivic contrast and voice leading; (6) concentration on middle range of instrument; (7) cool expression; and (8) "inside" playing, with chord-scale relationships sometimes implying blues scales.

Young's unique manner of playing critically affected the development of cool sax styles, notably those of Stan Getz, Gerry Mulligan, Paul Desmond, and Lee Konitz. Young also influenced Charlie Parker quite decisively, particularly in his use of irregular phrase lengths, swinging eighth-note lines, motivic contrast, and incorporation of blues inflections.

charlie parker

Charlie Parker was possibly the greatest, most consistently brilliant jazz improviser of all time. Parker's overall influence on jazz history even equaled Arm-

Charlie Parker (Courtesy Institute of Jazz Studies, Rutgers University).

strong's; both players generated a major jazz style while, at the same time, radically increasing the level of technical proficiency associated with their instruments.

Parker (1920-1955) was born in Kansas City, Mo. and, like most jazz players everywhere, worked his way through various local bands. In the early 1940s he joined Jay McShann's (b. 1909) orchestra where his playing reflected his admiration of Lester Young's style (hints of which can be heard on Parker's occasional tenor sax recordings). In the early 1940's, Parker worked in Harlem, developing bop with several other musicians including Dizzy Gillespie and Thelonious Monk. For the duration of the 1940s and the early 1950s, Parker played with various bop oriented ensembles, often including Dizzy Gillespie or Miles Davis.

Unfortunately, Parker's personal life was tragic, frought with alcoholism and drug addiction. Never fully appreciated by the public until late in his life, Parker refused to compromise his music in any way or affect a show business demeanor. In the early 1950s, though he continued to play publicly and record from time to time, his lifestyle grew even more erratic and unsettled. Eventually succumbing to his various addictions, he died in New York City at the age of 34, fanatically admired by his fellow musicians.

In his uptempo work, Parker expands most directly on Lester Young's style by adapting his smooth, swinging eighth-note lines to the more angular, oddly accented lines of bop. The influence of Young can also be heard when Parker plays slow, dreamy ballads like "Parker's Mood" (SCCJ) or "Embraceable You" (SCCJ). There, the blues inflections and cool, often irregular phrasing of Young are most obviously suggested.

In "Doggin' Around," Young filled an A section of the tune almost entirely with one eighth-note swing phrase. Parker's approach to rhythm changes in "Shaw 'Nuff" shows a similar tendency to long eighth-note lines. After the brisk motive in Am2, the rest of the A section is completed by one lengthy phrase. (See pp. 242-243 for a transcription of Parker's solo.) Whereas Young's long phrase in "Doggin' Around" swung in typical swing era fashion—smoothly contoured and laid back, with no unusual accents that might interrupt its overall flow—Parker's melody is disjointed, jumping at times to unexpected pitches. The uneasiness of Parker's line is increased by the accents that occur in unexpected metrical positions.

The continuous arpeggiations of the bridge provide a release from the angularity of the first two A sections. Throughout these arpeggiations, *chromaticisms* are emphasized as extended chord tones. They are often left hanging, a treatment that increases their poignancy.

From "Shaw 'Nuff," we can assemble these stylistic features characteristic of Parker's uptempo playing: (1) disjointed, irregularly accented melodic lines, mostly comprising eighth-notes with occasional arpeggiations; (2) little space between phrases; (3) melodic connections based on extremely subtle motivic interrelations and voice leading; (4) commanding, insistent tone quality; (5)

much use of melodic chord extensions; (6) intense, powerful expression; (7) frequent blues inflections; (8) concentration on middle and upper range of instrument; and (9) "inside" playing, with scale-chord relationships based on uncommon scales generated from use of extended chord harmonies.

Although "Shaw 'Nuff" and "Koko" (discussed in Chapter 4) display Parker's virtuosity to its fullest, his ballad playing powerfully evokes the feeling of the blues. Ranging from tenderness and mockery to fiery brilliance and driving impetuosity, Parker's style has decisively influenced all modern jazz musicians.

sonny rollins

Sonny Rollins achieves his big, dramatic tone by infusing the traditional, full-throated eloquence of Coleman Hawkins with the edgy raspiness sometimes heard in Charlie Parker. As a player nurtured on 1940s' bop, Rollins (b. 1930) brings to his style great technique in the form of unrelenting eighth-note lines with unexpected accents and shifting, irregular phrasing. Yet cool jazz had an effect on him as well, abating at least some of the technical fury characteristic of bop. As Rollins relaxes bop rhythm with a more flexible choice of note durations, he achieves a remarkable stylistic blend; for, although he possesses the speed and technique necessary to generate great excitement, he learned to unfold solos gradually and motivically, not allowing endless eighth-note lines to predominate mechanically.

Known as a hard bop player in the 1950s, Rollins began his career by playing with small groups in and around New York City, his home town. He eventually met Thelonious Monk, Bud Powell, and other important jazz musicians. After performing in a variety of bands, he established a major reputation with the Max Roach-Clifford Brown quintet, the last group in which he worked as a sideman.

Upon leaving the band in 1957, Rollins recorded several important albums, often without piano, that established him as the leading sax player of the day along with John Coltrane. Rollins has occasionally taken time off from public performance and recording to practice alone and rethink his improvisational directions. These periods of **woodshedding** prompted him to experiment with various jazz styles and substyles, including jazz-rock and jazz-pop. Still active, Rollins remains one of the finest improvisers in jazz.

Despite many fine solos with the Max Roach-Clifford Brown quintet, Rollins's sense of cumulative development on "I'll Remember April" is especially memorable. (See discussion of Clifford Brown in Chapter 6.) Afer Clifford Brown's trumpet improvisation, Rollins reverses the mood by beginning with pensive, slowly emerging phrases.

The first chorus of "I'll Remember April" is reminiscent, rhythmically, of Lester Young's "Doggin' Around" solo; the displaced phrases nudge the beat and are often delayed relative to the 4-bar norms. Such phrasing, as you will

Sonny Rollins (Courtesy Institute of Jazz Studies, Rutgers University).

see in Chapter 10's discussion of vocal styles, recalls the singing of Billie Holiday and is now associated with the jazz and pop singers that followed in her tradition.

Rollins also reveals fragments of the original tune throughout his first chorus. Yet, because he prefers paraphrasing the melody rather than reproducing it, his quotations are simplified to germane motives. This procedure, highly typical of Rollins's style, contrasts Parker, for example, who rarely refers to the tune in uptempo improvising.

Rollins's penchant for motivic improvisation is such that he often prefers tunes with strong, simple melodies he can easily allude to, for example, his recording of "Surrey with the Fringe on Top" or his own "St. Thomas." Rollins's ability to thread motives through his solos can be heard on "Blue Seven" (SCCJ), which exemplifies logical development in a jazz improvisation.

Typical of Rollins's attention to melodic development, the eighth-note phrases in the beginning of the A ' section foreshadow the bop runs that characterize the second chorus. After this allusion to bop style Rollins immediately backs away and returns to the floating phrases for the remainder of the first chorus.

A dramatic pause leads to the second chorus: the opening phrase is derived motivically from the original melody, as is typical of Rollins's work. After the strong melodic opening of the second chorus, Rollins proceeds to develop the tune motivically.

Rollins gradually increases the tension throughout the A section of chorus two, until C2B, where the longest bop phrases occur. Eventually, Rollins finishes the solo on a low A, a significant pitch in the original song. Rollins adds the final phrase of the solo as an afterthought, as if to remind the listener of the motives previously heard in the first chorus.

The following generalizations summarize Rollins's style as heard on "I'll Remember April": (1) wide variety of melody, from bop lines to floating phrases slightly reminiscent of cool jazz; (2) melodic connections based on voice leading and motivic development, some of which is quite subtle; (3) varied melodic rhythms; (4) highly irregular phrase lengths, from single notes to long bop phrases; (5) rich tone with occasional raspiness; (6) use of space between phrases; (7) use of entire range of instrument; (8) full range of emotional expression; and (9) mostly "inside" playing, with chord-scale relationships based on bop usages of extended chords and altered scales. This solo admirably reveals the sense of unfolding often present in Rollins's style, which remains one of the richest and widest-ranging in modern jazz.

gerry mulligan

> Gerry Mulligan and The Concert Jazz Band: "Blueport," from *The Essential Gerry Mulligan*, Verve V6-8567, Summer, 1960. Gerry Mulligan, baritone sax and piano; Nick Travis, Clark Terry, Don Ferrara, trumpets; Bob Brookmeyer, Willie Dennis, Alan Raph, trombones; Gene Quill, Gene Allen, Jim Reider, Bob Donovan, reeds; Bill Crow, bass; Mel Lewis, drums.

Gerry Mulligan (b. 1927) first attracted major critical attention with his participation as an arranger and player in the "Birth of the Cool" recordings with Miles Davis and Gil Evans. His playing, like Rollins's, matured during the bop era in the late 1940s. Unlike Rollins, however, Mulligan's improvisational concept was based on cool jazz, occasionally augmented with swing and bop phrases. In the 1950s he epitomized the West Coast sound, leading pianoless quartets that included trumpeter Chet Baker (b. 1929), valve trombonist Bob Brookmeyer, and alto saxophonist Lee Konitz (b. 1927). His Concert Jazz Band, which flourished in the late 1950s, recorded "Blueport" at the 1960 Newport Jazz Festival. Although he continues to play throughout the world with various musicians, he has recently been concentrating on composing, particularly for film.

Mulligan's style, simple and elegant, underscores the best features of cool jazz. Although unafraid to infuse swinging bop lines into his solos whenever they are appropriate, Mulligan more often reflects various fine-art techniques in his playing and arranging, especially the contrapuntal ingenuity of third stream music. However, Mulligan, at heart a freewheeling improviser, always maintains a fine balance between writing and improvisations.

The looser side of Mulligan's improvising style can be heard on the inspired "Blueport" recording. Throughout this exciting performance the band remains relaxed, never pushing too hard, but always disciplined and swinging. The lick used to kick off the solos recurs throughout the performance and reveals Mulligan's thematic approach to arranging. This 3-beat lick, when played in a 4/4 meter, produces a shimmering cross rhythm relative to the underlying beat.

Mulligan continues to develop this long, multichorus solo by the use of one basic idea: contrasting assertive quarter-note motives with serpentine bop lines. By subtly dropping hints in each chorus, Mulligan foreshadows the developmental ideas of the next.

Mulligan's style, as indicated in this solo, can be summarized as follows: (1) melodic variety, using patterns from simple motivic ideas to bop lines; (2) melodic connections based on motivic development and contrast, with attention to voice leading; (3) slightly irregular phrasing; (4) varied melodic rhythms; (5) overall cool tone with an occasional edge; (6) use of space between phrases; (7) emphasis on middle and upper range of instrument; (8) somewhat cool expression; and (9) "inside" playing, chord-scale relationships conservative with occasional exceptions.

john coltrane

John Coltrane Quartet: "Giant Steps," from *Giant Steps,* Atlantic 1311, May 4 or 5, 1959. John Coltrane, tenor sax; Tommy Flanagan, piano; Paul Chambers, bass; Art Taylor, drums.

John Coltrane (1926-1967), possibly the first truly original and artistically successful voice in saxophone playing since Parker and Young, was originally trained in bop. Like Rollins, Coltrane was able to adapt his technique to his own personal style, which evolved dramatically through the 1950s and 1960s. From bop through modal improvisation to free jazz, Coltrane insisted on self-growth, never allowing his playing to stagnate stylistically.

Born in Hamlet, N.C., Coltrane played with r & b groups during his youth

John Coltrane (Courtesy Institute of Jazz Studies, Rutgers University).

and eventually mastered bop sufficiently to perform with Dizzy Gillespie in the early 1950s. He became widely known soon after he joined Miles Davis's quintet in 1955, a period in which jazz critics viewed him and Sonny Rollins as competing for the position of leading tenor saxophonist. After various collaborations with Davis, Thelonious Monk, and others, Coltrane formed his own group in 1959, the great quartet with Elvin Jones on drums, Jimmy Garrison on bass, and McCoy Tyner on piano. Until his untimely death in 1967, Coltrane explored various modal and free jazz styles first with his quartet and then with other musicians, including tenor saxophonist Archie Shepp (b. 1937) and trumpeter Freddie Hubbard (b. 1938).

Coltrane's mastery of the hard bop, changes oriented style of playing is clearly demonstrated on his recording of "Giant Steps." This tune, perhaps Coltrane's most famous composition, combines the harmonic features of bop with unusual experimental twists. The name "Giant Steps" most likely signifies the use of thirds in both the melody and harmony. The bop orientation of the harmony is captured in the use of II-V-I and V-I changes, practically clichés during the bop era, whereas the experimental nature of the tune lies in how these changes are linked by major thirds. (For a transcription of the lead and further discussion, see p. 244.)

Coltrane plays a solo that is both emotional and remarkably facile on "Giant Steps." Because the harmonies change unusually quickly for an uptempo piece, any solo that attempts to articulate the changes necessarily features much arpeggiation. Hence, Coltrane's develops an arpeggiated motive whose first appearance consists of the pitches D-E-F♯-A, both in inversions and with other modifications. The long phrases and strings of eighth-notes reveal Coltrane's conception of the piece as a bop showcase, but with imaginative chord changes that in effect enrich the style.

"Giant Steps" testifies to Coltrane's bop mastery, but he is most well known for the power of his modal jazz playing. In "So What" (see discussions in Chapter 4 and in Chapter 6 under Miles Davis) we heard his exploration of the dorian mode in a context dissimilar from the changes oriented "Giant Steps," but still featuring the emotional cries on high notes and the sweeping, passionate runs. This style of modal playing is heard to best advantage on "Acknowledgement" from *A Love Supreme* (see Chapter 4).

"Acknowledgement," though modal, contains much playing outside the mode. After the bass establishes F dorian on the song's motive, F-A♭-F-B♭, Tyner enters with chords that reinforce the modal center. Coltrane's entrance also centers on F dorian, but after a few phrases he begins to veer off from pure reliance on the mode. Tyner and Garrison sometimes follow Coltrane's harmonic excursions, but just as often they react freely to them, as if to illuminate rather than track his musical path.

Throughout Coltrane's solo, F dorian, the location of the solo's beginning and the first statement of the motive, is perceived as the point of harmonic stability. Hence Coltrane refers his motivic and harmonic excursions to it. Yet, the very beginning of the tune had elaborated an E chord, implying that the F modal center might be treated very loosely.

Before the conclusion of Coltrane's solo, he plays the "A Love Supreme" motive at various transposition levels to reveal again how freely the F dorian is being interpreted. However, Coltrane begins from the F-dorian location of the motive before freely transposing it, and he returns to the F-dorian transposition level at the end of the section. An accented F-suspended chord from Tyner ushers in the vocal section, again in F dorian, before the abrupt change to E♭ dorian to introduce the next piece of the suite.

The climaxes of the solo highlight Coltrane's intensity and his preference for the high notes of the tenor sax. Coltrane seems to be reaching for unplayable notes, as if trying to express the inexpressible. This feature is as much a hallmark of his style as the famous blurred runs through the saxophone's entire range. This latter effect has been called "sheets of sound." Although the "sheets of sound" are less emphasized on "Acknowledgement," the technique can be glimpsed on Coltrane's "So What" solo, before his modal style had been fully formed. Coltrane's preoccupation with the higher range of the tenor possibly led to his later playing the soprano sax.

The following items summarize Coltrane's later modal jazz styles: (1) free melody, usually not formed into square phrases; (2) melodic connections based on motivic development and contrast, with voice leading more prominent in his earlier bop oriented work; (3) widely varying melodic rhythm, from long emotion-charged pitches to fast "sheets of sound"; (4) concentration on upper range and extreme upper range of instrument; (5) passionate expression; (6) full, rich tone with raspy edge; and (7) "outside" playing, featuring often very free chord-scale relationships.

The loose adherence to the F dorian mode in "Acknowledgement" foreshadows Coltrane's eventual drift into free jazz. Although Ornette Coleman had been advocating nontonal jazz since the late 1950s, Coltrane did not rush to embrace the fashionable free jazz style, but rather progressed naturally to it. Coltrane's free playing is generally well controlled and establishes him as a thinking musician. All in all, the intensity of his expression, his technical mastery, and his continual striving for new sounds have remained an inspiration to all jazz musicians.

ornette coleman

> Ornette Coleman: "Lonely Woman," from *The Shape of Jazz To Come,*
> Atlantic SD 1317, May 22, 1959. Ornette Coleman, alto sax; Donald
> Cherry, trumpet; Charlie Haden, bass; Billy Higgins, drums.

Ornette Coleman (b. 1930) has managed to remain influential and musically fertile since he first burst onto the jazz scene in 1959. The occasion then was

Ornette Coleman (Courtesy Institute of Jazz Studies, Rutgers University).

Coleman's appearance at New York's Five Spot with a group that played jazz more freely and radically than ever before. Eventually Coleman's early work, after some experimentation, culminated in *Free Jazz,* a landmark album that featured the first fully spontaneous free improvisations. Coleman's earlier albums were not quite so radical, but in them we can hear the music evolving in the direction of complete freedom from syntactic constraints.

For the remainder of his career, Coleman has worked sporadically, sometimes insisting on fees for records and appearances quite a bit higher than for other jazz musicians. Coleman has preferred to remain underemployed and underrecorded rather than sacrifice his artistic principles. He was once again in the jazz limelight during the late 1970s, combining his free style with funk rhythms, reemerging as an important and innovative player.

Coleman's recent music is structured on a theory he calls "harmolodics," but despite Coleman's own writing on the subject, the theory remains obscure.[1] Coleman is known for his strikingly original sound, created in part by his unique intonation (slightly raised or lowered pitches, similar to the blues inflections described earlier). Coleman utilizes this effect intentionally and in a perfectly controlled fashion; repeated listening will render his sound instantly recognizable.

"Lonely Woman" (SCCJ), which is less radical than most of Coleman's work, has become something of a jazz standard, although few others perform it publicly. Though in AABA form, it is not strictly metered in 32 bars. Instead, Coleman and trumpeter Don Cherry (b. 1936) intone it somewhat freely over the surging drum (playing in *double time*) and bass rhythms. The six phrases of the tune's A section are numbered and notated out of rhythm as follows:

(The last part of Coleman's solo, from the B section duet with Cherry, is loosely transcribed on pp. 245-246. The transcription is more approximate than usual, regarding both pitch and rhythm because of the nature of the composition.)

Throughout the solo, Coleman's passion and apparent abandon are controlled by attention to phrase balance and motive. The solo's dynamic character is especially compelling; the rise and fall of the melodic line with its carefully integrated structure and sense of formality balance the expressive and plaintive cries. In addition to these large-scale formal elements, intervallic motives that appeared first in the head are developed with great care.

These features summarize Coleman's style as presented in "Lonely Woman": (1) fragmented, angular melodies instead of long, spun out eighth-note phrases; (2) melodic connections based on motivic structure and large-scale gestures; (3) little if any use of conventional harmony and voice leading; (4) variety of melodic rhythm but avoidance of even-note phrases; (5) nasal, insistent tone; (6) rhythm loosely connected to background pulse; (7) concentration on middle and upper range of instrument; (8) passionate expression; and (9) unique intonation.

Tightly controlled as Coleman's playing is, his pitch structure and rhythmic fluidity create an impression of spontaneous expression. Repeated listenings confirm that Coleman has a sensuous, linear approach to the instrument. However, harmony in the conventional sense of chord-changes is not a factor in

---

[1]For example, see Coleman's explanation of harmolodics in *Downbeat*, Vol. 50, No. 7 (July, 1983), 54-55.

Coleman's music. Harmony in the sense of intervallic relatedness and control is a constant factor, though, while control of large-scale form depends more on large musical gestures such as dynamic climax, melodic shapes, and section-alization. Coleman succeeds in allying passionate expression to rigorous linear structure; his playing is emotional, powerful, and thoroughly individual.

In Chapter 8, I will examine a few of the other melodic jazz instruments. After the overview presented by Chapters 6, 7, and 8, I will offer a general summary of the development of melodic improvisation.

chapter
eight

other
jazz
instruments

The instrumentalists examined in this chapter have not dominated the melodic development of jazz to the extent that trumpeters, alto and tenor saxophonists, and clarinetists have. The techniques of guitars, trombones, violins, vibes, and synthesizers have been somewhat less broadly applicable, more often reflecting individual temperaments and idiosyncrasies. Within their own ranks development has been far reaching, but collectively they have influenced jazz far less than the instrumentalists considered earlier.

guitar

Quintette of the Hot Club of France: "Dinah," Ultraphone AP-1422, December, 1934. Django Reinhardt, Roger Chaput, Joseph Reinhardt: guitars; Stephane Grappelli: violin; Louis Vola: bass.

The Mahavishnu Orchestra: "The Dance of Maya," from *The Inner Mounting Flame,* Columbia KC 31067, 1972. John McLaughlin, electric guitar; Jerry Goodman, amplified violin; Jan Hammer, piano; Rick Laird, bass; Billy Cobham, drums.

Before amplification, jazz guitarists served mainly as rhythm section members. The guitar tone was too soft to compete with the horns that formed the front line of the small jazz ensemble. Still, the first great jazz guitarist, Eddie Lang (1904-1933), recorded many marvelous solos, often with violinist Joe Venuti.

Lang's playing style was imitated and then extended by the legendary Jean Baptiste "Django" Reinhardt (1910-1953), who achieved his reputation in an unusual group, the Quintette of the Hot Club of France, with the odd instrumentation of bass, three guitars, and violin. This band, which was formed during the meetings of a famous Parisian jazz club in the early 1930s played softly enough for the unamplified guitar and violin solos to shine through. The other great musician in this band was the violinist Stephane Grappelli.

Reinhardt, the first pioneering jazz musician who was not an American, initiated the period of true jazz internationalism. Europe was swept up by jazz in the early 1920s, thanks to the recordings and appearances of jazz groups that sometimes toured Europe before they had had much of an American impact. The hottest group in early jazz, at least in popularity, was the Original Dixieland Jazz Band (ODJB), who, direct from their triumphant appearance at Reisen-weber's restaurant in New York in 1917, sailed the Atlantic to appear at London's Palais de Dance from April 1919 to July 1920. Louis Mitchell's Jazz Kings were appearing in Paris as early as 1918. Thus, the roaring twenties sound of hot jazz triumphed in Europe as quickly as it had in America.

Europeans themselves soon learned to play jazz by listening to the touring American groups and their records. Because most of the touring groups appeared in Paris and London, these cities became the centers of European jazz, where the largest number of non-American jazz players could be found. The other parts of Europe were influenced by jazz, too, as bands traveled throughout the continent, even reaching the Soviet Union as early as the mid-1920s.

Although bop had some difficulty establishing a European audience, dixieland and swing were extremely popular there. Reinhardt, as a consummate swing musician, helped establish the popularity of this style in Paris. Part-gypsy Reinhardt had a rather freewheeling life style, which often led him to miss engagements and disregard starting times. However, he was much loved by other jazz musicians as well as by the public. His first recordings astonished other jazz musicians who did not expect to hear such good jazz coming from Europe so soon.

It was clear from Reinhardt's early recordings that he had listened to and absorbed the style of Eddie Lang. The quintet's first record with Reinhardt was "Dinah," issued in 1934. It remains one of Reinhardt's finest recordings, revealing his debt to Lang and demonstrating the early swing virtuosity of violinist Grappelli as well.

Reinhardt's two choruses of "Dinah" coyly balance diversity and unity. As swing style had been established by 1934, this solo reflects the fluid scales and arpeggios heard earlier in the work of Benny Goodman, but here adapted to the guitar. In order to achieve this fluidity, Reinhardt sometimes slides his left hand between pitches to connect them, rather than plucking each individual note. Another noteworthy feature of this solo is the quotation from the tune itself in the C1A' section. This quotation fits aptly into the solo and does not at all suggest a lapse of improvisational invention.

The bridge features the use of octaves, a virtuoso technique that quickly became standard on guitar and was often heard in the playing of Wes Montgomery (1925-1968). The octaves in the bridge are grouped into a pattern (on the pitches G, F, and E), which complements the extensive use of patterns elsewhere. Chords not yet heard in the solo nicely wrap up the improvisation and effectively usher in Grappelli's violin solo.

Reinhardt delineated swing style guitar as early as 1934, but Charlie Christian (1919-1942) was the first major guitarist to play electric guitar in jazz ensembles of more typical instrumentation. Christian's solos are remarkably elegant, as definitive of swing as Lester Young's or Benny Goodman's playing. Christian's guitar tone, with slight variations, was the established jazz guitar timbre until the late 1960s, when the jazz-rock stylists started to exploit the myriad possibilities of the new electronic equipment.

Christian's solo on "I Found a New Baby" (SCCJ), discussed in Chapter 4, displays his self-assured elegance. Here we find fully mature swing in a solo exemplifying the very best of that style. Throughout his solo, the lines are flowing and the voice leading is remarkably complex yet never out of control. Early signs of bop can be detected here, too, for although the swing arpeggios are ubiquitous, the chromaticism of the bridge is very typical of the lines we hear in Charlie Parker's solos. (For a transcription of Christian's solo on "I Found a New Baby," see pp. 247–248.)

Christian, who developed his reputation as a member of Benny Goodman's sextet and orchestra, seems perfectly poised between swing and bop. A relaxed sense of swing, perfect voice-leading control, subtle motivic manipulation, variety of phrase length, and imaginative harmonies characterize his style. Given his exemplary command of swing improvisation, Charlie Christian remains one of the greatest guitar players in jazz history.

Cool era guitar playing emphasized the use of beautifully voiced chords, but its improvisational styles remained rooted in swing and bop. Such was the influence of Charlie Christian that not much happened to change jazz guitar technique until the jazz-rock players of the late 1960s and early 1970s began restyling the sound. "Mahavishnu" John McLaughlin (b. 1942) who had epitomized early jazz-rock guitar, continues to be one of the most important players. His concept of the style includes the blues licks typical of 1950s and 1960s r & b guitar playing, and elements of non-Western musical traditions, especially East Indian styles. These stylistic features he adapted to the greater virtuosity and flexibility of jazz-rock.

McLaughlin played with Miles Davis for a brief time in the late 1960s and early 1970s, appearing on Davis's pioneering jazz-rock albums *In a Silent Way* and *Bitches Brew*. Having fully absorbed the jazz-rock innovations of Davis and his other sidemen, he left to form the Mahavishnu Orchestra, and later an "East-meets-West" group, Shakti, including three prominent classical Indian musicians.

One of the best pieces from the repertoire of the Mahavishnu Orchestra is "The Dance of Maya" from their first album *The Inner Mounting Flame*. In it, the various McLaughlin trademarks can be clearly distinguished: the blues, the modal jazz of the 1960s, the heavy-metal rock styles, the impassioned virtuosity, and the touches of "Hindu-pop" and third stream styles. The form of the piece is a large-scale ABA, with the B section featuring a McLaughlin solo that is similarly tripartite.

After McLaughlin develops an intense, wah-wah blues solo, the impulse of the beat is tripled by drummer Cobham's emphasis of each triplet eighth-note. The mode then changes from E mixolydian, a typical blues mode, to D dorian, as McLaughlin develops a single-line solo, not unlike the single-line styles of modal jazz horn players.

Note that McLaughlin at first remains totally within D dorian, then gradually adds other nondorian pitches. By beginning in the mode, then moving outside of it, he evokes Coltrane's method in "Acknowledgement." McLaughlin's melodic lines are almost boplike, except for the characteristic guitar slides that we heard earlier with Reinhardt. The high notes are sometimes given a bending, screaming rock characterization. (For transcriptions of portions of this performance, see p. 249.) The fast bop lines later became common in jazz-rock guitar and keyboard playing, heard in the work of pianist Chick Corea and guitarist Al Dimeola in their Return to Forever band.

Thus, in McLaughlin's work we can find elements of historical jazz guitar techniques amalgamated into one coherent framework. Most of the electronic effects now associated with rock and jazz-rock guitar originated in his groundbreaking style of the early 1970s, with both the Mahavishnu Orchestra and drummer Tony Williams's Lifetime band. Jazz guitar today continues to develop in two very different directions: the jazz-rock style associated with McLaughlin and the swing-bop style associated with Christian.

trombone

J. J. Johnson Quintet: "Boneology," from *Mad Bebop*, Savoy SJL 2232, December 24, 1947. J. J. Johnson, trombone; Leo Parker, baritone sax; Hank Jones, piano; Al Lucas, bass; Shadow Wilson, drums.

The trombone, though certainly common enough in all types of jazz ensembles, has never enjoyed the popularity of the other horns probably because of its unwieldy technique. The uptempo single-note lines pervasive in jazz wind styles are difficult to execute on the trombone because of the slide mechanism. Since this is especially true for the low register, agile trombone playing is essentially an upper register phenomenon. The difficulties of the slide mechanism have occasionally led trombonists to switch to valve trombone, which is fingered like a trumpet. (Because the trombone is pitched an octave lower than the trumpet, valve trombone can be readily learned by trumpet players as well.)

Although the vanguard soloists have rarely been trombone players, the instrument has persisted in jazz, probably because of its two important uses: in dixieland ensembles as a bass countermelody to the trumpet lead and in big band brass sections. The latter use especially highlights the instrument's rich, full-throated sound, similar in range to the male singing voice.

The first prominent trombone players were New Orleans musicians such as Kid Ory (1886-1973), who recorded with Louis Armstrong, among others. Not an especially inspiring soloist, Ory was the most famous of the New Orleans *tailgate* trombone players who were primarily ensemble musicians. (The term "tailgate" derived from the placement of the trombonist at the back of the parade band wagon where the instrument's slide was not impeded.) They can be heard anchoring the basslines in dixieland groups since the early 1920s. Their work

J.J. Johnson (Courtesy Institute of Jazz Studies, Rutgers University).

is best thought of as gutsy and rough-hewn, full of glissandos and lively punctuations.

Other fine trombonists, like Tricky Sam Nanton (1904–1946) with the Ellington band, created the smoother, swing trombone style that rapidly became the mainstream approach to the instrument until the 1940s. Swing trombonists that began to emphasize the higher register include Vic Dickenson (1906-1984), Dickie Wells (b. 1909) and Tommy Dorsey (1905-1956), the latter relying mainly on his beautifully liquid tone to play ballads for dancing.

Jazz trombone playing was shaken up by J. J. Johnson (b. 1924) in the late 1940s, although his technical developments followed logically from the work of the swing players. Johnson emphasized the high register and astonished everyone with boplike lines, at the time thought to be impossible on the trombone, that were reminiscent of Parker and Gillespie. After working in a variety of swing bands in the 1940s, Johnson made a series of important records in the late 1940s and early 1950s with small groups. Eventually he teamed up with fellow trombonist Kai Winding (1922-1983) to colead a two-trombone quintet in 1954.

From Johnson's small group sessions, the solo on his own tune, "Boneology," is particularly impressive. The tune pays oblique homage to Charlie Parker by referring to Parker's famous composition "Ornithology." Although "Boneology," like most bop tunes, is structured in 32-bar AABA form, it features an unusual harmony (bVI7) on bars 3 and 4. Otherwise, the changes are straightforward, emphasizing the circle of fifths, as bop harmonies often do.

Johnson strikes a wonderful balance between the Parker-like sixteenth-note passages and the inventive, melodic eighth-note sections. Note especially at the beginning of the A ' section how Johnson artfully lags behind the beat, gradually leading up to a bar of silence. Afterward, Johnson launches into a swinging, remarkably swift flourish that completes the section.

The phrase lengths are varied throughout the solo, thus balancing the effect of the straightforward AABA form with mostly customary chord changes. The typical bebop riff also can be found throughout, but its occurrence in Bm6 is noteworthy for the use of a ninth (C) and sharp eleventh (A natural), extended chord tones often heard in the work of Parker and Gillespie. (For a transcription of "Boneology," see p. 250.)

Johnson's improvisation on "Boneology" is surprisingly facile. Despite the inevitable references to Parker heard throughout, the gentle persuasiveness of Johnson's sound contrasts the more hard-edged Parker tone and creates a distinctive character of its own. Johnson's style was echoed in the modern era by Kai Winding, who, though slightly less facile than Johnson, relied heavily on swing and bop style. This concept of jazz trombone playing has persisted to the present time, especially in the 1970s, when Bill Watrous (b. 1939) displayed incredible dexterity by increasing the Johnson technique in both range and speed.

Jack Teagarden (1905-1964) seemingly spanned all periods and styles with his warm, friendly, blues oriented approach to the instrument. Although he eschewed the rough technique of the early New Orleans players, he became prominently associated with the New Orleans revival of the 1940s, performing often with Louis Armstrong and the fine swing-dixieland trumpeter Bobby Hackett. His singing has always been as relaxed and appealing as his playing. Teagarden's basic technique was based on 1930s swing trombone technique, but was imbued with a unique personality and feeling for the blues that was highly respected by avant-garde players as well.

Other trombonists considered the bop style more technically suitable for sax, trumpet, and piano, and thus aimed for a concept that more specifically fit the technique of the instrument, often recalling the tailgate trombonists of the past. Roswell Rudd (b. 1935) achieved prominence by applying a back-to-basics technique to free jazz in the 1960s. In the 1970s virtuosos like the German Albert Mangelsdorff (b. 1928), raised antibop trombone technique to a still higher level by incorporating **multiphonics,** a technique whereby the soloist can play two or sometimes three pitches at once. In the early 1980s, avant-garde trombonist George Lewis further developed "extended" techniques for the instrument.

vibraphone

> Lionel Hampton: "When Lights Are Low," Victor 26371, September 11, 1939. Lionel Hampton, vibes; Dizzy Gillespie, trumpet; Benny Carter, alto sax; Coleman Hawkins, Ben Webster, Chu Berry, tenor saxes; Clyde Hart, piano; Charlie Christian, guitar; Milt Hinton, bass; Cozy Cole, drums.
>
> Modern Jazz Quartet: "Django," Atlantic 2-603, April, 1960. Milt Jackson, vibes; John Lewis, piano; Percy Health, bass; Connie Kay, drums.

Jazz vibraphone ("vibes" or "vibraharp") playing derives from the occasional use of xylophones and marimbas in jazz during the 1920s. The latter two instruments, whose bars are made of wood, are unable to sustain pitches. The vibraphone, however, can be operated electrically; it is equipped with a pedal, like a piano damper pedal, that enables pitches to be sustained. The vibraphone is a somewhat limited jazz instrument, since it is difficult to bend or vary the sound of a note once it is struck. The piano possesses this characteristic, too, of course, but the vibraphone does not have the piano's flexibility of texture, range, or tone color.

Red Norvo (b. 1908), the first important xylophone and marimba player, did not switch to the more flexible vibraphone until later in his jazz career. Norvo's mallet style of jazz xylophone may be heard on the many excellent recordings he made during the 1920s. Similar to the guitar in its dependence on electricity, the vibraphone was not used in jazz until amplification became commonplace.

The first truly fine vibes player was Lionel Hampton (b. 1913). Hampton's reputation was established after joining Benny Goodman, Gene Krupa, and Teddy Wilson to transform the Benny Goodman Trio into the Quartet. He remained with Goodman from 1936 to 1940. A former drummer, Hampton was able to substitute for Gene Krupa on occasion, especially after Krupa left to form his own band. Once Hampton left Goodman, he exploited his own exceptional talent as a leader and showman, organizing jazz groups and appearing with his own big band as recently as the early 1980s.

Hampton's style is not unlike Goodman's swing clarinet style: elegant, often symmetrical, never straying too far from the changes, logical, and precise. Although his ballad style of playing is appealing too, with many superb recordings throughout his career, Hampton will always be best remembered for his up-tempo work. A good example of his economical playing can be heard on a studio recording arranged by saxophonist Benny Carter, "When Lights Are Low" (SCCJ).

Hampton begins with a nicely crafted, lyrical 4-bar phrase, balanced by a line with greater figuration and sense of pattern that completes the A section. The A' section, varying the regularity of phrasing heard in the first section by increased rhythmic unevenness, is highlighted by the delightful triplet run in A'm2. The precision of this run and its deft detour outside the prevailing Ab harmony are beguiling, especially after the straightforward nature of the solo until this point.

The changes of the tune grow more complex during the bridge. Hampton emphasizes a repeated-note motive, first heard at the end of section A', possibly to simplify the motivic structure as a counterbalance to the increased harmonic activity. Note that the changes of this section are negotiated primarily through arpeggios and that there is considerable regularity of phrase length. Within this regularity, interest is created by use of the repeated-note motive and the fine balance struck among the rising and falling lines of the phrases.

Most uptempo vibes work features two-mallet playing since it is quite difficult to handle four mallets, two in each hand, at fast tempos. The use of four mallets will permit chords, but most two-mallet solos consist of single-line melodies, with perhaps some occasional two-note harmonies. We see this characteristic in Hampton's solo, although there he finds it unnecessary to vary the single-line format at all.

Besides Hampton, one of the other most influential vibes players is Milt Jackson (b. 1923). Jackson has spent much of his career with the Modern Jazz Quartet (MJQ), led by pianist John Lewis. The two principal members of the quartet are often said to have balanced each other ideally: Jackson, the loose, swinging, uninhibited player creates a perfect foil for Lewis, the thoughtful, methodical musician, interested in fine-art and third stream music.

Jackson departed from Hampton's swinging elegance much in the way that Parker and Gillespie burst from the classical swing of Young, Hawkins, Goodman, and others. A brilliant example of his work can be heard on the MJQ recording of "Django" (SCCJ), a tribute to the great guitarist. The mournful flavor of the opening eventually yields to an uptempo, driving swing.

"Django" is slightly peculiar in that the changes used for the improvisations are not specifically those of the tune. Instead, they are derived from the tune and developed more fully for use in the solo sections. The sections in the improvisatory choruses are of irregular length but the changes are so artfully structured that they sound quite natural.

Unlike Hampton, Jackson seldom arpeggiates his lines; instead, he allows strong, scalar bop lines to predominate. These scalar patterns often include sixteenth-notes and altered extended chord tones as well. Although no motives are developed systematically and clearly in this solo, references to the original tune occur throughout. Much of the driving swing of this solo can be attributed to the boplike irregularity of phrase length; its coherence is a result of artful voice leading.

The performance is turned over to Lewis by a break in which the tune is quoted and played together by the whole ensemble. This thematic interlude caps Jackson's ebullience and skillfully prepares the mood for Lewis's more thoughtful improvisation.

Jackson consistently maximizes the expressive potential of his instrument. The two-mallet, single-note line does not at all restrain him from freely trying anything that comes to mind. Despite the fact that there is little motivic relatedness, the voice leading within the solo unifies the various phrases and provides Jackson with the opportunity to emphasize freewheeling swing and rhythmic drive.

Other prominent vibraharpists include Walt Dickerson (b. 1931) and Gary Burton (b. 1943). Burton, in particular, displays extraordinary ability in handling four mallets at once. His harmonic style has been strongly influenced by the major jazz pianists of the 1960s.

violin

> Jean-Luc Ponty: "Upon the Wings of Music" from *Upon the Wings of Music,* Atlantic SD 18138, 1975. Jean-Luc Ponty, electric violin; Patrice Rushen, keyboards; Dan Sawyer, electric guitar; Ralphe Armstrong, bass guitar; Ndugu (Leon Chancler), drums.

The violin has always had an uncomfortable association with jazz, probably because of the fine-art history of the instrument. However, the recordings of the Quintette of the Hot Club of France, whose work we first heard in examining Django Reinhardt, place the instrument in a refreshing perspective. In those recordings, violinist Stephane Grappelli (b. 1908) is complemented by acoustic guitars and bass, whose timbres seem well suited to accompany the violin.

Grappelli's gentlemanly approach to the instrument reflects his classical training. His refinement can be contrasted to the earthier technique of Stuff Smith (b. 1909), who tends to incorporate a greater variety of blues inflections. Grappelli was also fortunate in his association with Django Reinhardt in the 1930s. Their duets and band performances with the Quintette of the Hot Club of France vaulted Grappelli into the ranks of the top jazz players.

Grappelli's early style can be heard on "Dinah," recorded with Reinhardt (see previous discussion, this chapter). His solo is bouncy and deft throughout, but rather naïve, and certainly lacking the brilliant swing of Reinhardt. Like the guitar, the violin can slide between notes, but because there are no frets to interrupt the slide it can effect a true **portamento.**

Swing style arpeggios also occur in Grappelli's solo, but possibly since arpeggiation is somewhat more difficult to execute than scalar lines, fewer of them are found here than in early swing woodwind improvisation. Grappelli occasionally emphasizes blue notes, another element of early swing style. At their best, violinists such as Grappelli and Stuff Smith can swing hard, coaxing a strong rhythmic feel from the instrument.

Jazz violin styles, like those of the guitar, did not evolve much through the 1940s and 1950s, when the instrument's use in jazz was even less popular. Though occasionally heard in traditional jazz contexts, the violin was generally ignored by bop, cool, and funky players. Even in third stream music, its relationship to jazz was suppressed, and it was generally assigned the nonimprovisatory parts to play.

Nevertheless, during the 1960s Jean-Luc Ponty, who like Grappelli had studied Western classical music, became prominent as a boplike violin player at a time when there were very few jazz violinists.

. It was probably not until experimentation with electric violin that its use in jazz was taken more seriously. The electric violin offers a considerable contrast to the refined sensibility of the acoustic violin, since much of the resonant subtlety of the instrument is lost in the process of amplification. Yet, amplification contributed significantly to the acceptance of the instrument: the violin became more audible in a typical jazz and jazz-rock context, the overall sound of the instrument fitting the rock ambience especially well.

Jean-Luc Ponty (b. 1942) established himself as the premiere electric violinist in the 1970s, not long after he abandoned his earlier bop oriented style for rock. A harsh jazz-rock tone, an impassioned use of **double stops** (two notes at once), and a sliding, basically modal sense characterize his sound. Ponty's electric style can be heard to good effect on his searing solo from "Upon the Wings of Music." The album by the same title was helpful in establishing Ponty as the preeminent jazz-rock violinist.

On first hearing, Ponty's rough electric tone seems to resemble a synthesizer more than a violin. The timbral similarities between the old-fashioned fiddle and the faddish synthesizer probably helped earn the violin its welcome in the earlier days of jazz-rock. Also, throughout the solo we hear those typical scoops up to high notes that jazz violinists seem to favor.

Ponty relies heavily on the pitches of the Eb dorian scale, quite rarely playing outside the mode. Modal improvisation is quite common in 1970s jazz-rock and probably derived simultaneously from 1960s modal jazz and the use of modal harmonies in British rock tunes. The technique of sliding between pitches (portamento) is extended in Ponty's solo, a factor that increases the similarity between the amplified violin and the synthesizer. By bowing one of the *glissandi* with triplet eighth-notes, Ponty imparts a great deal of drive and excitement to his sound. He also relies on repeated patterns and complex syncopations throughout the solo.

While electric violin was very popular in the jazz-rock heyday of the 1970s, some violinists have been favoring the use of unamplified violin too, seeing advantages of both. The other strings instruments, cello and viola, are now also heard from time to time in a jazz setting. Some of the important jazz string players of today include cellist Abdul Wadud and violinist/violist Leroy Jenkins. Ornette Coleman also plays violin.

synthesizer

Synthesizers for musical use were developed in the early 1950s, some of the first having been built by RCA and the Bell Telephone Laboratories. The early models were very cumbersome, however, and totally unsuitable for live performance. Unlike acoustic instruments or amplified acoustic instruments, the synthesizer's sound is produced electronically: an oscillator supplies a voltage to an amplifier, from which it is routed to a speaker.

Later in the 1960s, the first synthesizers were built in which the player in a live setting could control the sound with some degree of freedom. During the 1970s, when synthesizers became cheaper and more compact, thanks to the miniaturization of the circuitry, the multikeyboardist, surrounded by stacks of electric pianos and synthesizers, became a familiar sight in rock bands. The Minimoog was perhaps the first convenient, widely used synthesizer, a standard keyboard accessory in rock bands and jazz groups in the early 1970s.

The mid-1970s witnessed the dual breakthroughs of polyphonic and digital synthesizers. The polyphonic models enabled the keyboardist to play chords, since several oscillators could function at the same time. Digital synthesizers were more flexible still, their numerical approximations of complex sound waves yielding a more precise method of timbral control. The convenience and flexibility of these synthesizers further popularized the practice of imitating the sounds of other instruments.

In the early 1980s the digital synthesizer was combined with the increasingly popular personal computer. The convenience of data storage on the computer's floppy discs increased the variety, complexity, convenience, and interaction of the digitally synthesized sounds with one another. The use of computer memory enabled the mixing of several tracks of digitally produced sound, simulating the use of a multitrack tape recorder.

Curiously, even the early jazz synthesizer solos reflected the instrument's potential. The synthesizer was then at the forefront of the developing jazz-rock style, the musicians were excited over the new instrument, and many imagi-

Herbie Hancock (Courtesy Institute of Jazz Studies, Rutgers University).

native solos were played. Herbie Hancock's solo on "Chameleon" established him as one of the finest live performers on the instrument. The solo was played on an Arp synthesizer, which was manufactured by a company specializing in synthesizers for live performance. (For a transcription of Hancock's solo on Chameleon, see pp. 251–254.)

Hancock's solo is so effective partly because of the beautiful balance among three distinct elements: free blues lines, repeated funky riffs, and nonpitched sounds. The bass line establishes the harmonic orientation of the piece by alternating Bb7 and Eb7, that is, the standard harmonies of the Bb blues. Hancock's solo responds to these blues harmonies with an emphasis on the Bb blues scale. When Hancock chooses to step out of the blues scale, he usually does so with a patterned riff.

Another strikingly effective deviation from the blues scale occurs toward the end of the solo, where Hancock gradually bends the pitch of the synthesizer (probably with a left-hand control device) a half step higher, thus simulating the upward blue note bend on a larger scale. The bounce back to the correct intonation comes across as the large-scale resolution of the inflected blue note.

In the last section, I mentioned the similarity in the sonorities of the electric violin and synthesizer. The typical scoops up to high notes often heard in jazz violin playing, when amplified, sound much like the synthesizer effects heard throughout the solo. Also like the electric violin are the occasional slides between notes, which on the synthesizer are controlled with a device known as "portamento," from the string effect of the same name.

Unlike the controlled voice leading and motivic structure that tend to unify bop and traditional jazz solos, the funky solo tends to be sectional, to feature a single idea until it settles in. Accordingly, Hancock begins his solo with a number of very funky blues licks, generously separated by space. Early on, a repeating pattern is gradually transformed by the addition of modulated sound. "Noise" or unpitched sound of this sort is usually produced by frequency or amplitude modulation of the signal. This modulated section is the first of two such passages that are similarly syncopated. The continuous dotted-quarter-notes of this section effect a fascinating cross-rhythm with the underlying 4/4 meter.

The band returns to climax the solo with some call-and-response exchanges between Hancock and the rest of the group. Here, Hancock plays solo breaks that climax in an effective liquidation of the ubiquitous blues licks into chromatic scale segments. This procedure winds up the solo in a logical and satisfying manner.

The synthesizer performs most advantageously when its unique timbral qualities are imaginatively exploited. Hancock's solo succeeds so well because it does what cannot be done on any other instrument, particularly the segments with the modulated sounds and the portamenti.

Since the mid-1970s, some synthesists have become less interested in the specialized use of the instrument and increasingly preoccupied with evoking the sounds of other instruments. Although this is an inexpensive way of simulating a larger ensemble, synthesizers will probably never replace the instruments being imitated. A trumpet player, for example, controls his tone and expression by directing the air flow from the lungs and diaphragm, tonguing each note in just the right way, and subtly adjusting his embouchure for each pitch. Depressing a piano key on a synthesizer can never totally simulate this process or reproduce the unique "feel" of a top player.

The most effective synthesizer music is likely to remain that which best exploits the indigenous qualities of the instrument. The sound control of the synthesizer becomes more subtle every year, the technology approaching truly impressive proportions. Yet, much of what a synthesizer does best can be heard on recordings from the 1970s. The future of synthesized sound remains a major stylistic question in jazz.

Modern jazz recordings, such as "Chameleon," continue to feature the significant aspects of jazz heard as early as the 1920s. Additive rhythm, use of a head and solos, a rhythm section backing up the lead instruments, and a blues flavor can all be heard in "Chameleon," updated here to reflect the popular music ambience of rock. Other fine jazz synthesists, such as Jan Hammer, Chick Corea, and Joe Zawinul, continue to extend its use in jazz.

jazz melodic styles summarized

In Chapters 6, 7, and 8 I examined some sample melodic solos that spanned a large range of jazz styles. These solos were primarily single-line improvisations, accompanied by rhythm sections and bands of various makeups. Within each instrumental category certain stylistic changes could be detected, generally based on extending the characteristics of the preceding style. Occasionally, too, stylistic reaction would set in, where conspicuous features of a preceding practice would be avoided.

Not surprisingly, general features applicable to all instruments in each jazz style have emerged: swing melodies often sound a lot alike whether played on clarinet, violin, or trumpet. In the following review, specific differences among instruments will be noted where appropriate.

New Orleans and Chicago Style Dixieland

Timbre: (1) generally more raucous and rough-hewn than later styles, with Beiderbecke's influence leading to at least some smoother playing; (2) more use of vibrato (especially Armstrong's use of terminal vibrato); (3) sax tone reedy, very rich; (4) use of trombone effects such as glissando; (5) much use of blue note inflections on all instruments; (6) comfortable instrumental ranges rather than exploitation of extreme registers; and (7) sharply articulated attacks, with forceful tonguing.

Phrasing: (1) square, often in 2- and 4-bar units; and (2) not much space between phrases.

Rhythm: (1) strongly tied to the basic beat; (2) much use of syncopation; and (3) choppiness produced by use of short, often syncopated melodic units.

Thematic continuity: motivically based with some voice-leading control, but aside from Beiderbecke, mostly rather simple.

Chord-scale relations: inside playing without exception.

Large-scale coherence: (1) motivic structure; and (2) balance of gesture (use of climax, etc.).

Swing

Timbre: (1) more refined and polished than dixieland; (2) less use of vibrato; (3) smoother, lighter sax tones; (4) more brilliant trumpet tones; (5) less use of specific instrumental effects; (6) instrumental ranges extended upward; (7) softer attacks and more legato playing; and (8) less use of blue note effects.

Phrasing: (1) in 2- or 4-bar units, but more varied in later swing styles (ballad playing featured more irregular phrasing); and (2) not much space between phrases.

Rhythm: (1) more swinging although less syncopation than dixieland; (2) uptempo reliance on eighth-note lines; and (3) ballads feature greater variety of rhythmic values.

Thematic continuity: less reliance on motive in uptempo solos, more reliance on voice leading; in ballads, motivic relationships more prominent.

Chord-scale relations: inside playing, but in later swing more experimentation with extended chord tones within melodic lines.

Large-scale coherence: (1) voice leading more often than motivic structure; and (2) gestural balance.

Bop

Timbre: (1) tougher, edgier sound than swing, often raspy; (2) little use of vibrato except on ballads; (3) little use of instrumental effects; (4) strong attacks combined with legato lines; (5) no use of blue note effects on uptempo pieces; and (6) instrumental ranges extended upwards, especially for brass instruments.

Phrasing: (1) highly irregular, perhaps to offset symmetrical AABA forms so often used; and (2) little space between phrases.

Rhythm: great reliance on eighth-note lines in uptempo pieces, ballads feature more rhythmic variety.

Thematic continuity: voice leading almost exclusively in uptempo pieces; motivic relations kept in the background.

Chord-scale relations: inside, but based on more complex scales that include extended chord tones.

Large-scale coherence: (1) voice leading with less reliance on use of climax followed by relaxation; and (2) balance of gesture.

Cool

Timbre: (1) softer, smoother, more relaxed sound; (2) mid-range of instruments emphasized; (3) almost no use of blue note effects; and (4) soft attacks and legato lines.

Phrasing: (1) irregular like bop; and (2) much use of space between phrases.

Rhythm: much greater variety than bop in uptempo and medium tempo pieces.

Thematic continuity: balanced between motivic and voice leading.

Chord-scale relations: inside playing, often with extended chord tones heard in bop.

Large-scale coherence: (1) motivic structure and voice leading; and (2) balance of gesture.

Hard Bop

Timbre: (1) continuation of boplike (hard-edged, brittle, instant) tones on various instruments; (2) use of upper registers; (3) return to blue note effects, blues riffs; and (4) wide variety of attacks and articulations.

Phrasing: somewhat more regular than bop phrasing, with return to 2- and 4-bar units.

Rhythm: more syncopated; trend toward simpler blues patterns; more variety than bop.

Thematic continuity: motives emphasized over voice leading, except in those players continuing in the 1940s bop tradition.

Chord-scale relations: more inside, often based on blues scale.

Large-scale coherence: motivic, use of climax-release, and gestural balance.

Free Jazz

Timbre: (1) emphasis on hard-edged, tough sound; (2) use of entire range of instrument, but upper range more prominent; (3) wide variety of attacks and articulations; (4) use of vocal sounds, cries, shrieks, etc.; and (5) extended techniques produced on individual instruments emphasized.

Phrasing: extremely irregular, often lack of steady pulse.

Rhythm: (1) free use of extreme rhythms, from held out notes to "sheets of sound" effects; and (2) syncopations.

Thematic continuity: motivic.

Chord-scale relations: outside playing, if a tonal center exists at all.

Large-scale coherence: gestural and motivic.

Modal Jazz

Timbre: (1) wide variety from tough, hard-edged bop to sweeter, cool jazz; (2) full instrumental ranges exploited; (3) some use of blue note effects, especially in ballads; and (4) individual instrumental characteristics somewhat emphasized.

Phrasing: highly irregular, 2- and 4-bar phrases rarely heard.

Rhythm: (1) wide variety of note values, though uptempo solos tend to emphasize eighth-notes; and (2) little use of beat oriented syncopation.

Thematic continuity: motivic.

Chord-scale relations: outside, often loosely based on a mode.

Large-scale coherence: motivic and gestural.

Jazz-rock

Timbre: (1) very hard-edged, raucous; (2) upper instrumental ranges emphasized; (3) use of blue note effects, particularly in funky substyles; (4) ambience of rock with many electric and electronic instruments in addition to more traditional instruments; and (5) high volume.

Phrasing: highly irregular in improvisation, but thematic heads often composed in 2- and 4-bar units.

Rhythm: (1) wide variety of rhythmic values, but eighth-notes emphasized in uptempo solos; and (2) highly energetic.

Thematic continuity: motivic.

Chord-scale relations: inside, though can become outside in high-energy modal rock performances; blues scale usages in funky styles.

Large-scale coherence: motivic.

chapter
nine

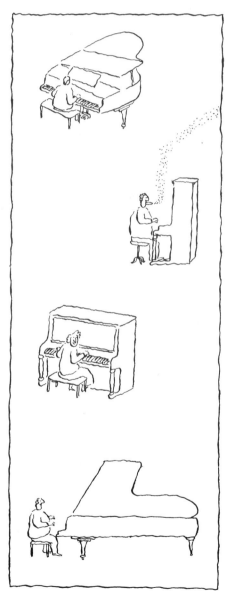

piano
styles

The piano is unique among the instruments in jazz in that it can function both as a part of a larger ensemble and as a complete "ensemble" of its own. As part of a larger ensemble, it is a member of the rhythm section, sometimes playing solos, but otherwise feeding harmonies to the other instruments and joining with the bass and drums in securing the band's rhythmic foundation. As a solo instrument, the left hand functions as a miniature rhythm section of its own by providing a rhythmic-harmonic foundation to the melodic lines of the right hand.

Right-hand melodies on the piano are often like those of the instruments studied in the preceding chapters. Yet, occasionally its melodies are more "pianistic," meaning that fast jumps and skips among groups of notes can be performed quite naturally, even simply. The melodies of early ragtime piano, for example, are awkward on most instruments other than the piano.

In this chapter I will concentrate primarily on solo jazz piano because the function of the ensemble pianist's right hand, during solo improvisation, is similar to that of the solo pianist's, while the left-hand part of the ensemble pianist is often simplified to accompanying chords.

early jazz piano

Early jazz piano evolved from nineteenth-century ragtime, a piano style that some writers[1] refer to as the first jazz style of all. Ragtime itself, initially a more syncopated, looser method of performing popular music and blues tunes, was pioneered by black musicians in the Midwest and the South. Early descriptions suggest that the first ragtime pianists, in "ragging" a piece of music, syncopated its rhythms, adding accents, off-beat rhythmic patterns, and other non-European musical features such as note clusters. Late nineteenth-century pianists who specialized in this style of playing traveled throughout the West and South, playing at bars, saloons, houses of prostitution, riverboats, or wherever they could find work.

Most likely, ragtime and blues pianists were one and the same throughout the 1880s and 1890s. As ragtime style coalesced in the late 1890s, blues and

[1]For example, see Taylor, Billy, *Jazz Piano,* Dubuque: Wm. C. Brown Company Publishers, 1982, p. 35ff.

boogie-woogie pianists probably distinguished themselves from the ragtime players by their somewhat earthier, more rhythmic technique and by their emphasis on the repetitive blues choruses. As blues musicians, they most likely accompanied themselves with singing.

Although ragtime was thought essentially to be a method of piano performance, bands played ragtime, too. Oral accounts of the early jazz players emphasize that many of the black brass bands in New Orleans throughout the late nineteenth and early twentieth centuries were playing marches as well as improvised pieces. Hence, it is likely that jazzlike liberties were taken with all their music.[2] Of course, without recordings of improvising brass bands it is difficult to establish the salient differences between "ragging" and "jazzing" a piece. Possibly a jazzed interpretation was more improvisatory, whereas a band that ragged tunes would merely syncopate the melodies.

In any event, by jazzing or ragging the square rhythms of the nineteenth-century marches and dance tunes, early jazz horn players gradually developed the New Orleans jazz style of the 1910s and early 1920s. Scott Joplin, one of the greatest ragtime composers, had played in marching bands as a youth, as did most of the early jazz wind musicians.

The piano nevertheless remained the instrument popularly associated with ragtime. Although the style had been largely improvisatory, musicians with formal education in writing and arranging music soon began to compose, codify, and compile ragtime tunes into piano sheet music for nonimprovising musicians. Probably as a result of this codification, march form came to be associated with the printed music, although the improvising ragtime pianists almost certainly played more freely. In any event, thanks to the wide dissemination of sheet music, ragtime piano became a national, perhaps even an international, craze from about 1900 to 1915, an event that prepared both the public and the musicians themselves for the looser, fully improvising jazz bands that defined the New Orleans and Chicago styles.

All in all, the ragtime and blues piano players of the late nineteenth century contributed critically to the stylistic formation of early jazz. Unfortunately, since these players were not recorded, it is necessary to turn to the sheet music, with its unavoidable formalizations, for the analysis of ragtime style.

scott joplin

> Scott Joplin: "Maple Leaf Rag," published by John Stark & Sons, Sedalia, Missouri, 1899.

Despite the fine work of James Scott, Charles Lamb, Artie Matthews, and many others, Scott Joplin (1868-1917) was the most popular of the ragtime

---

[2]See Schafer, William J., *Brass Bands and New Orleans Jazz*. Baton Rouge and London: Louisiana State University Press, 1977, pp. 2-38.

composers, writing and publishing the greatest rags of the era. Joplin, born in Texarkana, Tex., had studied classical piano as a youth, but, for a few years anyway, gave up his formal studies to travel as a blues and ragtime pianist. Carl Hoffman of Kansas City published Joplin's first rag, "Original Rags," in 1899, the same year in which the "Maple Leaf Rag" was published.

The tremendous popularity of the "Maple Leaf Rag" established Joplin as the premiere rag composer. During the rest of his life he wrote many outstanding rags, although, thinking of himself as a classical artist, he dreamed of establishing the genre as a fine art. Eventually, he composed a ragtime opera, "Treemonisha," which he staged by himself in 1915, but the work was a failure. Joplin, depressed and ill with syphilis, soon became unable to work and eventually died in a mental institution.

The "Maple Leaf Rag" (SCCJ) was one of the first rags to be formally composed and written down; it has remained the favorite ragtime piece for decades. In it many of the important features of early jazz piano can be observed, features that have remained present to this day in solo jazz piano.

As described earlier, most jazz styles separate the timekeeping and harmonic duties from the more melodic functions. Ragtime piano follows this principle by assigning the rhythm and harmony to the left hand and the melody to the right. At times the functions may be combined, but clear separation often prevails. In the first 4 bars of the "Maple Leaf Rag," the steady left hand supplies both beat and harmony. The right hand plays the engaging melody, syncopated by accents on rhythmically weak portions of the bar. The character of the melody is pianistic, falling easily under the fingers of the right hand.

The left-hand accompaniment in the opening 4 measures reveals an important texture heard in all ragtime piano pieces: the alternation between bass notes, played here as octaves, and chords, voiced in a somewhat higher register. This type of left-hand, harmonic-rhythmic accompaniment is known as **stride** and is commonly heard in solo jazz piano styles. In stride, most typically the left hand plays bass notes on the first and third beats and higher chords on the second and fourth beats. The stride pianist thus gives the impression of playing with three hands: bass, chords, and melody all clearly separated in register. This procedure can be heard in the next section of the rag.

The "Maple Leaf Rag" is written in march form. A march usually begins with two different sections, each typically comprising 16 bars, each repeated, and each with its own tune. After the second section has been played, the first will usually be repeated. This plan produces an ABA structure that, as a single unit, defines the main body of the march. It may be preceded by a 4-bar introduction, which Joplin chooses not to include in the "Maple Leaf Rag."

The composer usually follows the main body of the march (ABA) with an interlude to connect it to a new section called the "trio." The trio is almost always in the key of the subdominant (IV), which lies a perfect fourth above the key of the A section. The trio may have one or two tunes and sections associated with it, each usually 16 bars. After the trio the A section may be repeated a last time. Although many variations of this archetypal march form do occur, almost every written rag and march has a trio in the key of the subdominant.

The "Maple Leaf Rag" has the form ABACD, with CD being the trio section. There is no interlude or introduction and the D section returns to the original key of the A section. Each section, except for the second A section, is played twice, which is also typical of both rags and marches.

Ragtime, the immediate predecessor of improvised jazz, clearly reveals the relationship between the harmonic and formal foundation of European music and the rhythmic, melodic vitality of the African tradition. Written and unwritten rags form the basis from which the earliest recorded jazz styles developed: ragtime piano evolved into early jazz piano, while the marching bands evolved into the early jazz bands.

james p. johnson

James P. Johnson (solo piano): "Carolina Shout," Okeh 4495, October 18, 1921.

The styles of the earliest jazz pianists, such as Jelly Roll Morton and James P. Johnson, were similar to ragtime in two striking respects: use of march form and a solid left-hand stride accompaniment supporting a syncopated melody with jagged, short melodic phrases. The group of pianists who specialized in this style was known as the Harlem stride school, whose first major artist was James P. Johnson (1891-1955).

Johnson was born in New Brunswick, N.J., and raised in Jersey City and New York. Though essentially a popular and jazz pianist, he had a strong classical background and always remained interested in fine-art music. Most of his life was spent working in Atlantic City, New York, and other cities along the East Coast. He also toured extensively on the vaudeville circuit and even played in England.

Johnson wrote great popular songs, such as "Charleston," and other famous works, such as "Carolina Shout" (SCCJ). Many of the differences between "Carolina Shout" and classic ragtime are subtle, but a smoother, more linear jazz style can nevertheless be detected. For example, the right-hand melody articulates a long, jagged, descending phrase through the entire first 4 bars. A phrase such as this is certainly not unknown in ragtime, but it does suggest some differentiation from the earlier, rhythmic, more fragmented style found in the "Maple Leaf Rag."

Johnson soon adds new rhythmic complications to the left-hand part that would not have been found at all in published rags, though they might have been played by improvising rag pianists. For example, the repeat of the first section reveals a rather complex variation of left-hand stride. In a published rag, the first strain would have been repeated literally, and the left-hand complexity completely avoided.

The 16-bar sectional structure of "Carolina Shout" is also raglike, particularly with the inclusion of the trio in the key of the subdominant. Nevertheless, the longer, smoother phrases suggest the start of a slow evolution from ragtime to swing. Throughout, it seems clear that Johnson wished to overwhelm listeners with his Harlem-stride virtuosity, whereas many of the ragtime composers, particularly Joplin, took pains to insist that their works not be played too fast merely to create a flashy impression.

The Harlem stride school, which links the classic rag style to the classic swing style, features elements of both. The note clusters and the raw blues effects heard in many rags are avoided in stride, while the melodies effortlessly float between smooth swing and angular ragtime rhythms. Even the music of the later Harlem pianists, such as Fats Waller, continues to exhibit features of ragtime, in both the melodic styles and the stride rhythms. As you will see, the left-hand stride of ragtime forms a basis for many solo jazz piano styles.

jelly roll morton

> Jelly Roll Morton (solo piano): "New Orleans Blues" (called "New Orleans Joys"), Gennett 5486, July 17, 1923.

Like James P. Johnson, Jelly Roll Morton (1885–1941) was among the first pianists to develop a jazzlike style based on ragtime. His informal performance of the "Maple Leaf Rag" (SCCJ), full of the liberties most early improvising pianists took with written compositions, reveals the close relationship between ragtime and early jazz.

Morton was a colorful, unique jazz personality. A Creole who played often in the sporting houses of New Orleans, Morton claimed to have invented jazz in the early part of the century. An excellent pool player, braggart, and ladies' man, he often made a living from gambling and pimping, which were far more lucrative than merely playing the piano.[3] From 1907 to 1923, he traveled around the country, leading bands and playing solo *gigs* (jobs), often remaining for a few months in each city.

His early solo recordings for Gennett between 1923 and 1924 remain classics, equal in quality to the famous sides he soon recorded with his band, the Red Hot Peppers (SCCJ). For these recordings, Morton wrote some of the earliest great jazz arrangements and established himself as the first important jazz composer. Throughout the 1920s, he recorded voluminously, both solos and small-band arrangements. During the 1930s, unable to update his style to swing,

[3]See Lomax, Alan, *Mister Jelly Roll,* 2nd ed., Berkeley: University of California Press, 1973.

Jelly Roll Morton (Courtesy Institute of Jazz Studies, Rutgers University).

he commanded less and less attention. When he died in 1941 he was remembered by relatively few people.

Significantly different from the Harlem stride piano style, Morton's performances are less virtuosic and often include his so-called Spanish tinge, evidence of the early association of New Orleans jazz with music from the Caribbean or even South America. Morton's use of the Spanish tinge is also the first recorded

161

example of the "fusion" of Latin music and jazz. For example, his very early performance of "New Orleans Blues" is characterized by the following left-hand rhythm:

The Spanish tinge rhythm breaks the usual stride formula by syncopating the left-hand accompaniment, the upper chord entering on beat 2½. This pattern has the effect of simplifying a standard Latin rhythm and implying the *habañera* beat:

The upper chord, C#-D-F, is an early recorded instance of a *cluster*, a chord type usually associated with blues and boogie-woogie pianists. By playing the minor and major thirds together, pianists attempt to suggest blue notes, as if they are playing in the cracks between the piano keys. This is a sound that is not often seen in published rags or heard in the recordings of the Harlem stride pianists.

The work's multichorus format and the occasional breaks in the rhythm during which the left hand takes the melody also reflects the blues influence. These breaks occur during the first 4 bars of C3 and C4 before the Latin rhythm resumes in bar 5. A solo break during the first 4 bars of a 12-bar blues chorus soon became a standard jazz performance cliché, common in blues ever since. Morton liked to emphasize breaks in his arrangements.

Morton effectively finishes with a solid out-chorus, the seventh chorus of the performance, where the Spanish tinge finally yields to a satisfying "walking-chord" rhythm, each beat accented heavily and evenly. In so doing, Morton anticipates swing piano styles that avoid the 2-beat emphasis of stride and instead emulate the smooth feeling of 4 even beats.

One cannot leave this piece without taking note of the intricate right-hand rhythms of the sixth chorus. While the left hand maintains the tricky Spanish tinge beat, the right hand improvises lines of deft rhythmic complexity without interrupting or upsetting the rhythm of the left hand. Difficult to play and almost impossible to notate accurately, this sixth chorus perfectly prepares the driving, straight-ahead solidity of the out-chorus with its contrasting on-the-beat quarter-notes. Formally exquisite and beautifully performed, "New Orleans Blues" is one of the greatest solo piano recordings of the 1920s.

fats waller

Thomas "Fats" Waller (solo piano): "Handful of Keys" and "E Flat Blues," Victor LPT-6001, March 11, 1935.

Fats Waller (Courtesy Institute of Jazz Studies, Rutgers University).

Thomas Wright "Fats" Waller was the last of the great Harlem stride pianists and one of the finest pianists of the swing era. Elements of swing were prominent in his style, yet, in his solo work especially, many ragtime features remained. Apparently, band and ensemble performances prompted Waller to respond with smooth melodies typical of swing, but the striding left hand heard in his solo performances encouraged him to play bouncier ragtime licks in his right hand as well.

Waller (1904-1943) was born in New York City and, like many of the talented musicians raised there, thrived on its cosmopolitan atmosphere and its great diversity of musical activity. His father was a preacher who undoubtedly disapproved of Waller's early interest in ragtime and popular music. Still, while Waller was a teenager, he insisted on playing at the Harlem rent parties where he quickly developed his reputation. Finally heard by James P. Johnson, Waller was given piano lessons by the "king" of stride piano.

Waller began his recording career in 1922 and soon thereafter established himself as a songwriter. Often collaborating with lyricist Andy Razaf, Waller wrote hundreds of songs including many that remain popular today; for example, "Ain't Misbehavin'," "Black and Blue," and "Honeysuckle Rose." In the 1930s he became one of the most popular entertainers of the time, touring, writing songs, recording with bands, and appearing in feature and numerous short films. Unfortunately, alcoholism and obesity, combined with unrelentless activity and high living, led to his early death. A tremendous entertainer, Waller remains, with Louis Armstrong, beloved by the public for his humor and irresistible stage demeanor.

Waller's "Handful of Keys" most particularly recalls James P. Johnson and classic stride, while at the same time blending it with the looser feel of swing. The piece, however, projects more of a ragtime than swing feel because of (1) the marchlike form with a trio in the subdominant key, (2) the composed rather than improvised character of the sectional melodies, and (3) the stride accompaniment. The stride left hand racing along at such a fast tempo testifies to Waller's technique and the virtuosity of Harlem stride style itself.

The swing era character of the piece is exemplified by the song-form relationship of the first two sections, A (8 bars), A' (8 bars), B (8 bars), A" (8 bars). The B-section bridge even includes the rhythm-changes chord progression, further characterizing the piece as swing. Here is a summary of its rather elaborate formal plan:

Key: I   A(8) A'(8) B(8) A"(8)
            interlude (4)
Trio (IV):   C(8) D(8) E(16)
            interlude (4)
Key: I   F(8) F(8) G(8) F(10) sections B, D, and G are
            bridges with rhythm changes

The use of song forms and rhythm changes balances the vivacious ragtime feel of "Handful of Keys." Its sophisticated harmony, long phrases, and bright tempo also help establish the piece as Harlem stride. "Handful of Keys" admirably encompasses the 30-year pianistic evolution from ragtime to swing, though its eclecticism is not always typical of Waller's compositions.

An example of Waller's more casual swing style is the languorous "E Flat Blues," which, like Morton's "New Orleans Blues," is in 12-bar blues form. Waller's beautifully light touch enables the single pitches and chords to glide effortlessly from one to the next. The stride bass in this performance has been drained of all its old-fashioned ragtime drive and instead supports the lyricism of the right hand. Waller's frequent use of a chord on the first or third beat, instead of the usual single bass note, contributes to the smoothness of the left-hand rhythm. Occasionally the left hand simulates a walking bass by droning E♭ and B♭ pitches under fluent right-hand chords.

Another very important feature of solo piano in the swing era, rarely played by the older Harlem stride pianists, can be heard throughout the performance: intervals of tenths in the left hand played in a "walking" pattern. When falling on the first and third beats, in alternation with chords, the tenths produce a brilliant effect because the upper pitch of each tenth forms a counterpoint to the main melody of the right hand. The tenths either alternate with right-hand chords or, as in the example, are used in walking patterns. Tenths require a large stretch of the hand and thus are not found in printed ragtime.

The glistening runs at the beginning of the second chorus of "E Flat Blues" are another swing era piano innovation, heard in most of the players of the time, especially in those pianists with lighter touches like Teddy Wilson and Art Tatum. These runs are often used to provide fills between more melodic phrases.

The catchiness of the short melodic fragments of "E Flat Blues" can be attributed to Waller's great ability as a songwriter. Their use also suggests that much of the piece was composed beforehand, that it was in no sense a spontaneous improvisation. Nevertheless, Waller retains his excellence in more improvisatory settings too, effectively bridging the style of James P. Johnson's ragtime oriented stride to the mature swing styles of later pianists.

earl hines

Earl "Fatha" Hines (solo piano): "Rosetta," Bluebird B-10555, October 21, 1939.

Earl Hines first established himself as a major talent by performing superbly on the Louis Armstrong Hot Five recordings in the late 1920s. He was the musician most responsible for developing a linear, fluid concept of jazz piano; that is, he applied the style of Armstrong's trumpet playing to the keyboard. While his swinging jazz piano concept dominated the 1930s and 1940s, Hines himself continued to perform magnificently until the late 1970s.

The dramatic change of style that Hines initiated in the mid-1920s can be appreciated by comparing the earlier Armstrong records, with pianist Lil Hardin, to the later Hot Five selections with Hines. The graceful, easygoing sense of forward movement he contributes to the band presages the swing style of the 1930s, even while the other sidemen remain entrenched in the New Orleans sound.

From Pittsburgh, Hines (1905–1983) was raised in a musical family, studied classical piano, and played his first gigs in his hometown. In 1923 his musical

Earl Hines (Courtesy Institute of Jazz Studies, Rutgers University).

travels brought him to Chicago where, by playing with the Carroll Dickerson band, he met Louis Armstrong. He performed with Armstrong for several years, but decided to continue with his own groups after Armstrong departed for his career as a big band soloist. Soon, in the 1930s, Hines was leading big bands as well, and he continued to do so for many years.

Hines directed a historically important band in the early 1940s, with Charlie Parker and Billy Eckstine, a band that contributed to the evolution of bop style. In the late 1940s he rejoined Louis Armstrong, remained until 1951, then afterward continued to perform throughout the world, either as a soloist or as a leader of small groups, for the rest of his life. A phenomenal technician whose improvisations are consistently inventive, Hines's ability never seemed to diminish. He was indeed one of the finest jazz pianists of all time.

While Hines's playing never sounded stale, he achieved his greatest distinction during the swing era. He was able to play with great suaveness, as on "West End Blues," although be tended to be a rhythmic and adventurous player, more so than Teddy Wilson, for example, who among all others exemplifies the smooth swing pianist. The contrast between them can be heard effectively on their solo piano recordings of "Rosetta," Hines's most famous swing tune. (See next section for a discussion of Teddy Wilson's performance of "Rosetta.")

After an introduction in which unusual harmonies eventually converge to F major, the key of the piece, Hines establishes a bouncy stride to accompany an embellished version of the tune in the right hand. The tenths in the left hand are used to excellent effect, the thumb providing a counter line heard off and on throughout the entire performance with various modifications. Here is an outline of this left-hand effect:

The stride is broken during the first half of the bridge, where the left hand instead undertakes fuller, more developed countermelodies. The jaunty swing feel soon returns, however, providing an effective contrast between the first and last halves of the bridge.

Hines interpolates an ingenious interlude before continuing on to the second chorus. Because he avoids pinning a cadential ending onto the interlude, it seems to continue for more than its actual 4 bars; only retrospectively can the beginning of the second chorus be ascertained. Hines's adventurousness continues with some rhythmic trickery during the C2A' section, followed by a rather hectic and unsettled bridge. Although Hines playfully hints at reducing the tension by returning to stride accompaniment, he keeps us off balance throughout the remainder of the second chorus.

On the whole the performance is engaging, swinging, and constantly surprising, as if Hines is overflowing with too many ideas to cram into a three-minute recording. Hines was able to maintain such incredible inventiveness throughout his entire career. No other jazz pianist demands so much critical listening while simultaneously expressing the joy of adventurous improvisation.

teddy wilson

Teddy Wilson (solo piano): "Rosetta," Brunswick 7563, October 7, 1935; "Between the Devil and the Deep Blue Sea" (second take), CBS CL-2428, November 12, 1937.

Teddy Wilson, undoubtedly one of the greatest swing pianists of all time, was born in 1912 in Austin, Tex. Like Earl Hines, he was fortunate to have had a solid training in both classical piano and music theory. Following in Hines's footsteps, he traveled to Chicago in the 1920s, where he was influenced by Louis Armstrong and by Hines himself. By 1933 he was playing with Benny Carter (b. 1907) and shortly thereafter met Benny Goodman. At the urging of record producer John Hammond, Goodman hired Wilson, thus forming the Benny Goodman Trio, the first major jazz group that was racially mixed.

Wilson remained with Goodman from 1936 to 1939, then left to lead his own big band, which was a commercial failure. During the 1930s, however, he was fortunate to have arranged the music and assembled the musicians for the famous studio sessions with Billie Holiday, Lester Young, Benny Goodman, and others that remain the best small band swing recordings ever produced. For the remainder of the swing era, he played with various bands, then moved to the West Coast. In the 1960s and 1970s he became active once again, his technique only slightly less formidable, but with the same wonderful control and exquisite taste that have always marked his playing.

Probably the fooling, tricky quality of Hines's performance of "Rosetta" is the first thing we miss in Wilson's elegant but more restrained performance of the same tune. The slower tempo leaves Wilson more time to think and, hence, more time to devise passages characterized by tenths and complex harmonies. The first 4 bars of the bridge of the first chorus, for example, contain an ingenious passage in which the right-hand melody dissolves into an upward run leaving the left hand free to take over the tune. When the right hand reassumes the melody, during the last 4 bars, the left hand complements it again at the very end of the bridge. Further, the return of the right-hand melody for the last 4 bars is unsettled somewhat by the anticipated G♭7 (or D♭m) harmony on the fourth beat of C1Bm5. This harmony, a D♭-F♭ tenth played in passing between D-F and C-E♭, demonstrates the sophistication of Wilson's harmonic embellishments.

The lavishness of the interpolated runs reaches new heights with Wilson, who uses them frequently to connect more melodic passages. The runs tend to form links between phrases or sections, as for example the run just mentioned, played by the right hand at the end of the first 4 bars of the C1B section. One of the most beautiful of these runs connects the second chorus to the third. These figurations, used by most swing pianists, quickly became a feature associated with the style.

Which "Rosetta," Hines's or Wilson's, is the better performance? So similar as marvelous examples of classic solo piano swing, they are equally dissimilar in their temperaments. Hines has a lot more fun than Wilson and insists on challenging the listener with unexpected transitions, changes of mood, and varieties of texture, but Wilson projects an extremely engaging elegance and sophistication, with greater emphasis on the more old-fashioned values of musical excellence. In their own way, both performances are equally superb.

The tempo of the "Between the Devil and the Deep Blue Sea" is too fast for the comfortable use of tenths on the first and third beats of the stride pattern throughout, but Wilson frequently breaks from stride into walking tenths, a normal swing device found in most pianists with large enough hands. Further, a stride pianist will sometimes use an easier pattern in which the left hand remains stationary, especially in as fast a performance as this.

A stationary stride can be produced by breaking the tenths themselves, a technique heard throughout the bridge where the distance from the bass note to the top of the chord is usually a tenth. The resulting sound is thinner than that of the more usual stride accompaniment, but it can be used for a short while for contrast, even if its effect diminishes rapidly when maintained for too long. (For a transcription of the fourth chorus of Wilson's "Between the Devil and the Deep Blue Sea," see pp. 255-256.)

art tatum

Art Tatum (solo piano): "Aunt Hagar's Blues," Capitol M-11028, July 13, 1949.

Art Tatum's technique was incredibly dazzling. He could play stride about as fast as technically possible, yet in a more complex way than ever before. Possessing one of the lightest touches of all the major pianists, Tatum tended to play softly and smoothly, without much dynamic variation, a practice that enhanced his naturally gentle touch.

Tatum (1910-1956), born in Toledo, Ohio, was blind at birth because of cataracts. Fortunately, after a series of operations, he was able to gain partial vision in one eye. His professional career, begun in his early teens, was centered in the Toledo area until 1932 when he was finally heard in New York. After his first solo recordings were made in 1933, Tatum found himself in great demand as a performer. Though he worked in a trio with bassist Slam Stewart and guitarist Tiny Grimes for several years, beginning in 1943, Tatum continued to be recognized chiefly as a solo pianist. In the mid-1950s he recorded voluminously for jazz producer Norman Granz. Unfortunately, Tatum died soon thereafter, probably from the effects of alcoholism.

The following points summarize Tatum's piano technique.

1. Throughout the development of stride piano, 3- and 4-note chords were normally played on the second and fourth beats, while the first and third beats evolved from octaves and single notes to tenths. Tatum, in addition to frequent use of tenths, sometimes played stride with full chords on all four beats.

2. Throughout the development of stride, pianists made greater use of rapid embellished runs to connect the more melodic material of the phrases.

Art Tatum (Courtesy Institute of Jazz Studies, Rutgers University).

Tatum used these runs more frequently than anyone else. Moreover, his were the most technically elaborate ever.

3. The speed of uptempo stride piano gradually increased over the years of its development, from ragtime to Harlem stride to swing. Tatum's stride piano was the fastest ever.

4. Finally, jazz harmony slowly developed a more sophisticated application of extended chords and nondiatonic progressions. Tatum's harmony was the most complex of all swing stylists.

Tatum's "Aunt Hagar's Blues" is one of his greatest recordings, far surpassing most others in depth of expression and structural inventiveness. If Tatum had a flaw, it was his facility, so natural and ingrained that it sometimes bordered on the glib and formulaic. However, any such glibness is missing from "Aunt

Hagar's Blues." Here the technical polish and incredible dexterity always present in a Tatum performance are regulated by thoughtfulness, an impression that he is thoroughly involved in the improvisation. Few other recordings of his combine these elements more effectively.

The opening sonority of "Aunt Hagar's Blues" establishes a daring, somber mood that at the same time recalls the blues. The sonority (a Db b9)(13) chord) is voiced to emphasize the cluster of pitches comprising the root, seventh, and flat ninth. The melody in the right hand, while avoiding the cluster, emphasizes the same dissonance (the normal voicing of the chord is inverted there so that the Ebb lies below the melodic Db). During the opening measures, Tatum continues to highlight various half-step voicings reminiscent of early down-home blues playing, but still subtly controlled by Tatum's usual harmonic cleverness and sophistication.

During the fourth chorus, the last before the restatement of the theme, Tatum, rather than simplifying his playing, surprises us with an unexpected move: he returns to an emphasis on the half-step interval. This passage momentarily liquidates the harmony of the blues changes, rendering it more ambiguous than even the opening chord of the recording.

Although Tatum effectively unifies the various elements of the piece by the use of a half-step intervallic motive, the overall effectiveness of the performance is probably more based on Tatum's expert pacing of the transitions through the different textures. For example, the changes of mood between the opening 4 bars of a given chorus and its final 8 bars are always effectively controlled. This particular plan of Tatum's recalls the use of the first 4 bars of a blues chorus for an instrumental break.

Throughout the performance, Tatum's sense of timing is perfect. For although many of his various textures are magnificent in their own right, an exquisite moment exquisitely timed will always impart an immeasurably greater effect. Combining imaginative thematic materials, original chord voicings, controlled timing, velvety touch, delightful dexterity, and heartfelt expression, "Aunt Hagar's Blues" is one of the greatest achievements of solo jazz piano.

bud powell

Bud Powell Trio: "Somebody Loves Me," Roost 2224, January 10, 1947. Bud Powell, piano; Curley Russell, bass; Max Roach, drums.

Earl "Bud" Powell is generally thought of as the finest of the bop pianists. Born in New York City, Powell (1924–1966) began the study of piano early on and was soon professionally involved in music. His father had been a pianist and his younger brother, Richie, later became the pianist with the Max Roach–Clifford Brown Quintet. Powell was among the musicians to be present at the beginning of bop in the early 1940s. Perhaps the dominating presence of Charlie

Parker at Minton's influenced Powell's piano style, comprised largely of up-tempo bop lines, although much of the sound of Tatum can be heard on Powell's elegant figuration and slower work.

"Somebody Loves Me" is a fine example of Powell's style. The harmony of the tune is reworked to good effect. The melody itself is generally rendered in a "locked hands" style, both hands maintaining the same rhythm through a chordal harmonization of the tune. (This style later became associated with pianist George Shearing (b. 1919).) Once Powell begins his improvisation, the left hand takes a back seat with sporadic accompanying chords, similar in effect to a drummer's bass drum bombs. The chord changes are thus articulated far less explicitly than in swing jazz piano styles. The melodic lines themselves feature Parker-like accents, sudden twists and turns, and high-speed virtuosity. Many of these lines include a decorative triplet, which, though probably originating with Parker, is highly characteristic of Powell and can also be heard in the virtuosic style of Oscar Peterson (b. 1925).

thelonious monk

Thelonious Monk (solo piano): "I Should Care," Milestone 47004, April 12, 1957.

In view of his never-to-be-equaled swing-stride piano style, Art Tatum left jazz pianists no real path on which they could hope to travel further. It seemed that no one could ever outdo Tatum, who even while improvising was technically equal to fine-art piano virtuosos who had been practicing the same pieces for years. In the early 1950s pianists began reacting against Tatumesque devices, trying to guide jazz piano along other, less explored routes.

A totally new approach to the piano did not come along until the innovations of Thelonious Sphere Monk (1917–1982) who, with the possible exceptions of Tatum and Basie, is probably the most recognizable jazz pianist of all time. Monk was born in Rocky Mount, N.C., and raised in New York City. A largely self-taught musician, Monk played piano and organ in church. He also had acquired some European classical technique in his youth, but early on abandoned it in favor of jazz in which he fashioned a witty and thoroughly individual style.

Monk was a developer of bop, a participant in the afterhours jam sessions at Minton's with Gillespie, Parker, and Clarke in the early 1940s. However, Monk was rarely asked to record with them. At the time when the first bop records were being produced, Monk had already begun avoiding the facile up-tempo lines of the other musicians. His unique, drier style seemed to spurn, quite consciously, the "pianistic" facility of Tatum and Powell.

Monk's alternate approach to jazz dramatically foreshadowed the interest in minimalism and objectivity fashionable in several Western cultural milieus since

Thelonious Monk (Courtesy Institute of Jazz Studies, Rutgers University).

the 1950s. For in Monk's performances we are consciously drawn into each note, to judge it, to place it in contexts, and to enjoy its unique occurrence at that moment in that piece. Monk's decision to eschew traditional jazz piano values beset him with a great problem: to create worthwhile music with only a few pitches required that each pitch be imbued with especial significance. Hence, Monk could not rely on dazzling the listener with flashy, previously worked-out licks.

Monk's unique phrasing indeed works magically in his solo recording of "I Should Care" (SCCJ). Great popular and jazz performances sometimes consist of no more than one chorus of the chosen song, especially on ballads. Monk chooses to play one chorus on "I Should Care," with no introduction, save for a single low E. The song itself is in 32-bar, AA' form (i.e., with 16-bar first and second halves).

A low E introduces the first chord of the piece and the first pitch (D) of the tune. After ringing for a while, the chord is followed by a run to low A. Two more chords follow, in much more rapid succession, which support the next two melody notes of the song. The three melody notes heard thus far (D-C♯-C♯) are the song's hook, set to the lyric "I Should Care." Monk's rendering of the hook, though out of tempo, emphasizes and even exaggerates its long-short–long basic rhythm. These three notes, moreover, are harmonized with chords whose voicings are rather unusual. Distinctive chord voicings are among the most individual elements of Monk's style.

The next phrase of the song is presented with clearer rhythm, is voiced in a more typical manner, and occupies the middle register of the piano. These changes, which contrast the presentation of the first three notes of the tune, dissipate the tension created by the highly unusual opening. Moreover, the tune becomes more recognizable at this point.

The third and fourth phrases reverse the relationship of the first two phrases. We also hear the first occurrence of what will be a prominent textural motive throughout the performance: sharply struck chords, in which some pitches are held while others are released. This technique, associated more with twentieth-century fine-art music, was never so pervasively (or persuasively) applied to jazz until Monk used it. It is still uncommon, probably because it necessitates slower and more hesitant playing, contrary to the predilection of most pianists.

In the brief coda following the presentation of the tune, Monk's unusual harmonies eventually converge on a concluding (D6) chord, an unexpected use of a pop cliché that fondly recalls the more "mainstream" jazz tradition.

Throughout "I Should Care," Monk uses few pitches, but instills them with reference, meaning, and expressiveness. Nothing is wasted, nothing is superfluous, and nothing is missing. Like all great solo pianists, Monk effectively controls the large-scale timing with accurate performance and expert delivery. Within the universe suggested by the first few chords, Monk contructs a witty, yet profoundly elegiac performance.

bill evans

Bill Evans Trio: "The Two Lonely People," from *The Bill Evans Album*, Columbia CG33672, CBS 64533, May 1971. Bill Evans, piano; Eddie Gomez, bass; Marty Morell, drums.

Cool jazz piano styles developed as an overt reaction against swing style piano and bop as it had been evolving since ragtime. Most of the modern trends,

Bill Evans (Courtesy Institute of Jazz Studies, Rutgers University).

including Monk's, tended to avoid stride, which perhaps too closely evoked the dance band rhythms of the past. Yet without it, or some variation of it, a rhythm-section left hand was not easily obtainable. For this reason, uptempo solo piano performances declined in the 1950s, with most of the major pianists playing their uptempo material with a rhythm section to supply the beat. The jazz piano styles of the 1950s and 1960s were typical in this respect, though Bill Evans, one of the fine pianists of the 1960s and 1970s, would still sometimes perform uptempo piano solos.

Evans (1929-1980) was from Plainfield, N.J., and unlike most jazz musicians of his time, was the product of a comfortable, middle-class family. He grew up listening to swing and bop, occasionally playing piano in some local bands. After high school Evans attended a small Louisiana college, a rather unlikely place for a future jazz musician. The Korean War placed still another obstacle in the way of the young musician's development, for Evans was soon drafted.

In 1956, Evans finally succeeded in reaching New York and began gigging around the city. He was fortunate to have a record of his playing issued by Riverside Records, which ultimately led to his joining Miles Davis's quintet in 1958. His early album with Davis, *Kind of Blue,* established Evans as one of the great pianists of the 1960s.

You first heard Evans on "So What" (see pp. 62-64) where he played a short solo. There, and throughout *Kind of Blue,* Evans tended to highlight the modal aspects of the performance with sparse, lean playing. He often sprinkled his solos and his comping with the more dissonant intervals of a major and minor second, intervals that were more characteristic of the modal jazz sound.

A fine example of Evans's work can be heard in the trio performance of "The Two Lonely People." Opening with a lush, rubato performance of the melody, Evans displays his famous chord voicings that soon became the foundation of much jazz harmony in the 1960s:

Approaching a cadence to a tonic in F minor at the end of the first phrase of the piece, Evans decided upon a standard IV-V-I progression. Yet, the voicings of the chords are as unique to Evans as Monk's voicings were to him. Chords voiced in fourths are very characteristic of modal jazz, since, curiously enough, chordal pitches voiced in fourths often sound less tonal than the same pitches voiced in thirds. For example, C-E-G-A-D, a C chord, voiced bottom to top, with added 6th and 9th, sounds quite differently when voiced E-A-D-G-C, a more modal chord whose pitches are all separated by intervals of a perfect fourth. Voicing chords in fourths avoids the use of fifths between alternate pairs of notes and negates many of the implications of conventional tonality, especially with respect to voice leading. No pianist was more influential than Evans in establishing voicings such as these.

Much of Evans's excellence comes from his ability to link unusual voicings smoothly, as if hiding their distinctive personalities by finding ways of making them join perfectly together. However, the complexity and individuality of his voicings become transparent when an attempt is made to duplicate or transcribe them.

Evans's swinging solo on "The Two Lonely People" is almost entirely based on a linear melody. The left hand does very little except provide occasional harmonic support. Yet even here, some of the left-hand voicings emphasize the intervals of a second that complement the harmonic sense of the introduction. The rhythmic feel of the right hand is quite exciting, with occasional 2/4 rhythms superimposed on the 3/4 measures. At the end of the solo Evans returns to the kind of out-of-tempo passage that was heard in the opening. With this he brings the piece to a sensitive and poignant close.

Evans was probably the main influence on piano styles in the 1960s, for his harmonic and melodic approach can be heard in most of the best pianists of that era. His playing remains the touchstone of modern jazz piano, with unmatched sensitivity and beautiful control. His performances, so apparently easy and unassuming, reflect great subtlety, eloquence, and refinement of thought.

horace silver

Horace Silver: "The Preacher," from *Horace Silver and the Jazz Messengers,* Blue Note BST-81518, February 6, 1955. Horace Silver, piano; Kenny Dorham, trumpet; Hank Mobley, tenor sax; Doug Watkins, bass; Art Blakey, drums.

Since the 1950s, three distinct styles in jazz piano have emerged: the modern modal school of Bill Evans, the funky school of Horace Silver (b. 1928), and the free school of Cecil Taylor. Silver was the most imaginative of the major funk players in the 1950s and has remained at the forefront of this blues influenced style ever since. His playing vividly recalls the right-hand licks associated with the oldtime blues and boogie-woogie pianists, although his left hand avoids their repetitive, rhythmic accompaniments.

Silver adapts the earlier blues figures to a more modern setting in part by avoiding the boogie-woogie bass patterns that by the 1950s would have seemed hopelessly dated. Further, in reacting against the bop players, he learned not to play too many notes, instead letting a few funky figures separated by generous space resonate through the texture. In this sense, too, his playing avoids the continuous melodic and sometimes mechanical licks of the oldtime blues players. Finally, Silver has a fine sense of melody, a real knack for devising catchy little figures in his improvisations. This ability is reflected in his many songs, some of which have become jazz standards, like "The Preacher." Silver can be heard at his best on the Jazz Messengers' albums from the 1950s and with his own quintets of the 1960s and 1970s.

herbie hancock

> Herbie Hancock: "Maiden Voyage," from *Maiden Voyage,* Blue Note 84195, 1965. Herbie Hancock, piano; Freddie Hubbard, trumpet; George Coleman, tenor sax; Ron Carter, bass; Anthony Williams, drums.

Herbie Hancock's early development can be heard as an expansion of Bill Evans's basic style. A modern jazz pianist who rarely played uptempo solo piano, Hancock features wonderfully complex and sensitive chord voicings that over the years have been as eagerly appreciated as Evans's. Unlike the older pianist, however, Hancock's work in the 1960s flirted with atonality and free jazz, though even at its most extreme, some kind of modal tone center seemed to emerge from the texture.

For years Miles Davis's rhythm section with Hancock (b. 1940), drummer Anthony Williams, and bassist Ron Carter was considered the finest in jazz. When Hancock improvised, the inventiveness of his own playing was enhanced by the uncanny sense of communication among the three players. Most any of the Miles Davis records of the 1960s make this clear, but Hancock's own *Maiden Voyage* album, a truly inspired record, enables him to function in a more assertive role as a leader. This album was recorded with the Miles Davis rhythm section, with the new trumpeter Freddy Hubbard (b. 1938) filling Davis's place. Hancock composed all the tunes for the album.

"Maiden Voyage," the title tune, features a solo by Hancock that is unusually responsive to the mood of the song. After Hubbard ends his trumpet solo, Hancock begins with an almost military motive as if to call attention to himself. The line then evaporates into unusually voiced chords. Carter and, to an even greater extent, Williams follow the twists and turns of Hancock's solo as if it had been written out and rehearsed in advance.

Williams not only finds unusual ways of keeping the beat pattern going, but also stops playing entirely during moments when Hancock begins a particularly expressive falling phrase. Unlike Evans, Hancock occasionally injects a swinging, hard-edged, almost boplike texture into his melodic line, but its use is fully integrated into the texture; never is it an extraneous element. Hancock's melodic diversity recalls the great piano players of the bop and swing eras.

Hancock's projection of Evans's harmonic style is enhanced by his more ambitious textural and tonal sense. Evans thinks like a soloist, while Hancock seems to listen to and anticipate his accompaniment more perceptively. Whereas Evans works with a sense of absolute stylistic command, Hancock always seems to be reaching, trying to come up with something new.

This continual searching perhaps led to Hancock's eventual disillusionment with the modern modal style, which he thought had become too intellectual and not responsive enough to the audience.[4] In the early 1970s, he found a release in the repetition, heavy beat, and electronic orientation of jazz-rock funk. "Chameleon," one of his finest efforts in this style, was discussed in Chapter 8.

chick corea

Chick Corea, yet another fine musician discovered by Miles Davis, played with Davis's quintet in the late 1960s. Originally from Boston, Corea (b. 1941) worked with Davis for a much shorter time than did Herbie Hancock, who had been the quintet's pianist for many years. Corea was quickly swept into the jazz-rock experiments of the late 1960s, though he also recorded some free jazz in the early 1970s that demonstrated ability in that area. In general, Corea's harmonic language has been far less influenced by Evans than Hancock's, instead leaning more toward rock, Latin, and Spanish music. Though some of his piano work recalls Hancock's rich harmonic style, Corea tends to avoid really funky, gutsy playing.

Corea's strongest improvisation and composition can be heard on the 1970s Return to Forever albums. There he plays some excellent solos, on both electric keyboards and acoustic piano, that reveal his fascination with perfect fifths and long, harmonically modal areas reinforced by rock rhythms. The key to his harmonic style can be found in the "Children's Songs," whose simplicity contrasts the longer works on his albums. On the "Children's Songs," his modal style is reduced to its purest form and the influences of Latin and Spanish music can be more easily discerned.

Despite the prevalence of modal sound in Corea's work, it is not an exclusive preoccupation. Many of his pieces (e.g., "You're Everything" from the *Light as a Feather* album discussed in Chapter 4) reveal a complex harmonic language that includes traces of Evans's voicings, but with the Latin and rock touches that remain characteristic of Corea's unique sound.

cecil taylor

Cecil Taylor: "Enter Evening," from *Unit Structures,* Blue Note 84237, late 1966. Cecil Taylor, piano and bells; Eddie Gale Stevens, trumpet; Jimmy Lyons, alto sax; Ken McIntyre, alto sax, oboe, and bass clarinet; Henry Grimes and Alan Silva, bass; Andrew Cyrille, drums.

[4]See Hancock interview in *Contemporary Keyboard,* Vol. 1, No. 2 (Nov.-Dec., 1975), pp. 18ff.

Chick Corea (Courtesy Institute of Jazz Studies, Rutgers University).

Cecil Taylor is indeed one of the most important free jazz pianists. His power, energy, and unlimited drive produce a fascinating, if often foreboding, wall of intense soundblocks. From Long Island, N.Y., Taylor (b. 1933) is one of the few prominent jazz artists who came to the music via fine-art music—twentieth-century contemporary music in particular. Though he had played some popular music professionally in the New York area, he also attended the New York College of Music and the New England Conservatory. After leaving the Conservatory in 1954, Taylor devoted himself to modern jazz and soon abandoned the more traditional tonal approach.

Sections of Taylor's improvisations are frequently interrelated by motivic and intervallic similarity as well as by gesture. The motives may be ordered and logically developed to contrast the large-scale rippling figurations that abound elsewhere.

The sensitivity of "Enter Evening" (SCCJ) contrasts the often intensely powerful playing heard in Taylor's music, since the sounds of the instruments and Taylor's solo itself are carefully integrated into an evocative and gentle mood. The rumblings of the drums and bass suggest a more traditional jazz ensemble, even when they are accompanying the oboe. Some of the sounds in Taylor's music resemble figures heard in much post-1950s fine-art music, especially the quick waves of notes that dance animatedly over the keyboard.

Often, in Taylor's group performances, there is no real distinction between solo and accompaniment: all the players contribute to the overall texture. For example, Taylor's accompaniment of the other musicians in "Enter Evening" leads naturally and sensitively into his own solo statement. Taylor begins his solo simply, with small note patterns. These note patterns then grow into the more characteristic waves of sound, building to an inventive climax of considerable agitation. Then, without a break, the climax subsides into the gentle single note lines and light arpeggios that were heard at the beginning of the solo. After the other instruments return, the languorous beginning of the piece is recapitulated. (For a partial transcription of Taylor's solo in "Enter Evening," see pp. 257-258.)

As you may have noticed in listening to Ornette Coleman (Chapter 7), continued references to pitch sets can cogently organize an improvisation, but only when the large-scale gestures and other expressive nuances convincingly support them. Taylor, among all free jazz pianists, most effectively unites these elements. His music, like Monk's, breathes with the freshness of new ideas and new gestures, and usually avoids the swing and bop melodic lines that provide most jazz pianists with the basis of their technique.

piano styles summarized

Ragtime: ca. 1890-1920

Right-hand texture: short, syncopated figures, joined to create longer melodies of instrumental and pianistic character; occasional chords and melodies in octaves.

Left-hand texture: stride bass (bass notes or octaves on beats 1 and 3, chords on beats 2 and 4); patterns often slightly transformed; occasionally joins right hand for cross-hand textures.

Harmony: generally diatonic; much use of I and V chords, though chromatic harmony is also frequently heard (for example, the bVI chord).

Form and structure: marchlike, often ABA(trio:)CDA, with trio in the key of the subdominant; each section, usually 16 bars long, is repeated.

Harlem Stride: ca. 1920-1940

Right-hand texture: syncopated melodic figures but occasionally more use of longer lines; rhythms still tied to basic beat.

Left-hand texture: ragtime bass but occasional use of tenths and walking rhythms.

Harmony: still simple, predictable, mostly diatonic, but with occasional chromaticisms.

Form and structure: marchlike, like ragtime, but frequent incorporation of AABA structures; faster, flashier tempo.

Swing-Stride: ca. 1930-1950

Right-hand texture: single note improvisation much like swing style melodic improvisation; far less syncopated than ragtime; looser, more use of long eighth-note lines; brilliant runs used to fill between phrases.

Left-hand texture: stride bass, but bass notes often in tenths; use of walking tenths and occasional cross-hand textures.

Harmony: mostly diatonic, but seventh chords predominate in left hand with ninth chords occurring from time to time.

Form and structure: strophic AABA, AA', or blues forms; tempos range from slow to very fast; improvisations structured by voice leading and motivic relationships.

Late Swing-Stride and Bop: ca. 1940-1955

Right-hand texture: mostly single-note lines, often of eighth-notes in up tempo performances, though wide range of note values found; highly ornamental, often complex runs of sixteenth- and thirty-second-notes.

Left-hand texture: stride bass, but frequent use of tenths and even entire chords on beats 1 and 3; seventh chords on beats 2 and 4, but also frequent use of extended chords; walking tenths; more complicated cross-hand textures.

Harmony: more chromatic, diatonically based harmony extended; right-hand runs feature much chromaticism.

Form and structure: strophic AABA, AA', or blues forms; motivic relationships and voice leading; very slow to extremely fast tempos.

Hard Bop: ca. 1955-1965

Right-hand texture: blues licks and figures; catchy tunes; use of space between phrases.

Left-hand texture: occasional chords, as punctuation; rhythm section usually required for meter.

Harmony: blues based; much use of extended ninths and elevenths.

Form and structure: strophic blues structures and much use of song strophic structures as well; tempos generally slower than bop.

Modern Jazz: ca. 1960-

Right-hand texture: wide variety of melody, from simple, short syncopated figures to long modal lines; occasional chording.

Left-hand texture: supports right hand, but no stride; much of use of cross-hand textures (e.g., locked chords), since meter is maintained by the rhythm section.

Harmony: very complex, ranging from extremely chromatic harmony to outside playing on long modal tone centers; many voicings in fourths.

Form and structure: strophic at times, otherwise freely modal; motivic relationships more prominent than voice leading.

Free Jazz: ca. 1960-

Right-hand texture: unpredictable, ranging from short to long melodies, use of chords, special effects (e.g., knocking on piano body, strumming strings with fingers).

Left-hand texture: equally unpredictable, often supports right hand gestures; avoidance of meter effecting patterns.

Harmony: atonal or loosely based on a mode.

Structure: based on large-scale gesture and intervallic relationships; often no meter; dramatic contrasts of large-scale gesture.

The piano styles summarized above are the most prominent in jazz so far. Monk's style, by the way, is unique, fitting neatly into no category, but incorporating aspects of free jazz intervallic control with unusual bop harmonies, and oddly voiced and distinctive angular melodies. Boogie-woogie is a blues oriented style on the periphery of jazz. It features much use of blues progressions, mechanical, rhythmic bass patterns with 8 even eighth-notes to the bar, and right-hand blues licks.

chapter
ten

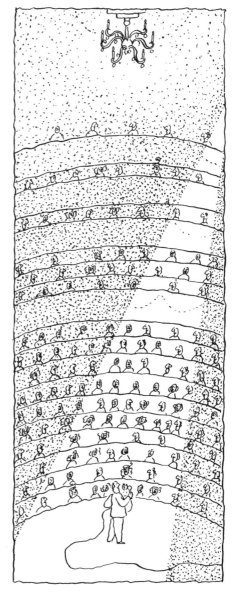

jazz
singers

What specific quality or qualities must be present in a singer's vocal style for he or she to be considered a jazz singer? Improvisation is certainly the most obvious response, although it is not quite satisfactory. Many singers, properly thought of as jazz singers, rarely improvise in the same way as instrumentalists. Indeed, improvising both words and music at once is rarely heard because of the difficulty of devising lyrics for spontaneous melodies.

One type of vocal improvisation that circumvents the problem of inventing appropriate lyrics is scat singing (first mentioned in Part One). In scat singing, nonsense syllables, such as "doo-wah-bah-dah," rhythmically grafted onto improvised melody, attempt to imitate common horn jazz lines and licks. Louis Armstrong's "Heebie Jeebies" is often credited as the first scat vocal recording, and it is sometimes claimed that he invented scat upon forgetting the lyrics during that particular recording. Colorful as the story is, it seems more probable that forms of scat singing were to be heard in the performances of the blues singers and pianists, perhaps as early as the nineteenth century. In any event, while scat is certainly an important style of jazz singing, other jazz vocal styles exist as well.

The blues was the first jazz vocal style, although blues singers were soon differentiated from the later jazz singers. As was pointed out in Part One, both instrumental and vocal jazz were greatly influenced by the blues. In the days of the first blues recordings, from Mamie Smith's "Crazy Blues" in 1920 until at least the end of the decade, many great jazz musicians were employed as accompanists for singers. Cornetists such as Armstrong and Joe Smith, pianists such as Fletcher Henderson, and many others commonly played blues recording sessions. Various blues vocal techniques were also adapted to dixieland style, as was pointed out earlier.

Still, the blues, while certainly influencing jazz as a whole, probably affected jazz singing even more demonstrably than its instrumental styles. The early blues singers, during the 1920s, established their reputations prior to the invention of microphones and PA systems, so, like fine-art singers, volume and projection were necessary assets. Of all the fine blues singers of this period, the greatest was Bessie Smith, whose richness and breadth of tone are evident on even her oldest recordings. With Smith's work we can begin to detect the qualities that later differentiated jazz, pop, and blues singers.

bessie smith

Bessie Smith: "Lost Your Head Blues," Columbia G 31093, March 18, 1926. Bessie Smith, vocal; Joe Smith, cornet; Fletcher Henderson, piano.

Bessie Smith (1895–1937) to this day remains probably the most beloved of all "classic" blues singers. A protégé of the great blues singer Ma Rainey, Smith frequently appeared in traveling vaudeville shows before embarking on a solo career. Her first blues recordings for Columbia Records, "Down-Hearted Blues" and "Gulf Coast Blues," were hits in 1923, though by the end of the decade her popularity waned as classic blues vocalists found themselves less in demand. Almost forgotten, she began to work in minor musical shows that toured the country. She was on such a tour when she died in a car crash in Clarksdale, Miss.

Smith's "Lost Your Head Blues" (SCCJ) is one of her finest recordings. The solid accompanists, Fletcher Henderson on piano and Joe Smith on cornet, respond to Smith's laments with many expressive and perfectly turned phrases. Henderson's rolling accompaniment adeptly supports the main voices, while remaining unobtrusive.

"Lost Your Head Blues" begins with a 4-bar introduction followed by 5 choruses of the customary 12-bar stanzas. (The vocal line of the first chorus can be seen in Example 3.3.) The first phrase of the lyric fits the first two bars of song, while C1m3 and C1m4 are left free for the answering commentary of Joe Smith's cornet. In C1m5 and C1m6 the same phrase is repeated, but with a new harmonization of the IV chord. Rather than repeating the same melody exactly, the singer instead heightens it with slight embellishments and greater expressive detail, such as the slide into the first note of the phrase.

In the last phrase of the first chorus, the dramatic statement of the song is finally presented. (Typically, the third phrase of a blues lyric clarifies the problem set out in the first two phrases.) Although the lyric of the third phrase differs from the one heard in the song's opening, the vocal melody reflects that of the first two phrases. This single musical phrase, constantly altered throughout the performance, is so strong that the singer can freely modify it without seeming to veer significantly from the song itself. In general, constant modification and embellishment of various phrases are important factors in distinguishing jazz and blues singing from less ornamental pop singing. Bessie Smith's performance culminates in the sublime final chorus in which the tune undergoes its greatest modification when she intones the powerful "Days are lonesome, nights are long."

Three other features of her performance remain characteristic of subsequent jazz singing. First, in jazz singing, the phrasing of the song must always be very loose. For example, sometimes the phrase begins on the downbeat, as in the previous example, while at other times it begins as a *pickup,* that is, on the fourth beat. This practice of varying the placement of the phrase relative to the beat gives a free quality to the performances that contrast the on-the-beat feel of nonjazz singing. In later styles, beginning with such singers as Billie Holiday in the 1930s, the placement of the melody is often delayed as much as a full bar. However, slight delays and embellishments of this kind are more typical of 1920s blues singing.

The second aspect of Bessie Smith's performance that figures significantly in jazz and blues singing is the offbeat, syncopated placement of important notes and their lyrics. Examples include the placement of the words "not" and "down," the latter being the last word of the first chorus. Jazz singing epitomizes the freedom of loose phrasing allied to inventive syncopation.

The third feature of jazz and blues singing evident in Smith's performance is the use of slides, blue notes, and other melodic pitch inflections and ornaments. Although these features have become embedded in all popular singing, they are especially prominent in blues performances.

These three key aspects of jazz singing quickly became synonymous with jazz oriented American popular music and were later appropriated by most rock styles. The extent to which a pop singer is a jazz singer depends most on the prominence of these three features. A singer can then strengthen a jazz reputation by both scat singing and sprinkling his or her repertoire with the popular songs most preferred by jazz musicians. Aside from scat, the three features of jazz singing, first nurtured by the classic 1920s blues singers, were brought to maturity during the swing era by such artists as Billie Holiday.

billie holiday

> Billie Holiday and Eddie Heywood and His Orchestra: "All of Me," Columbia K9 3214, March 21, 1941. Billie Holiday, vocal; Shad Collins, trumpet; Leslie Johnakins, Eddie Barefield, alto saxes; Lester Young, tenor sax; Eddie Heywood, piano; John Collins, guitar; Ted Sturgis, bass; Kenny Clarke, drums.

Billie Holiday was the touchstone of jazz singing. At the peak of her vocal powers in the 1930s and 1940s, Holiday usually performed with small jazz groups, though she made several big band recordings, too. Her recordings in the mid-1930s with studio pickup bands that included Lester Young, Teddy Wilson, and others are among the great treasures of swing era jazz. Holiday (1915-1959) lived a complex and tragic life, strewn with both poverty and drug addiction. Born in Baltimore of unwed parents, she was raped while still a child and compelled to work as a prostitute during her early teens. The tragedy of these times is perhaps reflected in her ability to convey a song lyric with a depth of emotion seldom equaled by other vocalists.

Holiday's reputation as the jazz singer's singer derives from her greatest

Billie Holiday (Courtesy Institute of Jazz Studies, Rutgers University).

strength—the freedom of her phrasing—actualized much more fully in her work than in the recordings of the blues singers. This freedom results primarily from delaying the entry of each phrase, a stylistic device now sometimes called *back phrasing* by other popular and jazz singers. In back phrasing it is important that the song's melody be sufficiently loose to accommodate rhythmic distortion without strain. In fact, this is a criterion by which many traditional jazz tunes are judged. Moreover, a good jazz melody must be resilient enough to hold up well under back phrasing. Finally, if the melody and lyric are unusually strong, then improvised variations of the tune do not negate the identity of the song. "All of Me" (SCCJ), by Seymour Simons and Gerald Marks, is a memorable tune that stands up well to Billie Holiday's interpretation.

Holiday's persona and vivid presence are greatly enhanced by the expressivity and the plaintive timbre of her voice. Unique timbre, a feature of most great jazz musicians, enables an audience immediately to distinguish and identify a performer. Holiday's powerful, expressive delivery far outshines the slicker interpretations of the pop singers of her time. A Holiday interpretation of even the most banal lyric seems to be imbued with meaning.

Holiday's style has been a seminal one in the subsequent history of jazz, since the popular singing styles of many fine performers reflect the influence of her back phrasing. Holiday also epitomizes the swing era in her general suppression or at least underemphasis of blue notes. This feature links her style to the popular song tradition rather than the blues tradition of the 1920s. Not surprisingly, she recorded few blues songs.

"All of Me" is representative of Holiday's many great recordings. An added bonus on this performance is the presence of Lester Young, whose style influenced and was influenced by Holiday. The comparison of their performances is revealing, since the relaxed, lyrical quality of their expression can be equated.

The following is an excerpt of a transcription of Holiday's performance of "All of Me."

The top line of Example 10.1 presents the first 8 bars of the original tune, while the first and last choruses of Holiday's performance appear in the middle and bottom lines. The song itself is constructed around a contraction of the opening motive, F-C-A (m. 1), into E-C#-A (m. 3), and finally into D-C-A (m. 5). These contractions parallel the chord changes F major, A major, and D seventh. In Holiday's out-chorus (Ex. 10.1, bottom line), the pitch A, common to all three appearances of the motive, is transferred to a higher register and emphasized.

While you listen to the recording, notice that this last chorus, a free melodic paraphrase, approaches the quality of an improvisation, but because of the song's strength does not disguise the tune in a forced or unnatural manner. Even the first chorus, which remains much closer to the original tune, is back phrased consistently. An interesting way to hear the back phrasing is to imagine or play the original melody, exactly as notated, along with the recorded version. The "accurate" performance of the tune seems stiff and hurried while Holiday's performance is much more expressive and languorous. In this way, good jazz phrasing can animate a song, heightening its intensity and feeling.

A great performer understands the need of always varying his or her material and, in so doing, widening its impact. Because the first lyric is to be repeated on the final chorus, an alternate lyric cannot be relied upon to provide variety. Hence, Holiday does not repeat her first interpretation in the final chorus, since this would rob the performance of its feeling of forward movement. Instead, she alters her rendition of the last chorus in two important ways. First, she sings with greater intensity, that is, the words are charged with more passionate expression than in the first, "prettier" chorus. Second, as was pointed out, the melody is actually sung more freely, duplicating fewer notes of the original tune.

In Holiday's out-chorus, the voice leading of her melodic lines is reworked simply and effectively. (For a voice-leading graph comparing the original song with the final chorus, see pp. 259.) Because Holiday avoids duplicating all of the voice-leading lines of the original melody, her out-chorus performance simplifies and intensifies the original song at the moment where this treatment is most appropriate. The intensification of the tune imparts a special poignancy to the final chorus and to the performance as a whole. Holiday's unique vocal timbre, her relaxed phrasing, and the depth of her expression are all present on this recording of "All of Me"; these qualities continue to be an inspiration to all jazz singers.

ella fitzgerald

Ella Fitzgerald: "You'd Be So Nice to Come Home To," Verve V/V6-4065, July 1964. Ella Fitzgerald, vocal; Roy Eldridge, trumpet; Tommy Flanagan, piano; Bill Yancey, bass; Gus Johnson, drums.

Ella Fitzgerald (Courtesy Institute of Jazz Studies, Rutgers University).

Ella Fitzgerald has continued to straddle popular and jazz singing deftly since her first hit recordings were made with the Chick Webb band in the 1930s. She has made many recordings since then, often appearing at jazz festivals and concerts with well-known big bands. Her most jazz oriented work, however, has occurred with smaller groups.

Equipped with great vocal dexterity, Fitzgerald (b.1918) incorporates a large pitch range, superb use of melodic ornaments, dramatic dynamic contrasts, brilliant runs, and scat into her performances. In fact, Fitzgerald's reputation as a jazz singer has been especially enhanced by her fine talent for scat, a technique avoided by Holiday.

On Fitzgerald's exciting recording of "You'd Be So Nice to Come Home To" (SCCJ), we can hear an occasional scat phrase, but most of the performance is devoted to a freewheeling improvisation of the melody with the original lyrics. Because the lyric itself, rather than a string of nonsense syllables, is fitted to the improvised line, the resulting tune is somewhat less instrumentally conceived than a scat melody.

For a lyric to be applied so freely, it is necessary that it be fairly easy to sing. The smooth, colloquial lyric of "You'd Be So Nice to Come Home To" enables Fitzgerald to show off her technique to excellent effect.

Fitzgerald's interpretation is far more florid than the melody of the original tune. This manner of singing, first mentioned in Chapter 2, is called "melismatic," in which one continuous syllable of lyric is sustained for several notes. In popular songwriting, excessive use of melisma usually creates a poor effect, as if the lyric and the tune were mismatched. Here, melisma provides an opportunity to attempt a tune-syllable match that is refreshingly free from the restrictions of popular song.

Despite Fitzgerald's exciting, wide-ranging performance, the almost flawless execution of her melismatic chorus suggests that it has been carefully worked out in advance as part of an arrangement that includes Eldridge's muted trumpet figures and the well-planned ending. Still, that Fitzgerald breathes so much life into the performance is a credit to her outstanding talent.

sarah vaughan

> Sarah Vaughan: "Ain't No Use," Roulette R 52060, 1961. Sarah Vaughan, vocal; Harry Edison, trumpet; Jimmy Jones, piano.

Sarah Vaughan (b. 1924), is another preeminent female jazz singer. Her leap to the limelight occurred during the heyday of bop when she sang with both the Earl Hines and Billy Eckstine big bands in the early 1940s. There, her associations with Parker and Gillespie established her reputation and refined her ability to sing with the looseness and unexpected vocal twists and turns of bop. As such, she seems to have concentrated more on jazz singing than Fitzgerald, who, after leaving the Chick Webb band, became firmly entrenched in more of a pop-jazz position. Vaughan has tried to maintain a close connection to the other jazz musicians of her generation as well.

Vaughan's performance of "Ain't No Use" (SCCJ) is an excellent example of her top-flight work. She maintains the mood exquisitely throughout the performance, leaving plenty of space between the supple phrases. The loose, roomy

Sarah Vaughan (Courtesy Institute of Jazz Studies, Rutgers University).

quality of her interpretation is highlighted by the equilibrium maintained between compressing certain phrases, to allow long spaces between them, and drawing out the more important ones.

Vaughan seems to relish exploring the colors and technical potential of her voice. Her fine sense of phrasing is underscored by dramatic contrasts in dynamics, ranging from very soft to quite loud passages. Her intonation, including the expressive use of vibrato and blue note effects, is perfectly controlled. Throughout the performance, we can hear well-planned silences between the phrases, a feature that helps provide a leisurely overall feeling.

joe williams

Joe Williams and the Thad Jones-Mel Lewis Jazz Orchestra: "It Don't Mean a Thing" and "Night Time Is the Right Time," from *Presenting Joe Williams and Thad Jones–Mel Lewis • The Jazz Orchestra*, Solid State SS 18008, 1968. Joe Williams, vocals; Thad Jones-Mel Lewis, leaders; Jerome Richardson, Jerry Dodgion, Eddie Daniels, Joe Farrell, Pepper Adams, saxes; Snooky Young, Jimmy Nottingham, Bill Berry, Richard Williams, trumpets; Bob Brookmeyer, Garnett Brown, Tom McIntosh, Cliff Heather, trombones; Roland Hanna, piano; Richard Davis, bass; Sam Herman, guitar; Mel Lewis, drums.

Of all the singers who have tried to bridge jazz and blues, few have been as successful as Joe Williams. After working with Coleman Hawkins and others, Williams (b. 1918) earned a major reputation as a replacement for Jimmy Rushing in the Count Basie band of the 1950s. He left Basie in 1961 to pursue a solo career while, at the same time, enlarging and enriching his style. His extensive solo career spans the past 25 years.

Among Williams's best recordings is an excellent collaborative album made with the Thad Jones-Mel Lewis big band in the late 1960s. Featuring great Thad Jones arrangements and excellent supporting solos by the band members, this record remains one of the finest big band vocal recordings of the time. Two outstanding performances on the album are Williams's surprisingly deft scat improvisation on "It Don't Mean a Thing" and the slow, intensely emotional blues "Night Time Is the Right Time."

On the scat performance, Williams uses squeals, grunts, and shrieks that extend high into a *falsetto* register. The rhythm section, usually the most impressive feature of the band aside from the arrangements, provides intensely swinging support throughout.

The solid feel of the rhythm section is also evident on "Night Time Is the Right Time," a 12-bar blues in which the arrangement builds with overwhelming effect. Listen to how dexterously Williams slides from his spoken first chorus into a gradually more intoned and impassioned vocal. This effect is akin to the style of preachers delivering sermons in black churches. (Not surprisingly, many jazz vocalists began their singing careers in church.) Roland Hanna's piano figures add flecks of color to these early, lightly scored choruses before the step-by-step addition of the band pushes them into the background. Thad Jones's arrangement concludes with huge walls of sound supporting Williams's climactic finish.

eddie jefferson

> Eddie Jefferson: "Body and Soul," from *The Jazz Singer,* Inner City IC
> 1016, January 19, 1959. Eddie Jefferson, lyric and vocal; Frank Gal-
> breath, John McFarland, trumpets; Matthew Gee, trombone; Bill Gra-
> ham, baritone sax; Musa Kaleem, tenor sax; Johnny Acea, piano; John
> Morrison, bass; Osie Johnson, drums.

Eddie Jefferson has finally been recognized as an important jazz vocalist,
an original artist who established an alternative singing style strongly disasso-
ciated from the Holiday-Fitzgerald-Sinatra mainstream. Jefferson (1918-1979)
was interested in vocal improvisation and also in composing lyrics to fit preexisting instrumental improvisations. To provide a change of pace from these carefully worked out lyric settings, Jefferson also mixed some scat singing into his
performances.

Jefferson's greatest performance strength was his tremendous vocal agility.
His flexible falsetto never seemed to strain or bury the lyric. The jazz solos he
set usually featured irregular phrasing, unlike the simple 4-bar phrases that are
often found in popular songs. Nevertheless, despite the difficulty of setting lyrics
to these freely wandering instrumental lines, Jefferson often found felicitous so-
lutions that incorporated odd though satisfying rhyme schemes.

Jefferson's first important setting was Coleman Hawkins's performance of
"Body and Soul." In that performance, the fluidity of Jefferson's lyric and voice
wonderfully evokes the warm feeling of the Hawkins original. The lyric is a particularly apt tribute to one of the first truly great sax players. In general, his work
is surprisingly refreshing, pleasing, and fun to listen to, as well as fine tributes
to some of the greatest jazz musicians and their improvisations.

lambert, hendricks, and ross

> Lambert, Hendricks, and Ross: various selections from *Lambert, Hen-
> dricks, and Ross,* Columbia CL 1403, 1960. Dave Lambert, Jon Hen-
> dricks, Annie Ross, vocals; Ike Isaacs Trio (personnel unspecified);
> trumpet, Harry Edison.

An important jazz vocal group broke onto the scene in the late 1950s; a
trio comprising Jon Hendricks, Dave Lambert, and Annie Ross. The group
mixed three distinct styles: first, an imitation of big band textures and arrangements; second, arrangements of preexisting jazz improvisations with added lyrics
(like those done by Eddie Jefferson); and third, traditional scat. This extremely
inventive group certainly provided much inspiration for the contemporary singing ensemble, Manhattan Transfer.

Among the fine efforts of Lambert, Hendricks, and Ross, particular attention should be called to Ross's solo on the ingenious tune "Twisted," the effec-

tive arrangement of "Cloudburst," and the scat singing on "Everybody's Boppin'." The quality of their lyrics in these interpretations is often as good as Eddie Jefferson's.

The big band imitations are somewhat more formulaic, but "Centerpiece" is very successful. Annie Ross's shakes, high pitches, and effortless phrasing convincingly evoke the sound of a lead trumpet above a most unlikely brass section consisting of two males voices. Throughout, riffs and other big band devices are amusingly and effectively referred to.

Lambert, Hendricks, and Ross refreshingly avoid standard pop tunes and their usual close vocal harmonizations, the Andrews Sisters sound that seemed so ubiquitous in the 1940s and 1950s. However, despite the sparkle of the clever arrangements and songs, the small range of their emotional expression probably results from the cool-jazz sound pervading their recordings and the intrinsic limitations of their stylistic concept.

frank sinatra

Frank Sinatra: "One For My Baby" from *In Concert—Sinatra at the Sands with Count Basie and the Orchestra,* Reprise 2FS 1019, 1965. Frank Sinatra, vocal; Bill Green, piano.

Frank Sinatra (b. 1915) should be included in the ranks of the jazz singers for his exceptionally free phrasing, his swinging big band recordings, his identification with outstanding songs, and his ability to convey the meaning and emotional content of a lyric. Add to these attributes his domination of the traditional pop vocal audience and respect by many jazz musicians and his importance remains indisputable.

Sinatra's swinging recordings have delighted listeners since the 1950s, though his earlier work with Tommy Dorsey was in a popular rather than jazz vein. The exciting performance of the Count Basie band in place of the sentimental string sound of most of Sinatra's studio recordings elevates the live double album *Sinatra and Basie at the Sands* to the status of a jazz vocal album, with many great performances of songs long associated with Sinatra.

Sinatra's ability to infuse a fine song with remarkable sensitivity is especially heard on Harold Arlen's "One For My Baby." Here, the absence of maudlin and often overdone backup textures enables Sinatra's voice to capture a more personal effect. His expression and loose Holiday-like phrasing are heard to greater advantage with Bill Green's simple, but effective piano performance, Sinatra's only accompaniment. The back phrasing on this performance is carried out effortlessly, with no strain or forcing.

Only one chorus of the song, in AABA form with an extended ending, is performed. In the A' section, the song deftly modulates from C major to E major, an unusual formal feature of the original music that further increases the leisurely and elegant mood set up by the performers. Arlen's song itself is a gem: it hovers freely over the beat and is easily adaptable to Sinatra's back phrasing. A sophisticated song written for a singer who can express deep emotion with economical means, it is far more complex melodically and harmonically than the straightforward tunes preferred by most improvising instrumentalists.

The song's melodic-harmonic complexity suggests fine-art music, but the stylish and conversational lyric dexterously balances the mood. The occasional use of blue notes as, for example, on the hook lyric "Ba—by" performed the second time, recalls the older blues tradition of Bessie Smith. Green's dark, bluesy chords, beautiful voicings, and perfect control effectively complement Sinatra.

Sinatra, along with most of the singers discussed in this chapter, has his roots in the big band era. When compared to the other singers of his generation, he remains closest to the Billie Holiday ideal of the jazz-pop vocalist.

As you have seen in Chapter 10, jazz singing is identified with four main characteristics: (1) loose back phrasing, (2) use of blue notes and occasional blues inflections, (3) free melodic embellishment, and (4) a repertoire of songs preferred by jazz musicians. Though many jazz singers are talented at scat singing, it is not a necessary ability. Billie Holiday, for example, was not a scat singer.

Of the four main characteristics, the first is by far the most important. Back phrasing has influenced all of American popular music, including rock. The classic blues singers, on the other hand, had not yet begun to phrase as loosely as the swing era singers. Hence, their work is somewhat more typical of the blues tradition than the pop-jazz tradition in which most jazz singers have functioned.

Singing today remains an exciting and popular jazz vehicle. Many contemporary artists, such as Betty Carter (b. 1930), have effectively assimilated past styles and combined them in new ways. Jazz vocalists and instrumentalists have always inspired each other; it seems very likely they will continue to do so.

Since Chapter 4, I have dealt entirely with the music—primarily with the major jazz artists and a few of their best recordings. Gradually, in more detail I have examined a few important instrumentalists and singers and investigated the various elements of the different jazz styles. With our deeper understanding and awareness of the music finally at hand, I am in a position to deal with the broader considerations presented in Part Three. First I will discuss the present state of jazz and then conclude by speculating on its future development.

part three

putting it together

chapter eleven

jazz from 1970 to the present

the hypotheses reconsidered

In Part Two, we examined the music itself. Now we can return to the hypotheses posed in Chapter 1. We shall begin by reconsidering the first hypothesis:

The large-scale features of jazz were established by 1930.

At first glance the hypothesis seems true. By 1915, jazz was distinguished from ragtime and other black music by its emphasis on hot rhythm and improvisation. Early New Orleans jazz featured group improvisation, but soon Chicago style and the influence of Armstrong and the other great soloists of the 1920s molded jazz into more of an individual's art. Later in jazz history, simultaneous improvisation would again become fashionable (during the dixieland revival or in free jazz, for example), but the two modes of improvisation—group and individual—were firmly established by 1930.

The big band concept was also firmly established by 1930. By then, the division of the ensemble into four sections: trumpets, trombones, saxophones (woodwinds), and rhythm (piano, guitar, bass, and drums) was customary. The use of the big band arranger to develop a unique sound for the group was also established by 1930, as was the procedure of writing for the four instrumental sections as units, often in counterpoint with one another.

By 1930 the swing beat began to dominate the sound of jazz rhythm, the same beat that remained the basis of almost all medium tempo and uptempo jazz until jazz-rock. At this point, we come to a weakness, the first of several, in hypothesis one. Jazz-rock revolutionized jazz by introducing to it a new sense of time: a driving straight eighth-note rhythm was substituted for the swing eighth-note rhythm. Before the era of jazz-rock, straight eighth-notes were usually heard only in Latin-influenced jazz. Of course, Jelly Roll Morton had introduced the "Spanish tinge" into his playing long before 1930, yet, it was not until the jazz-rock revolution that a driving eighth-note feel became the rhythmic norm.

For most of its history, jazz has relied on popular songs and blues for its thematic material. This was common practice long before 1930, if not before 1920. Even the jazz tunes of the bop era were based on the changes of popular songs and blues. This practice remained the norm until the 1950s, when some jazz styles began to avoid popular songs by substituting more complex thematic material and free improvisation. Thus, while the jazz repertoire had stabilized by 1930, it was amended in some styles beginning in the 1950s. This, too, weakens hypothesis one.

Throughout jazz history, the most important styles have been commercial. At first, in the 1910s and early 1920s, jazz was something of a "protest" entertainment—as rock in our time—embraced by young blacks while scorned by the white establishment. By 1930, however, the most "outrageous" features of jazz had been purged by those musicians seeking to maximize its appeal. The gentler, smoother swing style sounded at home alongside the more sentimental forms of popular music. Jazz was considered popular music until the 1940s and 1950s, when some styles began branching off onto more esoteric paths. Nevertheless, by 1930 jazz was well established as a popular entertainment, and despite the reorientation of some of its styles since bop, jazz has always retained something of its popular ambience.

Most of the instrumental techniques were established by 1930, too. Jazz trumpet playing especially, with the giant presence of Armstrong, had reached a remarkable technical level by then. Clarinet and saxophone tones were also mellowing thanks to the increasing popularity of the Kansas City style and its less edgy woodwind sound. Jazz piano technique was modernized in the 1920s, first by James P. Johnson and the Harlem stride school and later especially by Earl Hines with his prototypical swing style. Drummers in the late 1920s shifted their timekeeping duties from the snare drum to the ride and hi-hat cymbals.

On the other hand, some other instrumental techniques had not yet been modernized by 1930. Dixieland trombone playing was still in vogue, not yet replaced by the smoother swing style. Modern guitar techniques, first associated with Charlie Christian, required amplification, an innovation of the 1930s. In singing, too, the sophisticated use of the microphone, which antiquated full-throated projection as well as crooning through the megaphone, was uncommon until the Billie Holiday era in the mid-1930s. Jazz-rock changed the overall sonic presence of many instruments because of its loud, hard-edged, amplified sound. Despite these instances, however, the most important playing styles were entrenched by 1930. Even today, instrumentalists find that studying the jazz solos of the 1920s helps improve their technique.

From this examination of the first hypothesis, it seems clear that many of the large-scale features of jazz had been established by 1930, but since then several have undergone substantial modifications. To summarize the important changes in jazz since 1930 I might begin by pointing out the gradual loss of its popular audience, dating from the esoteric practices of bop. The inconspicuousness of the popular song, the angular melodies and the undanceable tempos of the bop era foreshadowed the radical changes of the musical repertoire and technique soon to come.

During the jazz "revolutions" of the 1950s, the potential popularity of many styles was sometimes undermined by the formal preoccupations of the musicians. Still, in that era, the basis of jazz rhythm, instrumentation, and its overall sonic presence remained. Jazz-rock then overturned these characteristics in an attempt to regain some of the youth audience. The style has not particularly thrived, since rock and r & b have remained the popular music of most young people. Thus, although hypothesis one is largely true—that the major stylistic features of jazz were in place by 1930—a slow evolution began to unfold during the next several decades until, by the late 1970s, much of the original stylistic basis had been overturned.

Perhaps the gradual evolution from the stylistic basis of 1930 accounts for the uncertain sense of direction detectable in the current jazz scene. This consideration raises the issues posed by hypothesis two:

> **Jazz developed as a folk music, rapidly became a popular music in the 1920s, then finally established itself as a fine art by around 1950. By the 1970s and early 1980s, jazz was unlikely to undergo any further significant evolution because it lacked the popularity necessary for continued vitality. At that time all of its previous styles became recognized as artistic vehicles for performance. Indications are, therefore, that jazz will not undergo any further significant evolution.**

Our examination of jazz styles in Part Two supports the first part of the second hypothesis: the folk element of jazz is unmistakable in its early recordings. As jazz became more acceptable during the 1920s, it metamorphosed into a thoroughly professional popular music and remained so from the middle 1920s through the early 1940s. In the bop era, jazz artists concentrated on elaborating the more esoteric, structurally sophisticated features of their music and shrunk from their previous roles as entertainers. In the 1950s, the musical leaders of several new styles disavowed any connection of jazz to entertainment and preferred to think of their music as an art. Nevertheless, much jazz today is still performed with popular artistic goals and aesthetics in mind.

Since the 1950s, the more recent jazz styles have united with other Western musical styles to form new hybrids. In the popular-music sphere, jazz has been allied to rock (jazz-rock), r & b (funk), and gospel ("gospel jazz" and hard bop). In the art-music realm we find free jazz and third stream (allied with fine-art music), and newer kinds of jazz, some of which are associated with musics of other cultures. Those musicians and audiences who prefer older styles of jazz sometimes refer to the more controversial hybrids as "not jazz."

Not all contemporary jazz is fine-art music in the usual sense of the word. While some of the newer types belong in the concert hall and are unsuitable for dancing, many other styles, based on popular music, are more comfortably performed in an informal atmosphere. Nevertheless, I shall consider contemporary jazz, in general, an art music since either it is created for quiet aesthetic contemplation or it projects involved and complex interpretations of music that is popularly based.

The second part of the second hypothesis, that jazz has reached a dead end because it lacks the popularity and vitality for meaningful evolution is indeed more controversial. The future can be better evaluated by a more extended discussion of the current musical scene in which evidence of both stagnation and heightened activity in jazz will be cited. Afterward, a specific hypothetical scenario for the future of jazz will be suggested. Finally, I will return, in the last section of the chapter, to reevaluate the second hypothesis and present the third hypothesis, which suggests that jazz has been the greatest American contribution to the world's musics.

problems in the current jazz scene

It is possible to argue that the jazz scene today is lethargic, that the public has lost interest in the newer jazz, and that there seems little chance of the music regaining its former popularity. Since the 1930s and early 1940s, the sales of jazz records have fallen relative to other music. No new jazz stars on the scene today dominate critical opinion or excite the record-buying public as Armstrong, Ellington, Basie, Davis, or Coltrane did in their day. Most jazz musicians from other countries copy the styles of the best-known American artists. Jazz fans, probably bored with the present, turn more and more to historical jazz, where they may find minor artists or the major artists' inferior recordings more stimulating than current avant-garde styles. Some contemporary jazz musicians respond to this interest in the past by concentrating on "nostalgia," evoking past styles, and ignoring modern trends.

Moreover, avant-garde musicians working today in improvisational styles sometimes avoid referring to their work as jazz. Surely the corpus of jazz styles from the early 1920s through the 1960s, though widely varied, is still recognizable as a coherent entity in some sense. Much of the music associated with free jazz styles since the 1970s, however, seems so distinct from the previous work that both musicians and listeners have sometimes hesitated to call it jazz. This situation by its very existence suggests that "jazz" as a term now denotes the former mainstream styles: dixieland, swing, bop, cool, and modal jazz. Jazz-rock, as its name implies, is a hybrid, both jazz and rock, rather than a mainstream jazz style. Much avant-garde jazz also departs radically from the original basis of mainstream jazz in such a way that "jazz," as the term is currently evolving, may soon no longer refer to a contemporary music.

Of course, lack of widespread popular support for new jazz styles cannot be equated automatically with artistic vacuity. There are far too many examples, in numerous Western art milieus, of great artists unappreciated by the public in their own time. Nevertheless, the relative lack of support today for the newer jazz as compared to jazz in its heyday of the 1920s and 1930s suggests at least one aspect of decline. As the audiences for jazz gradually diminish, artists are less encouraged to create, fewer new artists will enter the field of jazz, and hence many fewer significant works will result.

Of course, it can be argued that mass media and recordings have made the audience for all forms of art, including jazz and fine-art music, far larger than ever. Yet, this relatively large new audience does not necessarily mean increased financial support of the artists and the overall cultural acceptance of their art. Contrariwise, J. S. Bach was heard by few people, but he was considered important in his own time, was often published, and was rewarded financially for his efforts.

Even the most well-known jazz artists of today have little chance of obtaining the same relative recognition of the jazz greats of the 1920s, 1930s, and early 1940s. Of course, artists must strive to please themselves and to satisfy their personal goals. But to create only for oneself, and without external recognition will often decrease the chances of producing art of significance. Any new work is measured, ultimately, in terms of its impact on some audience.

Involvement with past styles is increasingly common in jazz, as it has been for years with fine-art music. Most of the public prefers to listen to dixieland, swing, and bop than to free jazz and other avant-garde styles. Perhaps this preference has tended to channel some of the younger jazz musicians into playing the older styles. Although it is laudable that past jazz masters and their efforts are finally receiving the critical acclaim they deserve, avant-garde artists sometimes find themselves nearly ignored. When public interest in new music slackens, record companies re-release and promote earlier records, sometimes by uninteresting and forgotten artists.

Because the lack of popular support for new jazz is so strikingly like the situation in avant-garde fine-art music, we can gain a perspective on jazz by examining them jointly. In the following subsections, I will suggest some reasons for the similar predicaments of jazz and fine-art music.

romanticism and artistic awareness

At some point in the histories of both fine-art music and jazz, artists decided that entertainment and public reaction were less important than pursuing their own goals and visions. Yet the public is slow to accept change, and even established artists will lose public support if their works are judged unpleasing. It is because of this slow acceptance of change that fine-art music programming relies on the same 200 pieces and jazz musicians revamp outmoded styles to attract public interest.

This situation, though unfortunate, can be traced to a prevalent attitude toward art in modern Western culture: that it must continually grow and evolve.

Each generation of artists examines the art form freshly, hoping to burst from its earlier conventions and restrictions. Unfortunately, an evolving art form may eventually outgrow the conservative tastes of large audiences, especially if the artists emphasize personal expression, novelty, and complexity, while eschewing entertainment.

This romantic attitude toward art, though implicit in the stylistic evolution of Western art from the time of the Renaissance at least, was explicitly realized during Beethoven's day in the late eighteenth and early nineteenth centuries. Beethoven, for example, insisted on the importance of the artist's personal and expressive needs and maintained that the audience must accommodate the artist's conception of the work. If the audience did not understand or like the artwork, the audience was deficient, not the artist.

The romantic attitude led, in the nineteenth century, to the well-known cliché of the visionary artist, years ahead of his time, who will only be understood long after his death. Abandoning themselves to this attitude, artists consciously tried to "advance" the art form, which usually meant introducing increasingly complex syntactic features.

The individualism of the romantic outlook was embodied later in the nineteenth century by composers who believed completely in their vision of the artwork and refused to compromise it in any respect. Wagner is an example of such a composer. In their need to establish a distinctive voice, then, the romantic composers stretched tonal-music syntax to an extreme, anticipating twentieth-century atonality and, eventually, the 12-tone method. As the public lost interest, the music became more specialized, appealing to a smaller and more devoted audience.

Public displeasure with jazz began during the bop era, though real disinterest probably did not set in until free jazz. (Because the modern age of Western fine-art music dates from the Renaissance and modern jazz dates from the bop era, perhaps by "modern" we mean the onset of artistic self-awareness.) Jazz-rock, though commercially broad based, appealed to rock fans far more than to the traditional jazz audience, so that the new style did little toward increasing the audience for jazz.

The first stages of artistic self-awareness in a musical style are possibly the most exciting moments in its entire development. One thinks of Beethoven and the early Romantics, Charlie Parker and bop, and the Beatles, the first of the artistically aware rock groups. Perhaps when the greatness of an art form crests, it begins to lose some of its popular appeal, that is, the art form begins to transcend the mass audience.

tonal evolution

Both jazz and fine-art music have undergone a complicated process of tonal evolution that effectively ended when the possibilities for tonal harmony had been largely exhausted. Schoenberg in particular experienced this end-of-an-era feeling in the early twentieth century. He eventually abandoned the use of tonality (except in a small number of works) and devoted himself to composing atonal music. Within this framework, he invented the 12-tone method as a means of providing a broad-ranging syntax applicable to a large number of works.

A similar genesis may be associated with free jazz. By the late 1950s and early 1960s, most of the possibilities for the construction of new harmonies had been exploited. No longer was it possible for musicians to follow Charlie Parker's example and explore the uncharted area of extended-chord harmonies. Logically, musicians who felt it important to innovate may have consciously or unconsciously chosen to abandon conventional tonality.

Without a tonal reference point it may be the case that popular Western audiences are not drawn to a musical style. Most of the atonal works in the twentieth century fine-art repertory are not nearly as popular as the tonal works. Brilliant atonal works such as Schoenberg's *Five Orchestral Pieces,* Op. 16, composed as long ago as 1909, are recorded and performed much less often than outstanding tonal works, such as Aaron Copland's *Appalachian Spring,* composed 1944.

Similarly, jazz audiences are more inclined to attend concerts featuring artists associated with the older, tonal jazz styles. In the 1984 Kool Jazz Festival in New York, for example, the headlining, mainstream musicians performed in the larger concert halls, such as Avery Fisher Hall and Carnegie Hall, while the experimental jazz musicians performed at Soundscape, a smaller and more remotely located loft.

Hence, it can be argued that once jazz, like fine-art music, reached the end of its tonal evolution, attracting a popular audience became difficult if not impossible for the avant-garde artists. Popular audiences have remained indifferent if not antagonistic to atonal styles throughout the twentieth century, and there seems little chance that this attitude will change. It may be the case, then, that new jazz styles have little chance of ever again becoming truly popular. Of course, good music may still result, though the likelihood diminishes as the audience dwindles.

recordings

Recordings have had a critical effect on the evolution of all twentieth-century Western music. Before the twentieth century, fine-art composers were encouraged to write new symphonies and quartets in part because recollection of the previous pieces had dimmed. Recording changed this situation dramatically. Once the new industry began issuing early cylinders and records of fine-art music in the late nineteenth century, the material chosen naturally included the most often played works of the time, for example, Beethoven symphonies, favorite opera arias, flashy violin encore pieces, etc.

The public eventually became well-versed in the late nineteenth-century repertoire and, hence, expected to hear these pieces at concerts. As the works grew increasingly familiar, it became more difficult to place newer music on the program. At the same time, once a Beethoven symphony was heard repeatedly and accepted as a masterpiece, then any nonmasterpiece was dismissed out of hand.

Similar behavior can be detected, too, among jazz fans who find themselves always returning to the great Ellington, Parker, and Armstrong recordings. Although these records, together with the work of the other jazz greats, constitute only a small fraction of the jazz available, most of the recordings by modern jazz artists are by no means masterpieces. As we become conditioned to the excellence of the established masterworks, it becomes more difficult to listen with an open mind to any music not at their level. Hence, our interest in modern jazz declines.

government support of the arts

If the popular audience cannot be inspired to support avant-garde jazz and fine-art music, government funding becomes necessary in order for the music to survive. In Europe, reasonably adequate levels of support have been made available for fine-art music and are currently being made available for jazz. Such financing is less common in America, where governmental arts spending is minuscule in comparison to budgeting in other areas. Moreover, most of the available money goes to symphony orchestras, public radio and television, opera companies and other groups who tend to support the performer at the expense of the creator, and established art at the expense of the innovative.

It is possible that the American people seem to care little about art because its society was never dominated by the nobility: a patron class that has considered artistic interest and support a responsibility since the middle ages. The traditional support given by nobility has been supplemented by European governments whenever patron interest has been insufficient.

America, by comparison, is a more informal country, whose citizens are far less likely to think of themselves as involved with the arts. Most of the eighteenth and nineteenth century literary and intellectual leaders of America were not associated with the propagation of formal, technical art at all. Our literary leaders did little to create much artistic awareness among the people.

Throughout the nineteenth century, important intellectual figures such as Mark Twain and Walt Whitman embodied a grassroots approach to art, that is, they preferred entertainment as such and shunned formal art as effete, decadent, and European. Even as recently as the late nineteenth century, major literary figures such as Henry James found the artistic atmosphere in America stifling. They often relocated to Europe, not unlike scores of unappreciated jazz musicians who have abandoned their native country over the last few decades.

Paralleling the American lack of interest in fine art was the country's early preoccupation with minstrelsy and circuses: performance vehicles that connoted informality, fanfare, and boisterous entertainment. What little fine-art music performance there was took place in the major cities, though less extensively than in Europe.

With such an unfortunate history of interest in formal art, America has conferred unequivocal success on very few fine-art composers or outstanding jazz musicians. The most successful have been those whose work can be connected to folk and popular music, for example, Gottschalk, Gershwin, Ives, Copland, Armstrong, Ellington, and Goodman. Hence, for both American jazz and fine-art music there has been little assured support among patrons or the government, nor is much likely to be forthcoming.

positive features in the current jazz scene

Perhaps the main point of the previous section is that avant-garde jazz and avant-garde fine-art music are in a similar predicament, both having been abandoned by the mainstream popular audience that prefers the earlier, tonal styles. It is arguable that broad-based popular support is irrelevant to the healthy existence of an artform. Jazz, taken as a whole, is thriving in a number of ways: a growing and enthusiastic audience for the older styles and an exciting avant-garde with a small, but dedicated following. In the following subsections, important contemporary artists will be cited along with examples of the increasing number of jazz festivals and other evidence of flourishing interest in jazz.

important artists

Jazz artists in the 1980s can be divided into three general categories: those who emphasize traditional jazz styles, those who work primarily in jazz-rock, and those whose work is more experimental. The traditionalists tend to focus on dixieland, swing, bop, or modal jazz. The experimentalists are often difficult to classify as jazz musicians per se, since their work often fuses improvisation with fine-art musical styles or integrates other artforms entirely.

Among the traditionalists trumpeter Wynton Marsalis (b. 1961) has attracted considerable attention. He is a fluent classical trumpeter as well as a jazz musician. Marsalis is the first artist to be signed by both the classical and jazz divisions of Columbia Records and has become the first artist ever to win Grammys for both classical and jazz recordings. His improvisational style alternates between bop and a more modal style characteristic of the 1960s. Historically oriented, Marsalis cares little for avant-garde jazz and cites the great musicians of the past as sources of musical inspiration.[1]

[1]Mandel, Howard, "The Wynton Marsalis Interview," Downbeat, Vol. 51, No. 7, July 1984, p. 17.

Branford Marsalis (b. 1960) has been attracting almost as much attention as his brother Wynton. As a tenor and soprano saxophonist, Branford has a style that recalls the 1960 modal work of Wayne Shorter (b. 1933). In fact, the quintet founded by the Marsalis brothers seems modeled stylistically on the Miles Davis quintets of the 1960s.

Richie Cole (b. 1948) and Phil Woods (b. 1931) remain two of the most popular alto sax traditionalists of the 1980s. Their styles are firmly rooted in the bop tradition of Charlie Parker and Sonny Stitt.

Trumpeter Jon Faddis (b. 1953) became well known in the 1970s as a protégé of Dizzy Gillespie. With a musical style stemming from the bop tradition of Gillespie and Parker, Faddis is currently leading a quintet popular at many jazz festivals.

French pianist Michel Petrucciani has recently become a major attraction at jazz festivals. His fine technique ranges over a various blend of earlier solo piano styles such as stride and bop. Pianist Keith Jarrett (b. 1945), though sometimes associated with free jazz, is perhaps best classified as a traditionalist. He works almost exclusively on acoustic piano with a free-flowing, thoughtful style that sometimes recalls Aaron Copland's work in the 1930s. Another pianist, Joanne Brackeen (b. 1938), combines a variety of influences, including the styles of Bill Evans and Chick Corea, but adds a graceful ability to effect smooth transitions between disparate sections of a work.

Joe Pass (b. 1929), a performer whose roots are in 1940s swing and bop, is an outstanding solo jazz guitar performer. He prefers interpreting the pre-1950s Tin Pan Alley repertoire.[2]

Among the important jazz-rock musicians is guitarist Al Di Meola (b. 1955), whose powerful technique drew considerable attention while he was performing with Chick Corea's Return to Forever band in the 1970s. He performs frequently on acoustic guitar as well. Pat Metheny (b. 1955) is also an excellent guitarist who seems established in the jazz-rock mode. He is currently experimenting with a guitar-controlled synthesizer.

Weather Report, though founded in the 1970s, continues to generate great excitement in the jazz-rock area. Keyboardist Joe Zawinul (b. 1932), one of the most imaginative synthesists in jazz, contributes the bulk of the band's repertoire. Miles Davis remains a pioneer in jazz-rock fusion as well. Although in 1984 his concerts began reflecting the more traditional sound of his classic 1950s and 1960s groups, his jazz-rock work since 1969 has always been important and innovative.

During the last decade or so, the experimental jazz field has spawned numerous exciting artists whose work is of considerable interest. The styles of these artists are sometimes difficult to categorize. A principal criterion in my choosing them as representative of experimental jazz is that improvisation is a major factor in their performances.

[2]Schneckloth, Tim, "Joe Pass on Guitar," Downbeat, Vol. 51, No. 3, March 1984, pp. 22-23.

Art Ensemble of Chicago (left to right): Lester Bowie, Don Moye, Malachi Favors, Roscoe Mitchell, Joseph Jarman (Courtesy Institute of Jazz Studies, Rutgers University).

Among trumpeters, Lester Bowie, one of the outstanding avant-garde figures in jazz, continues to work with the Art Ensemble of Chicago or as a leader of his own groups. His style is an amalgam of avant-garde licks interspersed with quotations of older jazz styles. Don Cherry continues as a vital presence in experimental trumpet playing, although he has switched to pocket trumpet. The instrument Cherry prefers is pitched an octave higher than the usual B♭ trumpet.

Among reed players, Anthony Braxton continues in the tradition of the Art Ensemble of Chicago with intelligent, engrossing performances rooted in free jazz. He has also developed a clarinet style refreshingly free from the swing and dixieland traditions of the instrument. Roscoe Mitchell and Arthur Blythe (b. 1940) are two other important reed players who were at first associated with the AACM.

Carla Bley's reputation as a composer, band leader, and pianist has been growing since her work with the Jazz Composers Orchestra Association in the mid 1960s. She has currently been working with a ten-piece ensemble whose style is extremely eclectic. Sun Ra (b. 1928), one of the most enduring and significant keyboard players and band leaders in free jazz, continues to engage in fascinating experiments with his large ensemble, the Arkestra. Another pianist, Muhal Richard Abrams, a co-founder of the AACM, remains an outstandingly gifted contributor to experimental jazz in the 1980s.

Ronald Shannon Jackson (b. 1940) is a first-rate percussionist who has previously worked with Ornette Coleman. Recently, his group, the Decoding Society, has been investigating an alliance between free jazz and funk. Ornette Coleman's band, Prime Time, is engaging in similar experiments. Other major musicians long associated with free jazz, such as Cecil Taylor, bassist Charlie Haden (b. 1937), and drummer Ed Blackwell (b. 1927) are continuing to produce much exciting music.

Laurie Anderson (b. 1947) is one of the most intriguing performers in contemporary music. She has been called a "performance artist" in lieu of a more precise label because her work encompasses music, photography, poetry, film, slideshows, and other media. Within the musical dimension her work includes elements of new wave rock, minimalism, pop, and jazz. Currently she can be seen performing on various violins, usually modified electronically, and numerous synthesizers.

As can be seen from the preceding review, many of today's leading avant-garde players have come from prior associations with Chicago's AACM (see page 17). In addition to the Art Ensemble of Chicago, the AACM has also launched the groups Air and the Creative Construction Company.

Throughout the United States, the music cooperative has been very helpful in establishing a stimulating environment for creative musicians. Roscoe Mitchell, though at first associated with the AACM, founded the Creative Arts Collective in East Lansing, Mich. Another AACM associate, trumpeter Leo Smith (b. 1941), founded the Creative Music Improvisers Forum (CMIF) in New Haven, Conn. Drummer Charles Shaw and others were among the founders of the Black Artists Group (BAG) in St. Louis. Other music collectives include the San Antonio Jazz Alliance, founded in 1983, and the California Outside Music Association (COMA). Many of these organizations have obtained funding from the National Endowment for the Arts as well as states' arts associations. It seems likely that such support for jazz, though small, will continue to grow.

jazz festivals

The first important jazz festival was the Newport Jazz Festival, organized by promoter George Wein in 1954. Though successful as a yearly event, the festival, in 1972, was reorganized by Wein in New York City to attract a wider audience. By 1984, its thirtieth anniversary, Wein's annual event had become large and extremely popular. Its name now changed to the Kool Jazz Festival, Wein sponsors concerts at Avery Fisher Hall, Carnegie Hall, Carnegie Recital Hall, and the new-music loft Soundscape. The more popular mainstream musicians perform at the larger concert halls while the experimental music is more appropriately handled at the more intimate location. Besides the Kool Jazz Festival, other jazz festivals in New York City include Highlights of Jazz and Jazztime. By 1984, Carnegie Recital Hall, long an important location for avant-garde fine-art music, had become a major outlet for experimental jazz as well.

By the mid 1980s jazz festivals had become common throughout the United States. Since 1975 the Kool Festival has sponsored shows in New York, Cleveland, Philadelphia, Cincinnati, St. Louis, Chicago, Detroit, Baltimore, and Houston. The yearly Jacksonville and All That Jazz festival began in 1980 and has been running yearly since then. The 1983 festival was extensively broadcast on PBS. The Philadelphia Jazz Society has also been sponsoring shows since 1980. Other U.S. cities with festivals that feature jazz include New Orleans, Charleston (SC), Cotati (CA), Conneaut Lake (PA), Atlanta, Greeley (CO), Boston, Wichita, Tiburon (CA), Sarasota, Chicago, and Kansas City. In addition to these local events, National Public Radio offers the American Jazz Radio Festival.

Jazz festivals have become increasingly common throughout the world. The annual Moers New Jazz Festival has continued since 1972. This is one of the few important festivals that focuses on avant-garde jazz. Another more eclectic festival is the annual Festival International de Jazz de Montreal, which started in 1980. An estimated crowd of 300,000 attended events in the 1984 edition. Other Canadian jazz festivals include the Ottawa Jazz Festival and various events in Toronto and Edmonton (Alberta).

Among other important festivals, India's Jazz Yatra is a biennial event; Germany features its Jazzfest Berlin; the annual Camden Jazz Festival can be heard in London; in Norway the Köngsberg Jazz Festival has been an annual event since 1965; Sweden's annual Umeå Jazz Festival began in 1968. The Montreux (Switzerland) Jazz Festival is one of Europe's best known. Portugal's Cascais Jazz Festival began in 1971.

It seems that many of the world's major cities are beginning to offer jazz festivals. The list cited above is only a sampling of the numerous festivals that can be found throughout the world. In fact, the festival scene has flourished so remarkably that the Jazz World Society is publishing a *Jazz Festivals International Directory,* already in its third edition.

professional education

In the last twenty years or so there has been an enormous increase in the number of schools offering professional education and scholarly study in jazz. Among the most important centers for jazz scholarship are the Rutgers Institute for Jazz Studies (Newark, NJ) and the Hochschule für Jazz in Graz, Austria. Each of these centers publishes a scholarly journal. (See the periodicals section in the bibliography.) The Rutgers Institute has an extensive collection of records, books, photographs, and other important jazz memorabilia.

There are numerous schools, colleges, and universities offering professional training in jazz performance. Among the best known are the jazz programs at the Eastman School of Music, North Texas State, Northern Illinois University, Duke University, New England Conservatory, and Kent State. For many years, pianist Mary Lou Williams was artist in residence at Duke. Now other colleges and universities have invited well known jazz musicians to become part of their faculties or serve as artists in residence.

Other schools and educational resource centers include the Berklee College of Music (Boston) and the Trane Stop Resource Institute (Philadelphia), dedicated to John Coltrane. The AACM in Chicago now offers jazz classes, as do other jazz collectives such as the Creative Music Foundation in Woodstock, NY. Pianist Barry Harris (b. 1929) has initiated the Jazz Cultural Theatre in New York. In Los Angeles, jazz can be studied at the Wind College. The Jazzmobile program, under the expert guidance of pianist Billy Taylor, has been successful in bringing jazz to the streets of New York. The University of Pittsburgh has recently established the International Academy of Jazz Hall of Fame.

Never before has jazz been studied so extensively. It seems clear that as the number of performing jazz musicians continues to grow, the number of outstanding players will continue to increase as well. There should be no danger of a shortage of jazz talent in the future.

the outlook for jazz

How can today's jazz scene best be summed up? On the whole, the situation is far from lethargic. In that sense, we can be relieved that much of the second hypothesis is certainly incorrect: interest and activity in jazz seem to be growing. Jazz is continually becoming more international; outstanding players are being produced by other countries in addition to the United States; the market for recordings is respectable; and the number of jazz festivals grows year by year.

Certain trends, nevertheless, may be more of a cause for concern. The greater interest on the part of the public is for the jazz masters of the past or for current artists performing in the older styles. With respect to the popular audience, interest in jazz was at its height in the 1920s and 1930s; thereafter, jazz gradually lost this audience until the 1970s when the older jazz styles again began to attract large crowds. This audience, however, remains uninterested in avant-garde trends. For example, attendance at the avant-garde concerts in the 1983 and 1984 Kool Jazz Festivals in New York was far smaller than the attendance for the mainstream artists.

Nor has a direction for the evolution of jazz definitively been secured by any group of players. Since the heyday of jazz-rock in the late 1960s and early 1970s, no leaders have emerged with the stature of an Armstrong, Ellington, Parker, or Coltrane to guide the music along with a sense of historical purpose. Instead, the new music scene is more of a potpourri of experiments and fusions among cultures and styles with flashes of excitement, but with no dominating trends. The growing interest in jazz is heartening, but the music, taken as a whole, lacks the direction it had in the first fifty years, 1920-1970.

It is possible that since the early 1970s jazz has succumbed to the kind of steady state posited by Leonard Meyer for fine-art music.[3] In a steady state there is no apparent stylistic progress; rather, numerous styles co-exist, competing for attention. According to Meyer, the stylistic evolution of Western fine-art music ran its course from the Middle Ages to perhaps 1960 before stylistic stasis became the norm. Perhaps the stylistic evolution so dramatically evident from New Orleans jazz to early 1970s jazz will no longer be a prominent trend in the future.

Is it possible for a new style of jazz to emerge that can once again provide a sure sense of direction and historical purpose to both musicians and listeners? One possibility is that the current experiments at combining jazz with musics of other cultures may provide such direction. At the same time, a cross-cultural jazz style may once again be associated with popular music and, hence, perhaps regain more of the popular audience. Jazz, by uniting the tonal–harmonic language of Western music with the rhythmic and emotional vitality of African music, was in fact first developed by such a large-scale cultural mix. Although the internal evolution of Western music reveals much intracultural pollinization, jazz was possibly the first major Western musical style, since the Renaissance at least, to be formed from the interaction of highly disparate cultures. When African music was first combined with European music by the innovators of pre-jazz black music, the syntaxes of each musical culture were vastly dissimilar. In the future, jazz might continue to develop this prominent characteristic and perhaps its greatest strength: cultural union, the blend of the syntaxes and the emotional dispositions of distinct musical traditions.

The appreciation of world musics by both musicians and listeners is easier now than ever, since recordings of different cultures' music are widely available. Western fine-art music is glancing at these cultures for inspiration too, but extensive improvisation has been a declining art in fine-art music for at least a century. Besides, improvising jazz musicians will most likely be affected by the music of other cultures in ways unlike nonimprovising fine-art musicians.

While experimenting with world music, jazz musicians might also explore mixed media more extensively, perhaps following the lead of popular music in developing short films to accompany the performances. Other more experimental multimedia presentations by such performance artists as Laurie Anderson may also help to restore a sense of direction to the jazz scene. Combining musical styles and various other media in this manner should become more and more common.

the folk music connection

By associating with other musical cultures, jazz will once again be connected to folk music, a potential source of inspiration and revivification. According to

[3] *Music, the Arts, and Ideas,* Chicago and London: The University of Chicago Press, 1967, pp. 134-169.

a provocative thesis advanced by Herder (an eighteenth-century German philosopher and critic), formal art should retain a syntactic connection to folk culture in order to remain vital and popular. If Herder's thesis is true, twentieth-century concert music and jazz may have lost their appeal for most people because they are too far removed from the syntax of folk and popular art. By appropriating and enriching the popular music of other cultures, on the other hand, jazz can echo its formative basis in American folk and popular music and, at the same time, attract an important and emerging audience: the increasingly large number of people who listen to world music.

As world popular music begins to develop cross-cultural characteristics, jazz musicians should be ready to apply their improvisational methods to whatever styles emerge. This new type of jazz will have the same relation to world popular music as did dixieland and swing to American popular music in the 1920s and 1930s. The older jazz styles, of course, elaborated the basic core of American popular song, ragtime, and the blues; jazz may reach its greatest audience when it extends an established popular music to a more elaborate, formal, and richly aesthetic level.

In the past, jazz has profited enormously from returning to its roots, that is, by revitalizing itself with the blues, gospel music, and rhythm and blues. In the future, jazz may look to new "roots," the music of other world cultures. This development may be undertaken by the growing number of non-American jazz musicians and, even more recently, non-Western jazz musicians. These newer artists will naturally look to their national musics for ideas. Still, as world music becomes a part of everyone's culture, there is no reason why American jazz musicians cannot remain at the vanguard, especially since jazz will probably retain the rhythm and feel of Afro-American and African music, developed here first by black Americans.

world-music jazz precedents

The dissemination of American popular music can be traced back at least to ragtime, which stimulated a surprising demand throughout the world. Soon after, the best Tin Pan Alley songs became internationally popular as well. Since the era of the Beatles in the 1960s, much American and English popular music has joined stylistically, with the same records popular on both sides of the Atlantic. In the 1970s, American–British style rock spread to other cultures.[4] Meanwhile, much recent pop, especially that with an artistic bent, appropriates stylistic devices from fine-art music.[5] Hence, an eclectic world-popular music that can serve as the basis for a jazz repertoire will most certainly emerge.

[4] Palmer, Robert, "Global Pop Takes Shape," *New York Times,* March 20, 1983, "Arts and Leisure," p. 25.
[5] Rockwell, John, "Popular Music Takes a Serious Turn," *New York Times,* June 26, 1983, "Arts and Leisure," p. 1.

The history of world-music jazz can be traced to the first non-American attempts at the style. Competent imitation began almost immediately after the founding of the first world-famous jazz bands in the 1920s. As we have seen, Django Reinhardt, a French gypsy, was already one of the finest guitarists in jazz by the early 1930s. A short time later, other original and truly fine European jazz musicians, such as Stephane Grappelli, were ranked with the best American players.

Even musicians in the Soviet Union were interested in jazz by the early 1920s. Since that time, Soviet musicians, by actively resisting the frequent bans on American records and music, have produced some very fine players.[6] World-music jazz can also be traced to the frequent alliances of jazz with Latin music and rhythms, for example, Jelly Roll Morton in the 1920s, Dizzy Gillespie in the 1940s, and the many musicians who popularized *bossa nova* in the 1960s.

Beginning in the 1970s with fusion music, American and non-American jazz musicians have tried to merge jazz with the music of other cultures, especially the folk and popular traditions of their own countries.[7] In the Soviet Union, jazz musicians have tried combining jazz with indigenous Russian folk music.[8] Other combinations of jazz with folk and popular traditions have become increasingly numerous since the 1960s. Right in step with this trend, the 1982 Kool Jazz Festival in New York featured a concert called "Jazz & World Music" at Avery Fisher Hall. At the 1983 Kool Jazz Festival, various world-music groups appeared frequently enough to require no special attention called to them. The hybrid musical styles heard in the work of Weather Report and others are examples of the same process that, with world music, may gradually become more universal.

world-music jazz

A world-music jazz will probably present listeners with a new aesthetic. Although the cultures involved are as yet unknown, it is likely that the world-jazz connection to popular and folk music will result in a renewed informality, similar to that of pre-bop jazz or jazz-rock. World-jazz should then reflect a pop ambience; it will be played by those musicians wishing to extend and enrich the current popular music scene.

The avant-garde jazz styles will probably continue to be pursued, much like the avant-garde styles of fine-art music. This music, more complex aesthetically and syntactically than world-jazz, will remain popular with a devoted coterie of

[6] Starr, S. Frederick, *Red and Hot, the Fate of Jazz in the Soviet Union*, Oxford University Press, 1983.
[7] Palmer, Robert, "Expatriates Return, All Jazzed Up," *New York Times*, May 29, 1977, "Arts and Leisure," p. 12.
[8] Starr, *Red and Hot*, pp. 279-280.

listeners, but will probably not engage a wide audience. Despite their different traditions and different styles of improvisation, avant-garde jazz and avant-garde fine-art music may also merge into one art form, since their aesthetic aims seem to be growing more similar. In all likelihood, these avant-garde musics will be performed at lofts and small concert halls or at university music concerts.

The art-music aesthetic of jazz, advocated in Part Two and undoubtedly foreign to the Afro-American originators of early black music, will probably be, in general, too formal for world-jazz. This music should be experienced by getting into its rhythm, by physically participating at some level, by letting oneself ride with the sound. In the 1920s, popular jazz was practically synonymous with dancing largely because of its dizzying rhythms. The rhythmic vitality of such music can be deadened by contemplating it with the revered aura associated with fine-art music; such concentration robs the music of its pulse.

The first attempts at a world-music jazz have, so far, not produced a music that requires a more formal aesthetic anyway. Nor have the musicians played for large audiences capable of understanding their experiments. Afro-Americans required decades if not centuries to produce an art of the greatness and vivacity of jazz. Nowadays, because of film, recordings, and live broadcasts, innovations in popular musical styles spread very quickly, but time will still be needed for truly great musicians, and audiences, to emerge with rich multicultural backgrounds.

Hence, to produce cross-cultural jazz of real brilliance, adequate time for musicians to develop naturally and fully in more than one culture will be required. Popular and folk music are syntactically the most simple, so the basic cross-cultural nexus will most likely occur at their levels. Jazz musicians will then enrich the syntax to a more elaborate and complex level, that is, jazz musicians will place the music in an improvisatory context where it can transcend the compelling, but more rudimentary popular style.

the influence of jazz

Jazz has already influenced world music significantly. It is played by musicians throughout the world: in Eastern Europe and the Soviet Union, in Africa, and even in Japan, where it is extremely popular. Tokyo jazz clubs, for example, often feature Japanese jazz musicians jamming with touring Western artists.

Because of the popularity of American entertainers, songwriters, and jazz musicians from 1920 to 1950, jazz permanently altered the course of the world's popular music. To some extent it even homogenized it, often to the chagrin of Western ethnomusicologists who found it increasingly difficult to sample "pure" music from other cultures.

Since 1950, of course, rock has been the American musical style most heavily reflected in popular music around the world. But the acceptance of rock was prepared by the prior popularity of American jazz before 1950. Rock and jazz are like brothers, both products of the blues and black popular music conjoined to European form and harmony. When jazz ceased to be fashionable, rock began to dominate the popular music of the world.

Aspects of jazz style can also be detected in the art music of other cultures, although there its influence has been far less dramatic. The concept of an evolving art music tends to be more developed in the West than in other cultures, where it is often tradition-bound, showing little stylistic change over time. Since the connection of much of the world's art music to its past is difficult to break, these musics reflect twentieth-century trends to a much lesser extent. The jazz influence on non-Western art music is considerably less substantial than its influence on popular music.

Virgil Thomson suggests that America matured too late to join the flowering of the European classical tradition, and maybe too late to partake significantly in its decline. Therefore, according to Thomson, America's contribution to world music lies in jazz and perhaps folklore.[9] Jazz was originally a product of American folklore, of course, and has been enthusiastically received for a far longer time than any other music this country has produced. Jazz can be heard in practically every major city in the world; it is the essence of quality night life, entertainment, and cultural diversity.

Jazz is the most easily identifiable, most widely influential American contribution to the world's music culture. The conditions for producing jazz were only available in America and America has not produced another art music with the same degree of cultural influence and wide recognizability as jazz.

The third hypothesis is unquestionably true. No other country had the ethnic mix required for the development of jazz. No other American art music is played with such fervor everywhere, nor is there any other American art music that had not been first developed in Europe by Europeans.

In fact, of the American music of all styles produced in this century, ranging from Ives, Copland, Gershwin, and Fats Waller to B. B. King, Stevie Wonder, and Elvis Presley, that which sounds distinctly American, and not just Western, is the music that projects at least something of a jazz heritage. There is no doubt that jazz is the most significant contribution of America to the world's art-music culture.

[9] Thomson, Virgil, "Music Does Not Flow," *New York Review of Books,* December 17, 1981, pp. 47-51.

chapter
twelve

jazz
and the
other
arts

The position of jazz as an important product of Western culture is surely bolstered by its continuing critical influence on other Western art forms, including those only peripherally connected with music. For although jazz has altered the evolution of popular music and contemporary fine-art music quite significantly, it has also affected the content and sometimes even the form of dance, poetry, theater, film, and fiction.

The rage for jazz during the roaring twenties derived at least partly from its association with popular ballroom dancing fads, like the Charleston. After the depression, popular dance continued its hand-in-hand connection with jazz until the beginning of the bop era. Fine-art dancing—ballet, modern, and "jazz" dance—presents a somewhat different jazz connection; it is much more likely to be accompanied by modern jazz music.

Along the same lines, theater, especially the musical comedy, boasts considerable jazz associations. Much of the dancing in musical comedy has a jazz flair and is often supported by swing oriented scores. After a consideration of the influence of jazz on Western fine-art music and film in the next two sections, I will list some of the associations of jazz with dance and theater.

If we agree that music is, at the very least, structured sound, then no art is more like music than poetry. For this reason, it is not surprising that we can find intriguing parallels between jazz and poetic structure. Moreover, many poems have been written that either describe jazz, pay homage to jazz artists, or borrow the images and lexicon of jazz. The other arts are for various reasons somewhat more deficient in their ability to reflect jazz structure. Dance, for example, is not music, but an interpretation of music. It is primarily visual, not aural, representing a transfer of continuous sound into continuous motion.

Prose is not normally considered to be an aural art form either, but we can point out several instances of written pieces borrowing large-scale jazz forms. In general, however, prose is too discursive and referential to take on small-scale jazz elements unless it is especially formalized, for example, the work of James Joyce. Such prose may be more akin to poetry than to the usual plot narratives that characterize most fiction. Many prose works have been written that describe jazz artists and their lifestyles, however, although these works do not usually preoccupy themselves with reflecting jazz musical structure.

Since painting, photography, and plastic art, such as sculpture, are not only nonaural, but also do not unfold through time, the influence of jazz structure in these areas has been minimal. Nevertheless, certain artists still manage to incorporate a sense of jazz into their works: for example, Mondrian's well known "Broadway Boogie-Woogie" reflects the pulse of Manhattan night life; its colors and rhythms vibrate through the painting like a swinging jazz solo. The improvisatory process itself can be observed in the "action" painters, who apply themselves to their work with a jazzlike abandon. Of course, many painters, of various schools, depict jazz themes visually in their work, not unlike the way the jazz life is described in novels.

Filmmakers, unlike dancers, poets, and fiction writers, have rarely incorporated aspects of musical structure into their films. The most famous experiment in interpreting musical structure abstractly through film is undoubtedly Walt Disney's *Fantasia*. Like prose, film tends to be discursive; movies tell stories, hence the representational elements of the plot and characters are often emphasized at the expense of formal considerations. Like novels without plots, nonrepresentational films have not won a widespread following. There are numerous films, both features and documentaries, however, that highlight the life and work of the great jazz artists.

The following lists provide the reader with sources and representative examples of the influence of jazz (and other Afro-American music) on the other Western arts.

third stream compositions and concert pieces influenced by jazz

ANTHEIL, GEORGE (1900-1959): *Ballet Mécanique*, 1923-1924 (revised 1953); *Jazz Symphony*, 1925.

BABBITT, MILTON (b. 1916): *All Set for Jazz Ensemble*, 1957.

BAKER, DAVID (b. 1931): *Le Chat Qui Pêche* for orchestra, soprano, and jazz quartet, 1974.

BERNSTEIN, LEONARD (b. 1918): *Prelude, Fugue, and Riffs* for orchestra, 1949; *Symphony No. 2—The Age of Anxiety* for piano and orchestra, 1949; *Mass*, 1970.

COPLAND, AARON (b. 1900): *Symphonic Ode*, 1929; *Short Symphony*, 1933; *Statements* for orchestra, 1934; *El Salon Mexico* for orchestra, 1936; *Billy the Kid* for orchestra, 1938; *Appalachian Spring* for orchestra, 1944; *Clarinet Concerto*, 1948; *Four Piano Blues*, 1926-1948.

DVOŘÁK, ANTONÍN (1841-1904): *Symphony No. 9 in E Minor*, "From the New World"; *String Quartet in F Major*, the "American."

DEBUSSY, CLAUDE (1862-1918): "Golliwog's Cakewalk" from the *Children's Corner* suite for piano, 1908; "General Lavine—Eccentric" from the *Preludes, Book II* for piano, 1913.

GERSHWIN, GEORGE (1898-1937): *Rhapsody in Blue* for piano and orchestra, 1924; *Piano Concerto*, 1928; *An American in Paris* for orchestra, 1928; *Porgy and Bess*, an opera, 1935; *Three Preludes* for piano, 1936.

GOTTSCHALK, LOUIS MOREAU (1829-1869): various short piano works reflecting the melody and harmony of black spirituals; short piano works incorporating Afro-American rhythms.

GOULD, MORTON (b. 1913): *Symphonette No. 2*.

LIEBERMANN, ROLF (b. 1910): *Concerto for Jazz Band and Orchestra*, 1955.

MILHAUD, DARIUS (1892-1974): *La Création du Monde* for orchestra, 1923.

RAVEL, MAURICE (1875-1937): *L'Enfant et les Sortilèges*, an opera, 1925; *Violin Sonata*, 1927; two piano concertos in G Major and D Major, 1931.

SCHULLER, GUNTHER (b. 1925): "Little Blue Devil" from *Seven Studies on Themes of Paul Klee* for orchestra, 1959; *Concertino for Jazz Quartet and Orchestra*, 1961; *The Visitation*, an opera, 1967.

STILL, WILLIAM GRANT (b. 1895): *Afro-American Symphony*, 1930 (revised 1969).

STRAVINSKY, IGOR (1882-1971): *L'Histoire du Soldat* for chamber ensemble, 1917; *Ragtime for Eleven Instruments*, 1918; *Piano Rag Music*, 1919; *Ebony Concerto* for clarinet and big band, 1945.

documentaries and films featuring jazz artists

American Music—from Folk to Jazz and Pop, 1969 (various artists)
Anatomy of a Murder, 1959 (Duke Ellington)
Artistry in Rhythm, 1944 (Stan Kenton)
L'Aventure du Jazz, 1969-1970 (various artists)
The Benny Goodman Story, 1955 (Benny Goodman, et al.)
The Big Broadcast of 1937, 1936 (various artists)
Black and Tan, 1929 (Duke Ellington)
Born to Swing, 1973 (various artists)
Drum Crazy—The Gene Krupa Story, 1959 (Gene Krupa, et al.)
Du Tam-tam au Jazz, 1969 (historical, various artists)
En Remontant le Mississippi, 1971 (mostly blues performances)
The Fabulous Dorseys, 1947 (Tommy and Jimmy Dorsey)
The Glenn Miller Story, 1953 (various artists)
High Society, 1956 (Louis Armstrong)
Hit Parade of 1937, 1936 (Duke Ellington)
Hit Parade of 1943, 1943 (Count Basie)
Jam Session, 1944 (various artists)
Jammin' the Blues, 1944 (Lester Young and others)
Jazz Festival, 1949/56 (various artists)
Jazz in Piazza, 1974 (various artists)
Jazz Is Our Religion, 1972 (various artists)
Jazz on a Summer's Day, 1960 (the 1958 Newport Jazz Festival)
Jazz the Intimate Art, 1968 (various artists)
Make Mine Music, 1945 (Benny Goodman)
Mingus, 1968 (Charles Mingus)
Monterey Jazz, 1968 and 1973 (various artists)
New Orleans, 1947 (various artists including Billie Holiday and Louis Armstrong)
On the Road with Duke Ellington, 1974
Reveille with Beverly, 1943 (various artists)
Satchmo the Great, 1956 (Louis Armstrong)
A Song Is Born, 1948 (Benny Goodman and others)
The Sound of Jazz, 1957 (various artists)
Stormy Weather, 1943 (Fats Waller, Cab Calloway, and others)
Sun Valley Serenade, 1941 (Glenn Miller and the Nicholas Brothers)
Sweet and Low-Down, 1944 (Benny Goodman)

shorter documentaries (some made for television)

After Hours, 1961 (Chick Webb)
Barney Kessel Trio, 1962

The Blues, 1960s
Bobby Hackett, 1961
Celebration, 1966 (Oscar Peterson)
Chick Corea, 1961
Coleman Hawkins Quartet, 1961
Cool and Groovy, 1956 (various artists)
Dave Brubeck, 1970
Dizzy Gillespie Quintet, 1964
Duke Ellington and His Orchestra, 1962
Earl "Fatha" Hines, 1963/64
European Music Revolution, 1970 (Art Ensemble of Chicago and Don Cherry)
Finale, 1970 (Louis Armstrong's last Newport Jazz Festival appearance)
Introduction to Jazz, 1952 (various artists)
L'Invention, 1967 (Cecil Taylor)
The John Coltrane Quartet, 1963/64
Mann with a Flute, 1960 (Herbie Mann)
The Modern Jazz Quartet, 1964
Pete Fountain Sextet, 1962
Shelly Manne and His Men, 1962
Shorty Rogers and His Giants, 1962
Sonny Rollins Live at Laren, 1973
Stage Entrance, 1951 (Charlie Parker and Dizzy Gillespie)
Stephane Grappelli and His Quintet, 1946
Ted Heath and His Music, 1961
Theater for a Story, 1959 (Miles Davis with Quintet and Gil Evans Orchestra)
Woody Herman and The Swingin' Herd, 1963

jazz film scores (by composer)

CARTER, BENNY: many films with jazz-oriented scores, including *A Man Called Adam,* 1966 (starring Sammy Davis, Jr. and Louis Armstrong); *Buck and the Preacher,* 1972.
DAVIS, MILES: *Ascenseur pour l'echautaud* ('Elevator to the Gallows'), 1957; *Jack Johnson,* 1970.
ELLINGTON, DUKE: *Anatomy of a Murder,* 1959.
HANCOCK, HERBIE: *The Spook Who Sat by the Door,* 1973.
JARRETT, KEITH: *Mon Coeur est Rouge,* 1976.
MANCINI, HENRY: Pink Panther films (various years); background music to *Peter Gunn* television show (during 1960s).
ROLLINS, SONNY: *Alfie,* 1966.
SCHIFRIN, LALO: many films with jazz oriented scores, including *Cool Hand Luke,* 1967.
WEATHER REPORT: *Watched,* 1974.

musicals featuring jazz

Africana, 1927
Ain't Misbehavin', 1978
Anything Goes, 1934
Blackbirds of 1928, 1928
Dancin', 1978

Darktown Follies, 1913
Dixie to Broadway, 1924
Eubie, 1978
Forty-second Street, 1980
Girl Crazy, 1930

Lady Be Good, 1924
On the Town, 1945
Porgy and Bess, 1935
Purlie, 1970
Rhapsody in Black, 1931
Shuffle Along, 1921

Sophisticated Ladies, 1981
Sweet Charity, 1966
West Side Story, 1957
The Wiz, 1975
Wonderful Town, 1953

prominent jazz dancers

AILEY, ALVIN
ASTAIRE, FRED
BUBBLES, JOHN
CASTLE, IRENE and VERNON
CHARISSE, CYD
COLE, JACK
DUNHAM, KATHERINE

KELLY, GENE
LANE, WILLIAM HENRY ("MASTER JUBA")
NICKS, WALTER
NUGENT, PETE
POWELL, ELEANOR
PRIMUS, PEARL
ROBINSON, BILL "BOJANGLES"

jazz in fiction

BAKER, DOROTHY. *Young Man with a Horn*. Boston: Houghton Mifflin, 1961 (1st ed. 1938). Fine novel based on the life of Bix Beiderbecke.

CHAPMAN, ABRAHAM, ed. *Black Voices, An Anthology of Afro-American Literature*. New York: New American Library, 1968. An excellent selection of fiction, poetry, autobiography, and literary criticism. Also includes extensive bibliography.

CHAPMAN, ABRAHAM, ed. *New Black Voices, An Anthology of Contemporary Afro-American Literature*. New York: New American Library, 1972. A continuation of *Black Voices*. Contains works written or first published in the 1960s or early 1970s.

FITZGERALD, F. SCOTT. *The Great Gatsby*. New York: Charles Scribner's Sons, 1925. Classic novel depicting the "jazz age" of the 1920s, though not dealing with jazz specifically.

GOSLING, PAULA. *Solo Blues*. New York: Ballantine Books, 1981. Jazz murder mystery.

HENTOFF, NAT. *Jazz Country*. New York: Dell, 1965. Well-done novel for teenagers about the problems of being a jazz musician.

HOLMES, JOHN CLELLON. *The Horn*. Berkeley: Creative Arts Book, 1980 (1st ed. 1953). Excellent novel whose central character, Edgar Pool, reflects the archetypal swing-bop sax player of the 1940s.

HUGHES, LANGSTON. *The Best of Simple*. New York: Hill & Wang, 1961. Selected Simple stories.

RUSSELL, ROSS. *The Sound*. New York: Macfadden-Bartell Corporation, 1961. Novel about the jazz world during the bop era.

ŠKVORECKÝ, JOSEF. *The Bass Saxophone*. New York: Knopf, 1979. Taking place in occupied Czechoslovakia during World War II, this novel tells about a young saxophonist who sits in on bass saxophone with a touring German band.

ŠKVORECKÝ, JOSEF. *The Cowards*. New York: Grove Press, Inc., 1970. Novel about young jazz musicians in Czechoslovakia at the end of World War II.

jazz in poetry

HARPER, MICHAEL S. *Images of Kin. New and Selected Poems*. Urbana, Chicago, and London: University of Illinois Press, 1977. Striking poems with many references to musicians and jazz.

226

HAYDEN, ROBERT, ed. *Kaleidoscope. Poems by American Negro Poets.* New York: Harcourt, Brace and World, Inc., 1967. A very fine collection of poems.

HUGHES, LANGSTON. *Selected Poems.* New York: Vintage, 1974 (1st ed. 1959). Hughes's own selection of what he considered to be his finest poems.

KING, WOODIE, ed. *The Forerunners. Black Poets in America.* Washington: Howard University Press, 1975. An interesting anthology featuring a representative selection of poets.

STETSON, ERLENE. *Black Sisters. Poetry by Black American Women, 1746-1980.* Bloomington: Indiana University Press, 1981. An extensive, often fascinating collection.

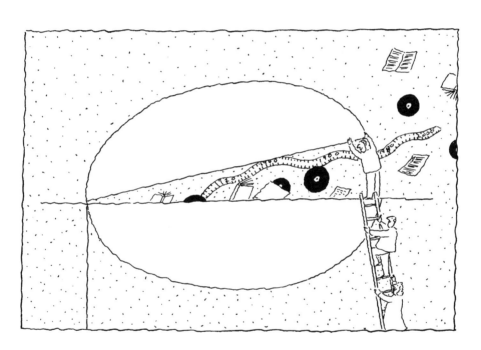

appendices

transcriptions

A range of styles has been chosen for this series of transcriptions. Not all styles for each instrument have been included since this would be unnecessary. Because these works have been discussed previously, the reader should refer to the earlier presentations for recording dates, personnel, etc.

bix beiderbecke: "jazz me blues"

[previous discussion: pp. 104–106]

1. The actual solo is shown on line (c), while the voices are schematized on lines (a) and (b). In the schematic presentation, the relative importance of a pitch is shown by the type of note value, viz., half-notes, quarter-notes, filled-in noteheads (without stems), and eighth-notes in decreasing importance.

2. The first two bars consist of the pitches A and F♯, which are members of the prevailing D7 chord harmony. Each pitch forms the beginning of a voice. In m. 3 the F♯ proceeds to the F of the G7 chord while the A continues, or is "prolonged." The idea behind prolongation is that the feeling or effect of the same pitch is continued through a new harmony or harmonies.

3. No pitches are left hanging for long—instead, all new voices are absorbed quickly into previous voices.

4. There is a tendency for most voices to move downwards.

5. There is a "principal voice," shown in half notes on line (a), that continues through the whole solo with an initial dip in m. 8 to Ab; in m. 9 the voice begins again on A, which is prolonged from m. 9 to m. 18 where it proceeds to Ab, and finally (in a skip) to F in mm. 19-20.

6. The voice-leading line, A-G-F, prominently occurs in both halves of the solo, but is reharmonized in the second half. This reharmonization prepares the extended cadence of the second half of the piece.

7. In the final cadence of this piece, the flatted third proceeds to the tonic pitch in a manner, derived from a typical usage in the blues, that suggests a replacement of the normal second degree to first degree cadence common in European tonal harmony. Certain melodic skips, like the flatted third to the tonic, because they occur so frequently in jazz, are often equivalent to normal step motion in the European harmonic tradition.

8. Another subtle aspect of "Jazz Me Blues" may be described as the unique identity of each voice; that is, no melodic continuation is ever duplicated. For example, A and Ab are a pair of pitches that often occur contiguously throughout the solo, but their rhythmic and motivic environment is constantly fresh. This feature is echoed in the melody line itself, which is ideally balanced between skips and steps.

louis armstrong: "west end blues"

[previous discussions: pp. 71–72 and 107–109]

1. In the beginning of the cadenza, Armstrong presents a single motivic reference to the song's opening, F#-G-Bb (M), which helps link the opening flourish to the solo's conclusion. These ascending triplets reach a penetrating high C; this suggests that this note may become significant later in the solo. From the high C, a virtuosic descending passage leads to the entrance of the full band on the Bb7(#5) chord. The inclusion of this pungent F# in the Bb7 chord anticipates the first note of the tune.

2. The drama of the cadenza is heightened by Armstrong's rhythmic control as well as by the large-scale shape of the cadenza itself. For example, the pitches accelerate to the high C (in measure 4), held out dramatically, after which a very fast passage follows, only slowing down toward the end of the cadenza. The cadenza starts high (m. 1), dips quickly (m. 2), then rises to its highest point (m. 4) before descending to its lowest point (m. 9). This dynamic large-scale shape is sharply contrasted by the relaxed presentation of the melody in the first ensemble chorus. Yet Armstrong, at the end of this chorus, echoes the triplets of the cadenza with a rising triplet figure in C1m11 that finishes on high Bb. The two highest notes, Bb and C, are thus presented as the culmination of two similar patterns and a link between them is established.

3. On his final chorus, Armstrong begins with motive M, transposed up an octave. By holding the high Bb for several bars, Armstrong prepares us for the insistently repeated 4-note figures that follow. In subsequent measures, Armstrong reiterates the high Bb and C, to reinforce their previous association. Armstrong's final bars provide one last low-register statement of the C-Bb idea just before the final Eb of the piece.

dizzy gillespie: "shaw 'nuff"

[previous discussion: pp. 110–112]

miles davis: "so what"

[previous discussions: pp. 114–116]

(continued)

1. "So What" consists of two 32-bar choruses, each AABA, with the B section a half step higher than the A. The A sections are in D dorian, while the B section is based on E♭ dorian.

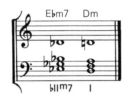

2. The relationship between the A and B sections is akin to the important jazz cadence ♭II–I. Hence, the change to E♭ dorian in the B section is more than just a change of mode; it is also a very large-scale change of harmony from a pervasive I or Dm7 in the A sections to a ♭II or E♭m7 in the B sections.

3. The general plan of Davis's solo consists of assembling a Dm11 chord (D-F-A-C-E-G) through the course of the solo. He begins by emphasizing the lower portion of the chord, C1Am1 to C1A′m5, followed by a hint of the high G and E in C1A′m6, and culminating first at the beginning of the second chorus and then most decisively at the beginning of the final A section. The E♭ dorian counterpart, the E♭m11 chord, is outlined assertively in the second B section.

benny goodman: "avalon"

[previous discussion: pp. 121–123]

1. The first 16 bars, harmonically structured by Bb7 (4 bars), Eb (4 bars), Bb7 (4 bars), and Eb (4 bars), are unified by a large-scale F-Eb-F-Eb corresponding to each of the chord changes. However, the F and Eb pitches are presented in a fresh melodic light at each recurrence, with no hint of mechanical planning on Goodman's part. The F-Eb pitch-pair returns frequently throughout the solo (mm. 12-15 and m. 24, for example), and is especially emphasized in m. 31 at its conclusion.

2. A large-scale voice leading succession proceeds from the high Bb, the first note of the solo. The same pitch is strongly articulated in mm. 7-9 and mm. 18-21, after which it begins a long descent to Ab in m. 23, G in m. 25, F in m. 30, and finally Eb in m. 32.

3. The Bb-Ab-G-F-Eb line occurs on a smaller scale throughout the solo, a technique often called "diminution"; for example, in mm. 1-2, mm. 30-32 (the beginning and the end), mm. 21-24, and, though incomplete (because the line finishes on F), in mm. 8-9 and m. 21.

4. The solo is organized around the Bb-Ab-G-F-Eb line, but it is never fully stated as an uninterrupted melody. Moreover, the pitch-pair F and Eb, emphasized in the first 16 bars, can be seen in a new light, as part of the larger scalar pattern.

5. The 5-note scale that effectively integrates the solo is derived from an important motive in the original song. Hence Goodman, without quoting the tune directly, explores the melody of "Avalon" by wrapping his solo around one of its important motives (**M**).

lester young: "doggin' around"

[previous discussion: pp. 123–125]

1. The "bluesy," relaxed quality of Young's playing extends throughout the solo. For example, whenever the Bb tonic harmony changes to the subdominant (IV) Eb in the third bar of the A section, a change that recalls the use of IV in bar 5 of the 12-bar blues progression, Young usually responds with lines that bend appropriately around various blue notes. The blues inflections are developed further in the A′ section, the first 4 bars of which seem completely disconnected from the beat of the rhythm section. The yearning character of this phrase is contrasted by the return to the swing style eighth-note lines to complete the A′ section.

2. Throughout the solo, Young juxtaposes assertive swing style lines with looser, blues-type phrases. For example, because the descending line at the beginning of the bridge is metrically irregular, floating gently over the beat, the return to eighth-note lines swings all the more effectively.

charlie parker: "shaw 'nuff"

[previous discussion: pp. 125–127]

1. The accented C and B in Am3 together imply an accent on the downbeat of Am4—instead, the B♭ is delayed and accented on the second beat of that measure. Similarly, the E♭ in that measure is the seventh of the F7 chord, resolving to the D, the third of the B♭ chord in Am5. Yet, this E♭ on beat 4½ is accented while the metrically strong downbeat D—its resolution—is not. Such unexpected and delightful melodic accents can be heard throughout the entire solo.

2. The treatment of the extended chord tones is an aspect of the voice-leading virtuosity always present in Parker's style. Throughout the solo, the pitches of most chords are led to proper connections in the following bars. When a pitch is left hanging and not immediately resolved to a proper pitch in the next harmony, Parker tends to return to it later and emphasize it in some way. For example, the high E♭ in Bm1 should resolve to a D within the D7 harmony, but does not. The E♭ returns and is strongly accented in Bm4 before the line proceeds to D and then C in Bm5. Subtlety of voice leading and motivic structure based on voice leading are common to most of Parker's solos. At the end of "Shaw 'Nuff," though, Parker abandons this logic, purposefully leaving the solo structurally incomplete to usher in Gillespie's statement.

john coltrane: "giant steps"

[previous discussion: pp. 130–132]

1. Ebmaj7 and Gmaj7 chords, harmonically prominent throughout, are melodically outlined in the first half.

2. In mm. 10-11, the B-A-D motive, developed sequentially, generates the melody for the remainder of the tune, yet this is the same motive that had joined m. 4 to m. 5, where it foreshadowed its use in the last half.

3. The bass line in the first half descends through whole steps that outline the prominent major thirds and tritones found in the last half.

4. Beginning on B and ending on Eb, the tune is tonally ambiguous. The large-scale harmonic movement, from B to Eb, is a "giant step."

ornette coleman: "lonely woman"

[previous discussion: pp. 133–136]

1. The last part of Coleman's solo, from the B-section duet with Cherry, is transcribed more approximately than usual, regarding both pitch and rhythm, because of Coleman's pitch slides and unique intonation. Flat or sharp pitches that are intentional variants of the usual tempered pitches are designated by an arrow specifying the direction of the inflection. The frequent curved lines before and after certain pitches signify the swooping attack and release that Coleman applies to so many notes.

2. At the end of the duet with Cherry, the motive C♯-D-A appears in mm. 17-20. The last three notes of the tune, these pitches link the second to the third phrase of the original song and appear, internally, in the third phrase as well. Coleman proceeds to spin out the C♯-D-A motive ingeniously. The placement of the C natural in m. 23 recalls the C-C♯ sound of the third phrase of the tune. In mm. 24-27, the high E and C♯ similarly paraphrase the third phrase.

3. The C♯-A idea is soon transposed to C-A♭ in mm. 33-34, then gradually raised again to C♯-A and D-B.

4. The climactic high A♭-G, identical to the climax of the song, moves the solo to its highest point. Also, like the song, it is placed in the penultimate phrase.

charlie christian: "i found a new baby"

[previous discussions: pp. 69–71 and pp. 139–140]

1. As an organizing element, the interval F–B, a tritone, is heard throughout the solo, with the B pitch particularly emphasized.

2. In the A″ section, the F–B tritone is explicitly articulated, with frequent repetition, although it was first outlined in Am4 to Am5, and in A′m3. The B pitch is further underscored in A′m5 as well as in Bm5.

3. It seems that whenever Christian comes to a D minor chord, after the A section, the pitch B, usually conjoined to the F, is articulated quite prominently. Yet, its use is perfectly controlled, and is never unpleasantly obvious.

4. As if to balance the F–B tritone, Christian articulates another tritone, G–C♯, on all of the A7 chords.

5. Whenever Christian plays a B during a G7 chord, he follows it soon with a B♭ during the C7 chord, an example of motivic voice leading, similar to Beiderbecke's, that imparts a strong feeling of command to the solo.

6. The wide variety of phrase length again foreshadows bop style, as does the bebop figure in A′m8 and the use of the extended chord tone, F♯, left hanging in Am8.

john mclaughlin: "dance of maya"

[previous discussion: pp. 140–141]

1. After the long opening vamp, the rhythm changes to a rocking blues beat, the bars alternating between a normal 12/8 and the unusual 8/8 division of $3+3+2$ beats. The aural effect of the second bar suggests 2-2/3 beats of a normal 4/4 bar, as if the last 1-1/3 beats of the bar were lopped off.

2. Here is the beginning of the D dorian section of McLaughlin's solo:

3. This outlines the transition back to the opening section of the piece:

j. j. johnson: "boneology"

[previous discussion: pp. 143]

herbie hancock: "chameleon"

[previous discussions: pp. 55–58 and 149–150]

(continued)

1. Unpitched sound (e.g., mm. 38–43) is transcribed approximately with only the rhythm suggested for the most part.

2. The funky patterns in m. 102 and on, which create a really good groove, are complemented by the drummer's moving to the bell of the ride cymbal. The repetitions help to drive the solo forward, but not at the expense of its funky earthiness.

3. Hancock's pattern in m. 116 and on is also a 3/4 rhythm superimposed on the basic underlying 4/4 of the bass line and rhythm section.

4. In m. 134 and on, the rhythmic component of the modulated sound becomes very complex, the 4:5 notation signifying that four notes are played in the time of five beats. Such a rhythm interlocks with the 4/4 meter in such a way that the pattern begins first on the downbeat, then on the second beat, and so on. In addition to the overall 4:5 rhythm, each large pulse is subdivided into three or four smaller note values, thus generating a multilevel polyrhythmic texture, evocative of the rhythmic textures sometimes heard in African music.

teddy wilson: "between the devil and the deep blue sea"
[previous discussion: pp. 167–169]

appendices

1. The first phrase, from C4Am1 to C4Am4, begins by emphasizing the A♭ blue third. The second phrase, also 4 bars, begins similarly, but cadences on F instead of C. In C4A'm1 the same pitch A♭ is reinterpreted as G♯, the raised second degree, as if Wilson were exploring the pitch by examining its different functions.

2. In the bridge, the pitch-pair G♯-A is heard again, reinterpreted in the context of A major. The G♯-A pitch-pair, heard throughout the chorus, is finally transformed to a nonconsecutive G-A in C4Bm5 and C4Bm6.

cecil taylor: "enter evening"

[previous discussion: pp. 179–181]

(Only the beginning and end of Taylor's solo are provided in the transcription.)

1. The solo is held together by a correspondence of gesture; practically all of the arpeggiated figures rise.

2. The single-note passage at the beginning of the solo is echoed by a similar passage in a higher register toward the end of the solo.

3. The opening single-note passage largely comprises fourths and tritones. Many of the arpeggiated chords have a similar construction, with emphasis on the perfect fourths that can be formed from the pitches E♭, A♭, D♭, G♭, and C♭. The single-note passage toward the end of the solo features just these pitches leading to a sustained E♭. In the passage immediately following, B♭♭ is added to the basic pitch set, much as it was at the beginning of the solo when it appeared with D♭, G♭, C♭, and F♭.

   4. The continued highlighting of fourths and chords containing E♭, A♭, D♭, G♭, and C♭ imparts a harmonic coherence to this solo.

billie holiday: "all of me"

[previous discussion: pp. 189–191]

The principal descending line of the tune is F–E–D. This same line is duplicated in the voice leading of Holiday's final chorus. At the same time, the intensity of her expression is extended by the addition of the new voice at the A pitch-level.

selected discography

The *Smithsonian Collection of Classic Jazz* and the Smithsonian's *Big Band Jazz, From the Beginnings to the Fifties* are highly recommended. Throughout this book, recordings that are contained in the *Classic Jazz* collection are marked SCCJ. This discography recommends other long-playing records as well including subsequent Smithsonian releases that feature specific artists. Whenever one of the following records contains a selection discussed in this book, it is indicated with the name of the cut in quotation marks.

louis armstrong

The Louis Armstrong Story, Vol. 1-4, Columbia CL 851-4. "West End Blues," "Hotter Than That," and "Heebie Jeebies."
Louis Armstrong and Earl Hines, Smithsonian Collection.

art ensemble of chicago

People in Sorrow, Nessa N-30.
Nice Guys, ECM 1-1126.

count basie

The Best of Count Basie, MCA2-4050. "Doggin' Around."

bix beiderbecke

Bix Beiderbecke—1924, Olympic 7130. "Jazz Me Blues."
The Bix Beiderbecke Story, Vol. 1-3, Columbia CS 844-6.

anthony braxton

New York, Fall 1974, Arista AL 4032.

clifford brown

Clifford Brown—The Quintet, EmArcy EMS-2-403.
Clifford Brown and Max Roach at Basin Street, Trip Jazz TLP-5511. "I Remember April."

dave brubeck

Time Out, Columbia CS 8192. "Blue Rondo à la Turk."

appendices

betty carter

The Audience With Betty Carter, Bet-Car Records, MK 1003.

charlie christian

Solo Flight, Columbia G-30779. "I Found a New Baby."

ornette coleman

At the Golden Circle, Blue Note ST-84224.
The Shape of Jazz to Come, Atlantic SD-1317. "Lonely Woman."

john coltrane

Giant Steps, Atlantic 1311. "Giant Steps."
Coltrane Live at Birdland, Impulse A-50. (The "classic" quartet)
A Love Supreme, Impulse A-77. "Acknowledgement."
Ascension, Impulse A-95. (Featuring 11-piece ensemble.)

chick corea

Light as a Feather, Polydor PD 5525. "You're Everything" and "Light as a Feather."
Where Have I Known You Before, Polydor PD 6509.

miles davis

The Complete Birth of the Cool, Capitol M-11026.
ESP, Columbia CS 9150.
In a Silent Way, Columbia CS 9875.
Kind of Blue, Columbia CS 8163. "So What."
Milestones, Columbia PC 9428.
Miles Smiles, Columbia CS 9401.
Porgy and Bess, Columbia PC 8085. "Summertime."

eric dolphy

The Berlin Concerts, Inner City IC 3017-2.

duke ellington

Duke Ellington 1938, 1939, and 1940, The Smithsonian Collection (Three 2-record sets). "Ko-Ko" and "Concerto for Cootie."
The Duke Ellington Carnegie Hall Concerts, vol. 1-4, Prestige P-34004, P-24073, P-24074, P-24075.

bill evans

The Village Vanguard Session, Milestone 47002.

gil evans

Into the Hot, Impulse A-9. (With Cecil Taylor.)
Out of the Cool, Impulse A-4.

ella fitzgerald

Ella Fitzgerald Sings Gershwin, Decca 74451.

dizzy gillespie

The Development of an American Artist, The Smithsonian Collection.
Dizzy Gillespie, RCA Victor LPV-530. "Woody'n You."
In the Beginning, Prestige P-24030.
The Greatest Jazz Concert Ever, Prestige PR 24024.

benny goodman

Benny Goodman Carnegie Hall Concert, Columbia OSL-160.
Solo Flight, Columbia CG 30779.

herbie hancock

Headhunters, Columbia KC 32731. "Chameleon."
Maiden Voyage, Blue Note ST-84195. "Maiden Voyage."

coleman hawkins

The Hawk Flies, Milestone M-47015.

fletcher henderson

Fletcher Henderson and Don Redman, Smithsonian Collection. "The Stampede."
The Immortal Fletcher Henderson, Milestone MLP 2005.

woody herman

The 3 Herds, Columbia JCL 592. "Four Others."

earl hines

Another Monday Date, Prestige P-24043.
Louis Armstrong and Earl Hines, Smithsonian Collection.

billie holiday

Billie Holiday/God Bless the Child, Columbia G 30782. "All of Me."

eddie jefferson

The Jazz Singer, Inner City IC 1016. "Body and Soul."

j. j. johnson

Mad Bebop, Savoy 2232. "Boneology."

james p. johnson

Father of the Stride Piano, Columbia CL-1780.

lambert, hendricks, and ross

Lambert, Hendricks, and Ross, Columbia CL 1403.

john mclaughlin

Inner Mounting Flame, Columbia PC 31067. "The Dance of Maya."

appendices

charles mingus

Passions of a Man—An Anthology of His Atlantic Recordings, Atlantic SD 3-600.

modern jazz quartet

Modern Jazz Quartet, Prestige 24005.

thelonious monk

Pure Monk, Milestone 47004. "I Should Care."
Thelonious Monk and John Coltrane, Milestone 47011.

jelly roll morton

Jelly Roll Morton 1923/24, Milestone M-47018. "New Orleans Blues."

gerry mulligan

The Essential Gerry Mulligan, Verve V6-8567. "Blueport."

fats navarro

Fat Girl—The Savoy Sessions, Savoy 2216.

king oliver

King Oliver's Jazz Band, 1923, Smithsonian Collection. "Dippermouth Blues."

charlie parker

Bird/The Savoy Recordings, Savoy SJL 2201. "Koko."
The Greatest Jazz Concert Ever, Prestige PR 24024.
The Very Best of Bird, Warner Brothers 2WB 3198.

joe pass

Virtuoso, Pablo 2310 708.

oscar peterson

In Concert, Verve 2683 063.

jean-luc ponty

Upon the Wings of Music, Atlantic SD 18138. "Upon the Wings of Music."

bud powell

The Amazing Bud Powell, Volume 1, Blue Note BST-81503.

django reinhardt

The Quintette of the Hot Club of France, Vol. 1-2, Crescendo GNP-9001, GNP 9019.

sonny rollins

Newk's Time, Blue Note BST-84001.
A Night at the Village Vanguard, Blue Note, BST 81581.

horace silver

Horace Silver and the Jazz Messengers, Blue Note 81518.

frank sinatra

Sinatra and Basie at the Sands, Reprise 1019. "One for My Baby."

bessie smith

Nobody's Blues but Mine, Columbia CG 31093. "Lost Your Head Blues."

art tatum

Art Tatum—Solo Piano, Capitol Jazz Classics Vol. 3, Capitol M-11028. "Aunt Hagar's
    Blues."
Masterpieces, MCA2-4019.

cecil taylor

Unit Structures, Blue Note BST-84237. "Enter Evening."

sarah vaughan

Sarah Vaughan and Count Basie, Roulette SR-42018.

fats waller

Fats Waller Piano Solos, 1929-1941, Bluebird AXM2-5518. "Handful of Keys."

weather report

Heavy Weather, Columbia PC 34418.

joe williams

Presenting Joe Williams and Thad Jones—Mel Lewis, Solid State SS 18008. "It Don't
    Mean a Thing" and "Night Time Is the Right Time."

teddy wilson

Statements and Improvisations, The Smithsonian Collection. "Rosetta."
Teddy Wilson and His All-Stars, Columbia KG 31617.

world saxophone quartet

Steppin' with the World Saxophone Quartet, Black Saint BSR 0027.

lester young

The Lester Young Story, Vol. 1-4, Columbia JG 33502, JG 34837, JG 34840, JG
    34843.

glossary of musical terms

accelerando: an acceleration of the tempo or beat.

accent: a special articulation of a pitch that makes it stand out. Usually the accented pitch is played somewhat sharply, though at times it may be played especially softly.

additive rhythm: an African technique of stringing short rhythmic patterns together to create longer ones.

antiphonal: see **call-and-response.**

appoggiatura: a relatively accented nonchord tone that is not usually approached or prepared by step.

arpeggio: an ascending or descending series of pitches that comprise a chord or harmony, usually played rapidly.

arrangement, arranger: a formal plan for a musical presentation in which an arranger usually composes the parts played by each musician. The arranger will decide what everyone plays except the improvising soloists. *See* **Head arrangement.**

atonal: Western music that avoids conventional tonal harmony.

augmented chord: a chord with the fifth degree raised a half step. For example, C-E-G♯-C is a C augmented chord.

augmentation: performing a motive or series of pitches in a slower rhythm.

back phrasing: The performance of a melody in which the phrases are delayed relative to the beat or the bar. For example, a phrase that normally begins on the downbeat of m. 1 and finishes on the downbeat of m. 3 may be delayed 2 beats, thus beginning on beat 3 of m. 1 and ending on beat 3 of m. 3.

bar or **measure:** a subdivision of musical time in which the basic beat is revealed; a bar of 4/4 time contains 4 beats with a quarter-note receiving 1 beat. Abbreviated "m." or "mm." for plural.

beat: the basic rhythmic pulse of music.

bebop: *see* **Bop.**

big band: a large jazz group usually comprising 3-5 trumpets, 3-5 trombones, 3-5 reeds, and 3-5 rhythm instruments. Most common during the big band era, ca. 1935-1945.

blue note: a flatted note, possibly with a sliding pitch frequency, that is played where an unflatted pitch might be expected; flatted third, fifth, or seventh degree of the scale heard most often.

blues: a black American musical form, usually 12 bars in length, with a specific harmonic pattern and often characterized by 3 distinct phrases, the first two identical. **Classic blues** was usually performed in the 1920s and 1930s by singers accompanied by a piano or a jazz band, and closely adhered to the 12 bar form. **Country blues** was an earlier and concurrent version of the form, often characterized by solo singers who accompanied themselves on guitar, and by more irregular harmony and melody.

bombs: irregular accents usually played on the bass drum.

bop or **bebop** or **rebop:** a jazz style developed in the 1940s and characterized by very fast or very slow tempos, extended-chord harmony, and improvised lines of eighth-notes that were often jagged and irregularly accented.

boogie-woogie: a solo piano style characterized by continuous eighth-note bass patterns and right-hand blues riffs; less commonly performed by bands.

break: a short pause by the entire band in which a soloist or a group of instruments executes a passage alone; usually 2 or 4 bars long and harmonized by a chord of tonic or dominant function.

bridge: see **release.**

bossa nova: a latin-jazz rhythm and style that became popular in the mid-1960s. It combined a relaxed jazz feeling with a samba-like rhythm.

cadence: the end of a phrase or section, characterized by a melodic resting point and usually reinforced by dominant-tonic or tonic-dominant harmony; the former sometimes called an **authentic cadence,** and the latter a **half cadence.**

cadenza: an out-of-tempo passage in which a soloist improvises freely and usually floridly.

cakewalk: a black dance popular around the turn of the century, in which couples compete for a cake by executing various struts.

call-and-response: a performance practice common in African music, jazz, and various Afro-American musical genres in which a leader calls out or plays prompting phrases. These phrases are then answered or echoed by the rest of the group.

Chicago style jazz: developed in the Chicago area by New Orleans musicians in the early 1920s. It featured small groups, a heavy march-like beat, bluesy playing, and often simultaneous improvisation.

circle of fifths: a harmonic progression in which the roots of the chords progress in fifths, usually in descending perfect fifths (G–C–F–Bb–Eb, etc.).

changes or **chord changes:** the harmonic pattern of a song, usually the basis for improvisation.

channel: see **release.**

chops: (1) slang for embouchure (see **embouchure**); (2) slang for strong technique, power, or endurance.

chord: three or more pitches that together comprise a harmony. See **harmony.**

chord changes: see **changes.**

chorus or **strophe:** (1) the entire set of changes for an improvisation played by a band or soloist exactly one time through; (2) loosely used to mean a solo of any number of strophes; (3) the more familiar section of a song that contains the hook and strongest melody; it usually follows the verse. Most jazz solos are improvisations on the changes of a song's chorus.

chromatic: pertaining to the use of all 12 pitches rather than the 7 pitches of the major, minor, or most common modes.

classic blues: a blues style flourishing from roughly 1920 to 1940 and performed by professional singers with band or solo piano accompaniment. Most great classic blues singers, like Bessie Smith, were women. The music itself was usually in standard 12-bar blues form.

clef: a sign at the beginning of a **staff** (single line of music) that reveals the correspondence of the staff's lines and spaces to the musical pitches.

cluster: closely spaced pitches struck at once.

comping: chording by a pianist or guitarist to back up another soloist.

concert pitch: the actual sound produced by an instrument, whether it customarily transposes or not. See **transposition.**

contrapuntal: see **counterpoint.**

cool: a jazz style developed in the 1950s and characterized by a relaxed sound, ample melodic space, a small range of emotional expression, and sometimes formal complexity and experimentation. Often identified with **West Coast** jazz.

counterpoint: a musical technique of combining two or more musical lines or melodies so that they blend harmonically, yet retain their melodic integrity.

cross-rhythm: an effect produced by the simultaneous articulation of two or more distinct and conflicting rhythms.

cut: when one soloist outplays another, the "winning" musician is said to have "cut" the loser.

diatonic: referring to the pitches of some major scale.

diminution: a technique whereby a motive or series of pitches is played either more quickly or on a smaller-scale level of structure than the original series.

dixieland jazz: jazz played in the **New Orleans** or **Chicago** styles of the 1920s.

dominant: the harmony built on the fifth degree of the scale. In jazz it may also denote the dominant-seventh chord on the lowered second degree of the scale which often resembles the true dominant in its harmonic function.

dominant-seventh chord: a 4-note chord with the bottom-to-top intervallic arrangement (in half steps) of 4-3-3. Hence an A dominant-seventh contains the pitches A-C♯-E-G.

dorian mode: a scale with the ascending intervallic pattern (in half steps) 2-1-2-2-2-1.

double stop: the playing of two pitches at once by a string player.

double time: a passage in which the tempo of the beat doubles. Usually the number of beats per harmony is also doubled so that the real-time speed of the changes remains the same.

downbeat: the first beat of a bar.

dynamics: degrees of softness and loudness in performance: pp, very soft; p, soft; mp, medium soft; mf, medium loud; f, loud; ff, very loud.

eighth-note: a pitch that receives half a beat in, for example, 4/4, 2/4, or 3/4 meters.

embellishment: the practice of ornamenting a melody with added notes, licks, etc. Also, the ornament itself.

embouchure: the way the mouth, lips, tongue, and teeth are positioned on the mouthpiece of a wind instrument.

enharmonic: a simplified spelling in musical notation; for example, a pitch correctly notated as E♯ could be spelled enharmonically as F.

extended chord: a chord in which five or more pitches are stated or implied, thus extending beyond the more common 7th chord, which contains four pitches.

extended chord tone: a pitch above the root, third, fifth, or seventh of the normal seventh chord: for example, C(7) contains the pitches C, E, G, B♭; C(9) extends the C(7) chord by adding a D, hence this pitch is an extended chord tone. Sometimes called a **tension.**

falsetto: the top range of the human voice, generally more nasal and thinner than the midrange register.

fermata: a sign placed over a note, rest, or chord to indicate that the pulse should stop and the pitch should be held out for a suitable length of time.

fifth: an interval of five letter-name steps, as in A up to E. A perfect fifth (e.g., A-E) has 7 half steps, a diminished fifth (e.g., A-E♭) has 6, and an augmented fifth (e.g., A-E♯) has 8.

fill: (1) a solo passage in which the drummer interrupts the basic pattern of the beat to provide contrast or indicate the end of a section; (2) an ornamentation played between the main phrases of the melody.

fours: when soloists **trade fours,** they improvise alternate 4-bar phrases.

fourth: an interval of four letter-name steps, as in A up to D. A perfect fourth (e.g., A-D) has 5 half steps, a diminished fourth (e.g., A-D♭) has 4, and an augmented fourth, or **tritone** (e.g., A-D♯), has 6.

free jazz: a jazz style developed in the late 1950s in which the musicians do not adhere to harmony or to thematic material based on songs, but instead improvise freely, often reacting to one another's musical statements.

frequency: the rate of vibration of a musical string, bore, etc., which in turn causes air molecules to vibrate and so imparts a specific pitch to our ears. Frequency is measured in hertz, which means "cycles per second." According to customary tuning, the A above middle C has a frequency of 440 hertz.

fret: a thin vertical bar on the fingerboard of a guitar, banjo, etc., that delineates the pitches.

funk: a jazz style, developed in the 1960s from the hard bop styles of the 1950s, in which jazz is combined with features of r & b.

fusion: a mixture of jazz and another style, but most often referring to the mixture of jazz and rock after the late 1960s.

ghost note: a pitch that is played very softly or sometimes just implied. It is generally notated with an "x."

glissando: a technique whereby a smooth slide is made between pitches so that the player or singer passes through all or most of the intervening pitches. Easily played, for example, on violin or trombone.

half: each section of an AA′ song; that is, the first and second halves. See **song form.**

half-note: a pitch that receives two beats in, for example, 2/4, 3/4, or 4/4 meters.

half step: the smallest distance of musical space in the Western European musical system; for example, the adjacent pitches E and F or G and A♭ are a half step apart.

half time: a passage in which the rate of the beat is halved.

hard bop: a number of styles developed in the 1950s that incorporated either an extension of bop style or gospel elements and blues.

harmony: a distinctive feature of tonal music, in which sets of pitches, called chords or harmonies, function through musical time by predominating, explicitly or implicitly, in the overall texture, often to accompany melody. In jazz, harmony is often supplied by the pianist or guitarist, who plays chords while the soloist improvises a melody.

head: (1) the song; (2) the A section of an AABA song. See **song form.**

head arrangement: an **arrangement** for a band that is devised by the musicians themselves in rehearsal and often, therefore, not written down.

hi-hat: a pair of cymbals usually operated by the drummer's left foot. When the foot is depressed, the cymbals produce a "chick" sound. The drummer will also play on them with the drumsticks. In swing beats, the hi-hat cymbals are often sounded on the second and fourth beats.

hook: the most familiar melodic phrase of a song. It is usually placed prominently at the beginning or end of the chorus, is melodically and lyrically catchy, summarizes the theme of the lyric, and supplies the song title.

hot jazz: uptempo jazz with much improvisation and often much syncopation.

inside: a slang term for improvising with pitches contained in the scales associated with the chord changes.

interlude: usually a short 2- or 4-bar passage that connects the sections of a longer work.

interval: (1) the distance between two pitches; (2) two pitches struck either simultaneously or consecutively.

inversion: (1) turning a chord upside down: for example, the inversions of an F7 chord (F-A-C-E♭) are A-C-E♭-F, C-E♭-F-A, etc. (2) The ascending melodic fragment of C-F-A♭, when inverted is the descending pattern C-G-E.

jam session: a musical session in which the musicians play together, improvising on tunes commonly known though usually without arrangements, predetermined personnel, or other formalities.

jazz-rock: a jazz style, developed in the late 1960s and early 1970s, that combined elements of jazz and rock, most often featuring jazz improvisation with rock instruments and rhythms.

Kansas City style: a regional jazz style flourishing in the 1920s and early 1930s. It emphasized riffs, the blues, swinging rhythm, and solo improvisation.

key: the harmonic and melodic focus of the composition at hand. For example, a piece that generally uses the pitches and the harmonic-melodic formulas of the C major scale is said to be in the key of C.

key signature: an arrangement of sharps or flats at the beginning of the staff that denotes the key. For example, no sharps or flats denotes the keys of C major or A minor; four flats—Bb, Eb, Ab, and Db—denote the keys of Ab major or F minor.

lead sheet: a notated, composed melody with harmonic chord symbols. Lyrics may accompany the melody.

leader: the musician who is in charge of the band.

legato: the technique of playing a series of notes smoothly, with no discernible space between pitches.

lick: (1) a short, often flashy, melodic figure, usually one beat to two measures long, practiced in advance by musicians for ideal placement in an improvisation; (2) loosely, any musical figure.

major chord: a **triad** with the bottom-to-top intervallic arrangement (in half steps) of 4-3. An F-major chord contains the pitches F-A-C.

major scale: an ordered series of closely spaced pitches with the ascending intervallic arrangement (in half steps) 2-2-1-2-2-2.

major-seventh chord: a 4-note chord with the bottom-to-top intervallic arrangement (in half steps) of 4-3-4. An E-major seventh chord contains the pitches E-G♯-B-D♯.

mallet: a wooden or plastic stick with a head of rubber, plastic, or wound yarn for playing a marimba, vibraphone, etc.

measure: abbreviated "m.," or "mm." for plural. See **bar.**

melisma: a florid singing technique in which one syllable of lyric is held through several pitches.

melody: a tuneful sequence of single notes, usually catchy and often simple enough to sing.

meter: a feeling of pulse that is produced by accenting regularly spaced beats. All meters are duple or triple, or a combination of both, depending on whether the metrical accents fall every 2 or 3 beats.

minor chord: a **triad** with the bottom-to-top intervallic arrangement (in half steps) of 3-4. An Eb minor chord contains the pitches Eb-Gb-Bb.

minor-seventh chord: a 4-note chord with the bottom-to-top intervallic arrangement (in half steps) of 3-4-3. A B-minor seventh chord contains the pitches B-D-F♯-A.

minor scale: an ordered sequence of closely spaced pitches of various forms. The **harmonic minor scale** has the ascending intervallic pattern (in half steps) 2-1-2-2-1-3. The *natural minor* or *aeolian mode* is constructed 2-1-2-2-1-2. The structure of the *ascending melodic minor* is 2-1-2-2-2-2.

mixolydian mode: a scale with the ascending intervallic pattern (in half steps) 2-2-1-2-2-1. Associated with the dominant-seventh chord.

modal: referring to a mode, a scalar arrangement of the pitches.

modal jazz: a jazz style, developed in the late 1950s, in which harmonies change infrequently and are elaborated by the use of modal scales or modes.

mode: a scale with specific intervallic arrangement. See **dorian mode** and **mixolydian modes.**

modulation: (1) a change of key that may be momentary or permanent; (2) a technique in electronic music in which the frequency or amplitude of a pitch signal is varied according to the shape of another voltage. This technique produces a complex sound in which pitch may be indeterminant.

motive: a short set of notes, usually from 2 to about 10 pitches, and often accompanied by a characteristic rhythm, that unifies the piece by providing a thematic referent.

multiphonics: a technique whereby a wind instrument player produces several pitches at once. The specific method varies depending on the instrument.

multitracking: a recording technique in which the tape is segmented into different tracks, usually 4, 8, 16, or 24. Then individual instruments, groups of instruments, or voices are recorded onto the different tracks. This allows the separate parts to be recorded at different times; the players adding new parts play along with the previously recorded parts by listening to them on headphones.

mute: a device for damping or modifying the sound of an instrument. Brass players insert cup mutes, straight mutes, harmon mutes, etc., into the bells of the instruments. String players have a muting device that clips onto the bridge of their instruments.

neighbor tone: one type of melodic **embellishment.** The neighbor tone is often not part of the harmony; for example, a C major triad supporting a melody E-F-E in which the F is a nonchord embellishing neighbor tone.

New Orleans style jazz: a jazz style maturing in the first two decades of the twentieth century after a long period of development in the New Orleans area. It features simultaneous improvisation, small groups, a heavy marchlike beat, bluesy playing, and often long harmonic sections focusing on one chord. The latter quality possibly derives from the ragtime pieces often used as a basis for improvisation.

nonchord tone: a pitch that is not a member of the prevailing harmony. For the most important types, see **appoggiatura, neighbor tone,** and **passing tone.**

obbligato: a countermelody that is usually voiced above the principal melody and contains faster pitches.

octave: an interval between consecutive pitches with the same letter name, as in the interval from middle C to the next C above or below it. Pitches an octave apart have a 2:1 pitch-frequency ratio.

oral tradition: the practice of teaching songs or melodies to others by ear. Hence, the pieces within a culture characterized by an oral tradition are at best partially notated.

orchestrator: see **arranger.**

ostinato: a repeating musical figure, often used as accompaniment. Similar to **vamp.**

outside: a slang term for improvisation in which the notes played may not be closely related to the accompanying harmonies.

out-chorus: the last chorus performed of a jazz piece, often more excited or frenzied to effect a sense of climax and finale.

passing tone: one type of melodic **embellishment;** for example, in a C major harmony supporting a melody E-F-G, the F is a passing nonchord embellishing tone between the two chord tones E and G.

pattern: (1) a set of pitches that is highly ordered, usually with a repeating structure such as, for example, descending triads (C-A-F, B-G-E, A-F-D); (2) a repeated rhythm.

pedal tone: a pitch that is sustained through a longer passage of music. Often occurs in the bass.

pickup: a pitch or small set of pitches that lead to the downbeat, usually at the beginning of a piece or tune.

phrase: a closed and relatively self-contained unit of melodic or musical structure. Melody is formed by linking phrases much like a speech is formed by linking a series of sentences.

polyphony: the use of **counterpoint.**

portamento: similar to a **glissando** but often not as long a slide.

quarter-note: a pitch that receives one beat in, for example, 2/4, 3/4, or 4/4 meters.

r & b: rhythm and blues; a catchall term for black popular music (called "soul" music in the 1960s).

ragtime: an early form (or precursor) of jazz, usually performed on solo piano, developed by black Americans in the late nineteenth century and characterized by constant syncopation in the right hand with a sort of **stride** bass in the left hand.

release: the bridge, channel, or B section of an AABA song. See **song form.**

rest: a symbol that denotes musical silence. A certain rest corresponds to each note value. Hence, a quarter-rest denotes one beat of silence in 2/4, 3/4, or 4/4 time.

rhythm: the temporal aspect of music, as determined by the arrangement of pitches and rests of various durations.

rhythm changes: the chord changes from the Gershwin song "I Got Rhythm." Often used as a basis for improvisation.

rhythm section: those members of a jazz group who concentrate primarily (though not exclusively) on supplying the beat. Usually includes bass, drums, keyboard, and/ or guitar or banjo.

ride cymbal: a large cymbal usually played with the drummer's right hand and most often used to keep a beat pattern going.

riff: a repeated melodic figure, often played by sections of a big band to accompany a soloist.

Roman numeral analysis: an analytical technique whereby harmony is indicated by the use of the Roman numerals I through VII to designate scale degrees. Arabic numerals are then affixed to the Roman numerals to show the type of harmony; for example, "V(7)" means the dominant-seventh chord on the fifth scale degree. See **scale degree.**

root: the principal pitch of a chord that names the chord itself; the lowest pitch when the chord is voiced in thirds.

rubato: (1) a musical technique in which the speed of the beat is highly flexible; (2) more commonly in jazz, a technique in which the soloist plays behind or ahead of the beat in a somewhat free manner; (3) an out-of-tempo passage somewhat like a cadenza.

run: a facile, usually fleet series of pitches, either ascending or descending, in which fragments of scales, arpeggios, or both may occur.

scale: an ascending or descending pattern of pitches, usually separated by whole and half steps, that is repeated in each octave.

scale degree: a pitch, usually of the major or minor scale, which abstracted from that scale denotes one of its harmonies. For example, scale degree II in the key of C major denotes the harmony D minor, since D is the second degree of the C major scale, and the pitches of the D minor triad (D-F-A) are diatonic in the key of C major.

scat: a technique of singing in which a tune is improvised with nonsense syllables; for example, boo, bah, doo, wha, wee, or bop.

second: an interval of two letter-name steps, as in C up to D. A diminished second (e.g., C-D♭♭) contains no half steps (**unison**), a minor second (e.g., C-D♭) contains one half step, a major second (e.g., C-D) contains 2, and an augmented second (e.g., C-D♯) contains 3.

section: a formal division of a song or piece. Song sections are usually 8 or 16 bars long. Sections of larger pieces have varying lengths.

sequence: a melodic pattern, repeated at least once on a different series of pitches; for example, E-G-F-E, then F-A-G-F, then G-B-A-G, etc.

seventh: an interval of seven letter-name steps, as in A up to G. A diminished seventh (e.g., A-G♭) contains 9 half steps, a minor seventh (e.g., A-G) contains 10, a major seventh (e.g., A-G♯) contains 11, and an augmented seventh (e.g., A-G♯♯)contains 12 and is equal to an **octave.**

sideman: a musician who is not the leader or a star player of the band.

sixteenth-note: a pitch whose temporal value is a quarter of a beat in, for example, 2/4, 3/4, or 4/4 meters.

sixth: an interval of six letter-name steps, as in G up to E. A diminished sixth (e.g., G-E♭♭) contains 7 half steps, a minor sixth (e.g., G-E♭) contains 8, a major sixth (e.g., G-E) contains 9, and an augmented sixth (e.g., G-E♯) contains 10.

Snader Telescription: produced in the early 1950s, these films were three-minute entertainments used for fillers on television.

sock-chorus: an **out-chorus,** but generally refers to a big band context where the chorus may be performed with more insistent rhythm. See **out-chorus.**

song form: (1) 32-bar AABA form in which the A is called the **head** or **chorus** and the B is called the **release, channel,** or **bridge.** Each section is normally 8 bars long. (2) 16- or 32-bar AA' form, with each section called the **first half** and the **second half.** The AABA and AA' units are collectively called the **chorus.** The chorus may be preceded by a **verse,** which is usually introductory in **Tin Pan Alley** songs. In rock-style songs the verse is usually repeated with an alternate lyric.

soundy: three-minute films that presented popular entertainers. They were produced for private viewing booths supplied to bars, hotel lobbies, etc.

Spanish tinge: a term Jelly Roll Morton applied to the incorporation of a Latin habañera beat into his jazz rhythm.

staccato: a manner of playing in which the pitches are detached and usually articulated crisply; the opposite of **legato.**

staff: an arrangement of five horizontal lines enclosing four spaces, that correspond to the musical pitches. For pitches that go above or below the staff, ledger lines provide a system of correspondence that links the more extreme pitches to the staff itself. See **clef.**

standard: a very well known and long-lived popular song.

stepwise motion: the connection of two pitches, often harmonic pitches in adjacent harmonies, by a whole or half step.

stoptime: a technique often heard in dixieland jazz in which, most often, the first beat of each bar is articulated by the band while the soloist improvises.

stride: a piano technique in which the left hand articulates bass pitches on the first and third beats, and chords, usually pitched higher, on the second and fourth beats. Often heard in the solo piano performances of ragtime, Harlem stride, and swing styles.

strophe: see **chorus.**

structure: musical architecture and form; the way a piece of music is elaborated compositionally or improvisationally.

subdominant: the IV chord; for example, a G major chord in the key of D major.

sweet: smooth, sentimental, dance oriented music, as opposed to **hot jazz.**

swing: (1) the feeling of forward impetus normally imparted by good uptempo jazz playing; (2) a jazz style, maturing in the 1930s, characterized by a swing feeling, smooth eighth-note lines, dancing, improvisation on popular songs, and big band performances.

swing beat: a beat heard in swing style jazz characterized by a rolling rhythm. (See *The Rhythm Section* in Chapter 2 for further discussion of swing beat.)

syncopation: a musical technique in which pitches falling on metrically strong portions of a bar are underplayed, while pitches falling on metrically weak portions of the bar are accented.

synthesizer: developed in the 1950s, this instrument produces pitches electronically; in **digital synthesis** the pitches are produced by transforming a closely spaced series of numbers into waveforms.

tag: a short, usually 2- or 4-bar ending to a piece.

tailgate: a slang term for coarse, dixieland style trombone playing. Derives from the placement of the trombonist at the back of the parade wagon where the slide is unimpeded.

tension: see **extended chord tone.**

third: an interval of three letter-name steps, as in A up to C. A diminished third (e.g., A-Cb) contains 2 half steps, a minor third (e.g., A-C) contains 3, a major third (e.g., A-C♯) contains 4 and an augmented third (e.g., A-C♯♯) contains 5.

third stream: a musical style that combines features of jazz with twentieth-century Western fine-art music.

timbre: the characteristic sound of a voice, instrument, or group of instruments.

time signature: two numbers appearing at the beginning of a musical composition that designate the meter of the piece and the value of note receiving one beat. A typical time signature is 3/4, which states that there will be 3 beats in a bar and that the quarter-note will receive one beat.

Tin Pan Alley: a nickname for a group of prominent New York City music publishing companies. Most of the finest American song composers from 1900 to 1950 were associated with Tin Pan Alley.

tonal: a Western musical system in which pieces are organized according to harmony within some key or with respect to some central pitch.

trading fours: see **fours.**

traditional jazz or **trad jazz:** music of the late 1940s dixieland revival.

transcription: a descriptive written representation of a jazz solo or arrangement.

transposition: moving a musical passage to another tone level; for example, C-E-F when transposed up 7 half steps becomes G-B-C. Transposing instruments read pitches whose names do not match the ones sounded. For example, a trumpet is usually pitched in Bb. This means that when a trumpeter reads and plays a C, the heard pitch will actually be Bb. Hence all the pitches played by Bb instruments sound a whole step lower than written.

triad: a major or minor chord with possible chromatic alternations. For example, C-E-G is a major triad, C-Eb-G is a minor triad, C-Eb-Gb is a diminished triad, and C-E-G♯ is an augmented triad.

trio: (1) the third section (usually) of a rag or march, always beginning in the key of the subdominant (IV); (2) a group of three instruments or voices.

triplet: a rhythmic device in which three pitches are played in the same time normally needed for two. For example, in 4/4 time, two eighth-notes and three triplet eighth-notes are both played in one beat.

tritone: the interval of 3 whole steps, as in A to Eb. Also called a "diminished fifth" or "augmented fourth," depending on which note is higher.

tremolo: rapid alternation most often between two notes. In piano music tremolos can occur between two sets of notes—even two chords.

trill: rapid alternation between a principal pitch and the pitch a whole or half step higher.

tutti: the entire ensemble playing together.

twelve-tone technique: a major twentieth-century compositional method devised by Schoenberg in which the 12 pitches of the chromatic scale are ordered into a row or set. The resulting tone row may then be transposed, inverted, retrograded (played backward), and retrograde inverted to produce 48 classic row forms. These rows are then used to construct the piece. In general, twelve-tone pieces maintain a series of aggregates, complete presentations of the 12 pitches, from the beginning of the piece to the end.

two-beat: a marchlike rhythm in which every other beat is accented. Often heard in dixieland jazz.

unison: (1) two or more instruments or voices playing the same pitch or part; (2) an interval of zero half steps.

vamp: a repeating musical accompaniment, often like an **ostinato.**

verse: see **song form.**

vibrato: a technique of rapidly varying the frequency of a note, so as to produce a warm, resonating effect.

voice: a specific line of pitches defined by voice-leading principles.

voice leading: the principle whereby the harmonic pitches of one chord are smoothly connected to the harmonic pitches of the next chord, often by stepwise motion. Harmonic pitches that are not thus connected are said to be "left hanging."

walking bass: a bass line that is produced by playing one note on each beat, heard often in swing style jazz and bop.

West Coast jazz: usually thought to be synonymous with **cool jazz,** since many of the leading "cool" musicians were from the West Coast.

whole-note: in 4/4 time, the pitch whose time value is 4 beats or a whole bar.

whole step: the interval of 2 half steps, for example, D-E, Ab-Bb, or B-C♯.

woodshedding: time spent practicing alone.

chronology

The following chronology correlates significant events in jazz history with other prominent events in both Western music and world history. Items relevant to jazz are marked "J." Musical items, marked "M," include important fine-art compositions and American popular standard songs. Under "H" you will find other major events in political history, science, and the arts.

1868

(J) Scott Joplin, Kid Ory, and Buddy Bolden born.
(M) Brahms, *A German Requiem.*
(H) Dostoyevsky, *The Idiot;* Johnson impeached by the House, cleared by the Senate.

1885

(J) King Oliver and Jelly Roll Morton born.
(M) Gilbert and Sullivan, *The Mikado.*

1892

(J) Johnny Dodds born.
(M) Bruckner, *Eighth Symphony;* Debussy, *Afternoon of a Faun.*

1897

(J) Sidney Bechet born.
(M) Richard Strauss, *Don Quixote;* Sousa, "The Stars and Stripes Forever."

1898

(J) Zutty Singleton born.
(M) Richard Strauss, *Ein Heldenleben.*
(H) Spanish-American War; China's hundred days of reform.

1899

(J) Joplin's "Maple Leaf Rag" published; Duke Ellington born.
(M) Arnold Schoenberg, *Verklärte Nacht.*

1900

(J) Louis Armstrong born.
(M) Puccini, *Tosca.*
(H) Boxer Rebellion in China; Conrad, *Lord Jim.*

1903

(J) Bix Beiderbecke born.
(M) "In the Merry Month of May" (Evans-Shields).
(H) Wright brothers complete first plane flight; Henry James, *The Ambassadors.*

1904

(J) Count Basie born.
(M) Puccini, *Madame Butterfly;* Mahler, *Sixth Symphony;* "Give My Regards to Broadway" (Cohan); "Fascination" (Marchetti).
(H) War between Russia and Japan.

1905

(J) Earl Hines born.
(M) Debussy, *La Mer;* "Daddy's Little Girl" (Morse-Madden).
(H) First Russian revolution; Eugene Debs founds The Industrial Workers of the World (IWW).

1909

(J) Benny Goodman, Lester Young born.
(M) Schoenberg, *Piano Pieces,* Op. 11; Ravel, *Daphnis et Chloé;* "By the Light of the Silvery Moon" (Edwards-Madden).
(H) Heredity found to be linked to chromosomes.

1913

(J) Freddie Keppard's Original Creole Band on tour of U.S.
(M) Stravinsky, *Le Sacre du printemps;* "When Your Irish Eyes Are Smiling" (Ball-Olcott-Graff); "You Made Me Love You" (Monaco-McCarthy).
(H) Proust begins *Remembrance of Things Past;* Russell-Whitehead, *Principia Mathematica;* Rutherford discovers proton as hydrogen nucleus.

1914

(J) Jelly Roll Morton playing throughout Midwest.
(M) "By the Beautiful Sea" (Carroll-Atteridge); "St. Louis Blues" (Handy); "When You Wore a Tulip" (Wenrich-Mahoney).
(H) Outbreak of World War I; Robert Frost, *North of Boston.*

1915

(J) Billie Holiday born; Freddie Keppard band plays in New York.
(M) Ives, *Concord Sonata;* "Alabama Jubilee" (Cobb-Yellen).
(H) Somerset Maugham, *Of Human Bondage;* Charlie Chaplin, *The Tramp;* Einstein, *General Theory of Relativity.*

1917

(J) New Orleans's Storyville closed; Original Dixieland Jazz Band appears at Reisen-weber's Restaurant in New York City and soon records first jazz record, "Livery Stable Blues"; Dizzy Gillespie and Thelonious Monk born.

(M) "Beale Street Blues" (Handy); "For Me and My Gal" (Meyer-Leslie-Goetz); "Indiana" (Hanley-MacDonald); "Over There" (Cohan).

(H) U.S. becomes involved in World War I; Chinese begin using vernacular in literature; Czar abdicates as Lenin and Bolsheviks seize power in Russia.

1918

(J) Freddie Keppard settles in Chicago.

(M) Stravinsky, *L'Histoire du soldat;* "After You've Gone" (Layton-Creamer); "Ja-da" (Carleton); "Swanee" (Gershwin-Caesar).

(H) End of World War I.

1919

(J) Original Dixieland Jazz Band begins London engagement at Palais de Dance; Louis Mitchell's Jazz Kings playing in Paris; Ernest Ansermet writes glowing review of Sidney Bechet.

(M) "Any Old Place With You" (Rodgers-Hart); "A Pretty Girl Is Like a Melody" (Berlin).

(H) Prohibition; Treaty of Versailles; League of Nations founded; Hesse, *Demian;* commercial airplane service begins, between London and Paris.

1920

(J) Mamie Smith records first blues record, "Crazy Blues"; Charlie Parker born.

(M) "Avalon" (Rose-Jolson-DeSylva); "Whispering" (Rose-Coburn-Schonberger); "Margie" (Conrad-Robinson-Davis).

(H) Commercial radio broadcasting begins; nineteenth amendment ratified, giving women the right to vote.

1921

(J) James P. Johnson, "Caroline Shout."

(M) "Ain't We Got Fun" (Whiting-Kahn-Egan); "All by Myself" (Berlin); "April Showers" (Silvers-DeSylva); "I'm Just Wild about Harry" (Blake-Sissle); "The Sheik of Araby" (Snyder-Smith-Wheeler); "Look for the Silver Lining" (Kern).

(H) Pablo Picasso, *Three Musicians;* Berg, *Wozzeck;* Wittgenstein, *Tractatus Logico-Philosophicus.*

1922

(J) Louis Armstrong joins King Oliver's Creole Jazz Band in Chicago.

(M) "Chicago" (Fisher); "China Boy" (Winfree-Boutelje); "Georgia" (Donaldson-Johnson); "Toot Toot Tootsie" (Rito-King-Kahn-Erdman).

(H) Revolution in Italy, fascists take over; T. S. Eliot, "The Waste Land"; James Joyce, *Ulysses.*

1923

(J) Jelly Roll Morton, "New Orleans Blues;" Ellington becomes established in New York; King Oliver's Creole Jazz Band, "Dippermouth Blues."

(M) Schoenberg, *Five Piano Pieces.* Op. 23, *Serenade*, Op. 24 (first 12-tone works);

"Charleston" (Johnson-Mack); "I Cried for You" (Arnheim-Lyman-Freed); "Linger Awhile" (Rose-Owens); "Who's Sorry Now?" (Snyder-Ruby-Kalmar).

(H) France begins occupation of the Ruhr; Hitler's beerhall putsch in Munich.

1924

(J) Bix Beiderbecke, "Jazz Me Blues" with the Wolverine Orchestra; Armstrong joins Fletcher Henderson band in New York; Bud Powell born.

(M) Gershwin, "Rhapsody in Blue"; "Fascinatin' Rhythm" (Gershwin-Gershwin); "I'll See You in My Dreams" (Jones-Kahn); "It Had to Be You" (Jones-Kahn); "Lazy" (Berlin); "Limehouse Blues" (Braham-Furber); "The Man I Love" (Gershwin-Gershwin); "The One I Love Belongs to Somebody Else" (Jones-Kahn).

(H) Stalin becomes Russian dictator; Thomas Mann, *The Magic Mountain.*

1925

(J) Fletcher Henderson, "Sugarfoot Stomp"; Bennie Moten band makes first recordings.

(M) Berg's *Wozzeck* premiered; "Always" (Berlin); "Dinah" (Akst-Lewis-Young); "Five Foot Two, Eyes of Blue" (Henderson-Lewis-Young); "Manhattan" (Rodgers-Hart); "Remember" (Berlin); "Sweet Georgia Brown" (Bernie-Pinkard-Casey); "Tea for Two" (Youmans-Caesar); "Yes, Sir, That's My Baby" (Donaldson-Kahn).

(H) Fitzgerald, *The Great Gatsby;* Watson, *Behaviorism;* beginning of electrical recording.

1926

(J) Jelly Roll Morton, "Black Bottom Stomp"; Duke Ellington, "East St. Louis Toodle-Oo"; Louis Armstrong, "Heebie Jeebies"; John Coltrane, Miles Davis born.

(M) Berg, *Lyric Suite;* "Baby Face" (Akst-Davis); "Bye Bye Blackbird" (Henderson-Dixon); "Mountain Greenery" (Rodgers-Hart); "Muskrat (or Muskat) Ramble" (Ory); "Someone to Watch Over Me" (Gershwin-Gershwin).

(H) Sound movies begin; Hemingway, *The Sun Also Rises;* first exhibition of Klee's work in Paris; Germany joins League of Nations; Schroedinger develops theory of waves.

1927

(J) Armstrong, "Potato Head Blues"; Trumbauer, "Riverboat Shuffle"; Ellington at Cotton Club, "Black and Tan Fantasy."

(M) Stravinsky, *Oedipus Rex;* "Ain't She Sweet" (Ager-Yellen); "Blue Skies" (Berlin); "I'm Coming Virginia" (Heywood-Cook); "My Blue Heaven" (Donaldson-Whiting); "My Heart Stood Still" (Rodgers-Hart); "'S Wonderful" (Gershwin-Gershwin); "Sometimes I'm Happy" (Youmans-Caesar).

(H) Television transmission; Lindbergh completes first solo flight across the Atlantic; Hitler, *Mein Kampf;* Heisenberg uncertainty principle; Lemaitre, "Big Bang" theory of universe.

1928

(J) Armstrong, "A Monday Night Date"; Ellington, "The Mooche."

(M) Webern, *Symphony,* Op. 21; Bartok, *Fourth String Quartet;* "Bill" (Kern-Wodehouse-Hammerstein); "I Can't Give You Anything but Love" (McHugh-Fields); "I'll Get By" (Ahlert-Turk); "Let's Do It" (Porter); "Makin' Whoopie" (Donaldson-Kahn); "Ol' Man River" (Kern-Hammerstein); "Sweet Lorraine" (Burwell-Parish); "You Took Advantage of Me" (Rodgers-Hart).

(H) Talking movies begin.

1929

(J) Fats Waller, "Handful of Keys"; Armstrong, "When You're Smiling."

(M) "Ain't Misbehavin'" (Waller-Brooks-Razaf); "Am I Blue" (Akst-Clarke); "Black and Blue" (Waller-Brooks-Razaf); "Liza" (Gershwin-Gershwin-Kahn); "Singing in the Rain" (Brown-Freed); "With a Song in My Heart" (Rodgers-Hart); "You Were Meant for Me" (Brown-Freed).

(H) Stock market crash; Faulkner, *The Sound and the Fury;* Dali, *Illuminated Pleasures;* Trotsky exiled from Russia.

1930

(J) Ellington's first hit: "Mood Indigo"; Ornette Coleman born.

(M) Stravinsky, *Symphony of Psalms;* "Body and Soul" (Green-Heyman-Sauer-Eyton); "But Not for Me" (Gershwin-Gershwin); "Embraceable You" (Gershwin-Gershwin); "Get Happy" (Arlen-Koehler); "Happy Days Are Here Again" (Ager-Yellen); "I Got Rhythm" (Gershwin-Gershwin); "Love for Sale" (Porter); "On the Sunny Side of the Street" (McHugh-Fields); "Rockin' Chair" (Carmichael); "Ten Cents a Dance" (Rodgers-Hart); "When You're Smiling" (Shay-Goodwin-Fisher); "Mood Indigo" (Ellington-Bigard-Mills).

(H) Penicillin discovered; Grant Wood, *American Gothic;* Keynes, *Treatise on Money;* cyclotron developed in U.S.

1931

(J) Armstrong, "When It's Sleepy Time Down South"; Ellington, "Limehouse Blues."

(M) "All of Me" (Marks-Simons); "As Time Goes By" (Hupfield); "Between the Devil and the Deep Blue Sea" (Arlen-Koehler); "Dancing in the Dark" (Schwartz-Dietz); "Just Friends" (Klenner-Lewis); "Lazy River" (Carmichael-Arodin); "Out of Nowhere" (Green-Heyman); "Star Dust" (Carmichael-Parish).

(H) Japan invades Manchuria; Spain establishes republic; nylon invented.

1932

(J) Ellington, "It Don't Mean a Thing"; Dorsey Brothers, "I'm Getting Sentimental Over You."

(M) Ravel, two piano concertos; "April in Paris" (Duke-Harburg); "Brother, Can You Spare a Dime" (Gorney-Harburg); "How Deep Is the Ocean" (Berlin); "It Don't Mean a Thing" (Ellington-Mills); "Lover" (Rodgers-Hart); "Night and Day" (Porter); "The Song Is You" (Kern-Hammerstein); "Willow Weep for Me" (Ronell).

(H) Neutrons discovered.

1933

(J) Billie Holiday records "Your Mother's Son-in-Law" with Benny Goodman; Earl Hines, "Rosetta."

(M) Bartok, *Second Piano Concerto;* "Don't Blame Me" (McHugh-Fields); "Easter Parade" (Berlin); "Forty-Second Street" (Warren-Dubin); "A Ghost of a Chance" (Young-Washington-Crosby); "I Cover the Waterfront" (Greene-Heyman); "It's Only a Paper Moon" (Arlen-Harburg-Rose); "I've Got the World on a String" (Arlen-Koehler); "Rosetta" (Hines-Woode); "Sophisticated Lady" (Ellington-Mills-Parish); "Stormy Weather" (Arlen-Koehler); "Yesterdays" (Kern-Harbach); "You Are Too Beautiful" (Rodgers-Hart).

(H) Hitler becomes Chancellor of Germany; Franklin Roosevelt inaugurated; Japan quits League of Nations; Roosevelt passes New Deal legislation.

1934

(J) Ellington, "Solitude"; Chick Webb, "Stompin' at the Savoy."

(M) Webern, *Concerto*, Op. 24; "Anything Goes" (Porter); "I Get a Kick Out of You" (Porter); "I Only Have Eyes for You" (Warren-Dubin); "Let's Fall in Love" (Arlen-Koehler); "My Old Flame" (Johnston-Coslow); "What a Difference a Day Made" (Grever-Adams); "Winter Wonderland" (Bernard-Smith).

(H) Stalin imposes policy of Socialist Realism.

1935

(J) Benny Goodman's stupendous success at the Palomar Ballroom in Los Angeles; Count Basie takes over Walter Page's Blue Devil band; Goodman, "King Porter Stomp"; Teddy Wilson–Billie Holiday, "Miss Brown to You."

(M) Berg, *Violin Concerto;* "Autumn in New York" (Duke); "Begin the Beguine" (Porter); "Blue Moon" (Rodgers-Hart); "Cheek to Cheek" (Berlin); "I Got Plenty o' Nuttin'" (Gershwin-Gershwin); "I'm in the Mood for Love" (McHugh-Fields); "The Most Beautiful Girl in the World" (Rodgers-Hart); "Solitude" (Ellington-DeLange-Mills); "Summertime" (Gershwin-Heyward).

(H) Congress passes Social Security Act.

1936

(J) Lester Young plays with Count Basie; Goodman, "Get Happy."

(M) Schoenberg, *Violin Concerto;* Prokofiev, *Peter and the Wolf;* "I Can't Get Started" (Duke-Gershwin); "In a Sentimental Mood" (Ellington-Mills-Kurtz); "I've Got You Under My Skin" (Porter); "Pennies from Heaven" (Johnson-Burke); "Pick Yourself Up" (Kern-Fields); "These Foolish Things" (Strachey-Link-Marvell).

(H) Spanish civil war; Mussolini conquers Ethiopia; Hitler remilitarizes Rhineland.

1937

(J) Height of swing era; Goodman, Basie, Ellington extremely popular; Basie, "One O'clock Jump"; Ellington, "Caravan"; Benny Goodman Quartet, "Avalon."

(M) Schoenberg, *Fourth String Quartet;* Shostakovich, *Fifth Symphony;* "Caravan" (Ellington-Tizol-Mills); "Easy Living" (Rainger-Robin); "A Foggy Day" (Gershwin-Gershwin); "Have You Met Miss Jones" (Rodgers-Hart); "The Lady Is a Tramp" (Rodgers-Hart); "My Funny Valentine" (Rodgers-Hart); "Where or When" (Rodgers-Hart).

(H) Japan declares war on China; Picasso, *Guernica.*

1938

(J) Benny Goodman at Carnegie Hall; Basie, "Doggin' Around."

(M) Webern, *String Quartet*, Op. 28; "Heart and Soul" (Carmichael-Loesser); "I Can Dream, Can't I?" (Fain-Kahal); "I Let a Song Go Out of My Heart" (Ellington-Mills-Nemo); "Jeepers Creepers" (Warren-Mercer); "Love Is Here to Stay" (Gershwin-Gershwin); "My Heart Belongs to Daddy" (Porter); "September Song" (Weill-Anderson); "Spring Is Here" (Rodgers-Hart).

(H) Hitler annexes Austria to Germany; Volkswagen produces first "Beetle."

1939

(J) Beginnings of bop at Monroe's Uptown House in Harlem; Charlie Christian plays with Benny Goodman; Coleman Hawkins, "Body and Soul"; Goodman, "Undecided"; Woody Herman, "Woodchopper's Ball"; Glenn Miller, "In the Mood."

(M) Webern, *Cantata, Op. 29;* "All the Things You Are" (Kern-Hammerstein); "Darn That Dream" (Van Heusen-DeLange); "God Bless America" (Berlin); "I Didn't Know What Time It Was" (Rodgers-Hart); "In the Mood" (Garland-Razaf); "Over the Rainbow" (Arlen-Harburg).

(H) World War II begins; Joyce, *Finnegan's Wake;* Steinbeck, *The Grapes of Wrath; Gone with the Wind* filmed.

1940

(J) Ellington, "Concerto for Cootie"; Artie Shaw, "Star Dust."

(M) "Fools Rush In" (Bloom-Mercer); "Harlem Nocturne" (Hagen); "How High the Moon" (Lewis-Hamilton); "I Concentrate on You" (Porter); "Pennsylvania 6-5000" (Gray-Sigman); "Polka Dots and Moonbeams" (Van Heusen-Burke); "Tuxedo Junction" (Hawkins-Dash-Johnson).

(H) Roosevelt becomes first three-term president; Hemingway, *For Whom the Bell Tolls;* plutonium, first nonnatural element.

1941

(J) Ellington, "Take the A Train"; Krupa-Eldridge, "Rockin' Chair"; Glenn Miller, "String of Pearls."

(M) "Bewitched, (Bothered and Bewildered)" (Rodgers-Hart); "Boogie Woogie Bugle Boy" (Raye-Prince); "Chattanooga Choo Choo" (Warren-Gordon); "I Could Write a Book" (Rodgers-Hart); "I Got It Bad" (Ellington-Webster).

(H) U.S. enters war after the bombing of Pearl Harbor; *Citizen Kane* filmed; first jet plane.

1942

(J) Beginnings of New Orleans dixieland revival; evolution of bop well underway; big bands depleted by draft; recording ban imposed by the American Federation of Musicians (AF of M).

(M) Schoenberg, *Piano Concerto;* "I've Got a Gal in Kalamazoo" (Warren-Gordon); "Skylark" (Carmichael-Mercer); "Tangerine" (Schertzinger-Mercer); "That Old Black Magic" (Arlen-Mercer); "There Will Never Be Another You" (Warren-Gordon); "White Chrismas" (Berlin).

(H) United Nations Alliance; first nuclear reactor.

1943

(J) Earl Hines band formed, including Parker and Gillespie; Ellington appears at Carnegie Hall.

(M) Bartok, *Concerto for Orchestra;* Britten, *Serenade for Tenor, Horn, and Strings;* "Do Nothin' Till You Hear from Me" (Ellington-Russell); "My Shining Hour" (Arlen-Mercer); "Oklahoma" (Rodgers-Hammerstein); "Star Eyes" (DePaul-Raye).

(H) Russians stop Germans at Stalingrad.

1944

(J) End of recording ban, begin early bop recordings; Tommy Dorsey, "Opus No. 1."

(M) Copland, *Appalachian Spring;* "Ev'ry Time We Say Goodbye" (Porter); "How Little We Know" (Carmichael-Mercer); "Moonlight in Vermont" (Suessedorf-Blackburn); "Sentimental Journey" (Homer-Brown-Green); "You're Nobody 'Til Somebody Loves You" (Morgan-Stock-Cavanaugh).

(H) Invasion of Normandy by allies; mechanical calculating machine produced by IBM.

1945

(J) Dizzy Gillespie big band formed; Gillespie-Parker, "Shaw 'Nuff"; Parker, "Koko."
(M) Bartok, *Third Piano Concerto;* Webern, *Second Cantata;* "It Might As Well Be Spring" (Rodgers-Hammerstein); "Laura" (Raksin-Mercer); "The More I See You" (Warren-Gordon); "New York, New York" (Bernstein-Comden-Green).
(H) Germany surrenders; first atomic bomb dropped on Hiroshima; United Nations formed.

1946

(J) Parker, "Ornithology," "A Night in Tunisia."
(M) Stravinsky, *Ebony Concerto* (for Woody Herman) and *Symphony in Three Movements;* Schoenberg, *String Trio;* "The Christmas Song" (Torme-Wells); "Come Rain or Come Shine" (Arlen-Mercer); "Stella by Starlight" (Young-Washington); "There's No Business Like Show Business" (Berlin).

1947

(J) Gillespie, "Two Bass Hit"; Herman, "Four Brothers."
(M) "Old Devil Moon" (Lane-Harburg); "On Green Dolphin Street" (Kaper-Washington); "Time After Time" (Styne-Cahn).
(H) India gains independence from Britain; Truman Doctrine; Tennessee Williams, *A Streetcar Named Desire;* Camus, *The Plague.*

1948

(J) First long-playing 33⅓ twelve-inch record; Gillespie, "Manteca."
(M) Boulez, *Second Piano Sonata;* "It's Magic" (Styne-Cahn); "The Night Has a Thousand Eyes" (Brainin-Bernier); "Red Roses for a Blue Lady" (Tepper-Brodsky).
(H) Zionists proclaim Israel's independence; transistor invented.

1949

(J) Miles Davis, Gil Evans, and Gerry Mulligan begin collaboration on the *Birth of the Cool;* Herman, "Early Autumn."
(M) Schoenberg, *Fantasy* for violin and piano; "Bali Ha'i" (Rodgers-Hammerstein); "Rudolph, the Red-Nosed Reindeer" (Marks).
(H) Mao Zedong organizes revolution in China; Arthur Miller, *Death of a Salesman;* George Orwell, *1984.*

1950

(J) Dave Brubeck begins collaboration with Paul Desmond.
(M) "From This Moment On" (Porter); "Luck Be a Lady" (Loesser); "Mona Lisa" (Livingston-Evans); "Syncopated Clock" (Anderson-Parish).
(H) Korean War begins.

1951

(J) Parker-Davis, "Star Eyes"; Dave Brubeck Quartet formed.
(M) Menotti, *Amahl and the Night Visitors;* Carter, *First String Quartet;* "Hello Young Lovers" (Rodgers-Hammerstein); "I Talk to the Trees" (Lerner-Loewe); "Getting to Know You" (Rodgers-Hammerstein).
(H) NATO formed; Truman relieves MacArthur of command.

1952

(J) Gerry Mulligan Quartet, Modern Jazz Quartet formed.

(M) Cage, *4'33"*; "Blue Tango" (Anderson-Parish); "Lullaby of Birdland" (Shearing); "My One and Only Love" (Wood-Mellin); "When I Fall in Love" (Young-Heyman).

(H) Hydrogen bomb tested; Ellison, *Invisible Man.*

1953

(J) Massey Hall jazz concert with Parker, Gillespie, Bud Powell, Charles Mingus, and Max Roach.

(M) "Ebb Tide" (Maxwell-Sigman); "Angel Eyes" (Dennis-Brent); "Your Cheatin' Heart" (Williams); "Rock Around the Clock" (Freedman-DeKnight).

(H) Eisenhower inaugurated; Korean War ended; McCarthy hearings on communist infiltration begin; death of Stalin.

1954

(J) Davis, "Walkin'"; Quartet formed by Kai Winding and J. J. Johnson; first Newport Jazz Festival; Joe Williams joins Count Basie.

(M) Boulez, *Le Marteau sans Maître;* "All of You" (Porter); "Fly Me to the Moon" (Howard); "Sh-Boom" (Feaster-Keys-McCrae-Edwards); "Shake, Rattle & Roll" (Calhoun).

(H) Viet Nam War begins; "Supreme Court, Brown vs. Board of Education of Topeka" against racial segregation in public schools; Ryle, *Dilemmas.*

1955

(J) Death of Charlie Parker; Coltrane joins Miles Davis Quintet; Davis, "There Is No Greater Love."

(M) "Autumn Leaves" (Kosma-Mercer); "Love Is a Many-Splendored Thing" (Fain-Webster); "Misty" (Garner-Burke); "Ain't It a Shame" (Domino-Bartholomew); "The Great Pretender" (Ram).

(H) Polio vaccine invented by Salk.

1956

(J) Clifford Brown dies; Goodman tours Far East; Gillespie tours Middle East; Davis, "My Funny Valentine."

(M) "Just in Time" (Styne-Comden-Green); "On the Street Where You Live" (Lerner-Loewe); "Hound Dog" (Leiber-Stoller); "Love Me Tender" (Matson-Presley); "Blue Suede Shoes" (Perkins).

(H) Hungary invaded by Soviet Union; neutrino discovered; Soviet Union and China split over ideological differences.

1957

(J) Thelonious Monk–John Coltrane, "Ruby, My Dear"; Miles Davis–Gil Evans, "Miles Ahead"; Cecil Taylor with Steve Lacy at Newport Jazz Festival.

(M) Bernstein, *West Side Story;* Stravinsky, *Agon;* "Witchcraft" (Coleman-Leigh); "Jailhouse Rock" (Leiber-Stoller); "All Shook Up" (Blackwell-Presley); "That'll Be the Day" (Allison-Holly-Petty).

(H) Soviet Union launches Sputnik; Chomsky, *Syntactic Structures.*

1958

(J) Stereo records marketed; Davis, *Milestones*.

(M) "Yakety-Yak" (Leiber-Stoller); "Thank Heaven for Little Girls" (Lerner-Loewe); "At the Hop" (Medora-Singer); "Chantilly Lace" (Richardson).

(H) Khrushchev becomes premier of Soviet Union; DeGaulle becomes president of France.

1959

(J) Ornette Coleman, *The Shape of Jazz to Come;* Davis, *Kind of Blue;* Coltrane, *Giant Steps.*

(M) "My Favorite Things" (Rodgers-Hammerstein); "Till There Was You" (Wilson); "Charlie Brown" (Leiber-Stoller); "Stagger Lee" (Price-Logan).

(H) Fidel Castro leads communist revolution in Cuba.

1960

(J) Coleman, *Free Jazz;* Coltrane, *My Favorite Things;* Charles Mingus, "Fables of Faubus."

(M) "Exodus" (Gold); "Paper Roses" (Spielman-Torre); "Chain Gang" (Cook); "You're Sixteen" (Sherman-Sherman).

(H) Independence of Belgian Congo; Soviet Union withdraws aid from China; Civil Rights Act; laser invented.

1961

(J) Davis and Evans at Carnegie Hall.

(M) "Al-di-La" (Donida-Drake-Mogol); "I Believe in You" (Loesser); "Let's Twist Again" (Appell-Mann); "The Peppermint Twist" (Dee-Glover).

(H) Yuri Gagarin, first manned space flight; Berlin wall erected; Peace Corps established; South Africa independent of Britain; Bay of Pigs invasion.

1962

(J) Classic Coltrane quartet formed with Elvin Jones, Jimmy Garrison, and McCoy Tyner; Bill Dixon-Archie Shepp, "Quartet."

(M) Britten, *War Requiem;* "Days of Wine and Roses" (Mancini-Mercer); "Breaking Up Is Hard to Do" (Sedaka-Greenfield); "Go Away Little Girl" (King-Goffin); "Surfin' Safari" (Wilson-Love).

(H) Vatican Council II; Cuban missile crisis.

1963

(J) Ron Carter, Tony Williams, and Herbie Hancock join Miles Davis Quintet; Davis, *Seven Steps to Heaven;* Coltrane, "Alabama."

(M) "Blowin' in the Wind" (Dylan); "I Wish You Love" (Beach-Trenet); "Puff, the Magic Dragon" (Lipton-Yarrow); "He's So Fine" (Mack).

(H) Assassination of President Kennedy; Nuclear Test Ban Treaty signed; Pop Art movement begins.

1964

(J) Coltrane, *A Love Supreme;* Davis, "Four"; Association for the Advancement of Creative Musicians (AACM) founded; death of Eric Dolphy in Berlin.

(M) "Walk On By" (Bacharach-David); "I Want to Hold Your Hand" (Lennon-McCartney); "Can't Buy Me Love" (Lennon-McCartney); "Baby Love" (Holland-Holland-Dozier).

(H) Passage of Civil Rights Bill; War on Poverty begins; Third World alliance begun by Nyerere.

1965

(J) Davis, "ESP"; Coltrane, "Ascension"; Albert Ayler, "Bells."

(M) "Mr. Tambourine Man" (Dylan); "The Shadow of Your Smile" (Webster-Mercer); "I Can't Get No Satisfaction" (Jagger-Richard); "Yesterday" (Lennon-McCartney).

(H) Martin Luther King leads civil rights march in Selma, Al.; Mariner 4 flies by Mars.

1966

(J) Davis, "Freedom Jazz Dance"; Cecil Taylor, "Unit Structures."

(M) "Impossible Dream" (Leigh-Darion); "See You in September" (Wayne-Edwards); "Good Vibrations" (Wilson-Love); "We Can Work It Out" (Lennon-McCartney).

(H) France leaves NATO alliance; Cultural Revolution begins in China; first heart transplant.

1967

(J) Death of John Coltrane; Davis, "Nefertiti."

(M) "I Say a Little Prayer" (Bacharach-David); "Light My Fire" (Morrison); "Ode to Billy Joe" (Gentry); "Penny Lane" (Lennon-McCartney); Beatles, *Sargeant Pepper.*

(H) Six Day War between Arabs and Israelis; Marquez, *One Hundred Years of Solitude.*

1968

(J) Davis, "Stuff"; Anthony Braxton, "For Alto" (solo saxophone); Jazz Composer's Orchestra records.

(M) "Fool on the Hill" (Lennon-McCartney); "MacArthur Park" (Webb); "I Heard It Through the Grapevine" (Whitfield-Strong); "Hey Jude" (Lennon-McCartney).

(H) Martin Luther King and Robert F. Kennedy assassinated; Soviet Union invades Czechoslovakia.

1969

(J) Davis, *In a Silent Way, Bitches Brew;* Art Ensemble of Chicago's first recording, "People In Sorrow"; Art Ensemble, Anthony Braxton, Leroy Jenkins, Archie Shepp, Steve Lacy, Leo Smith, and others, relocate to Paris.

(M) "Didn't We" (Webb); "Lay, Lady, Lay" (Dylan); "Leaving on Jet Plane" (Denver); "Everyday People" (Stewart); "Get Back" (Lennon-McCartney).

(H) U.S. astronauts walk on the moon; draft lottery established; DDT banned.

1970

(J) Davis, *Jack Johnson* and *At Fillmore;* death of Albert Ayler; start of New York City "new music" loft concerts.

(M) "Cracklin' Rosie" (Diamond); "Love Story" (Lai-Sigman); "Bridge Over Troubled Water" (Simon); "My Sweet Lord" (Harrison).

(H) U.S. intervenes in Cambodia; Allende, a Marxist, elected president of Chile, then killed in a coup.

1971

(J) Death of Louis Armstrong.

(M) "Here's That Rainy Day" (Van Heusen-Burke); "I Don't Know How to Love Him" (Rice-Webber); "Rainy Days and Mondays" (Nichols-Williams); "Joy to the World" (Axton).

(H) War between India and Pakistan; China joins UN; U.S. space probes to Mars, Mercury, and Jupiter.

1972

(J) Davis, *On the Corner;* John McLaughlin, *Inner Mounting Flame;* Chick Corea, *Light as a Feather;* Leo Smith, "Creative Music 1."

(M) "Where Is the Love" (MacDonald-Salter); "You're So Vain" (Simon); "American Pie" (McLean); "Alone Again (Naturally)" (Sullivan); " I Am Woman" (Burton-Reddy).

(H) Nixon visit to China; international convention bans germ warfare.

1973

(J) Newport jazz festival moves to New York City; Hancock, *Headhunters;* Cecil Taylor, "Indent"; multi-instrumentalist Sam Rivers's "Streams."

(M) "Bad Bad Leroy Brown" (Croce); "Let's Get It On" (Gaye); "Superstition" (Wonder); "You Are the Sunshine of My Life" (Wonder); "My Love" (McCartney).

(H) Beginning of "Watergate"; U.S. vacates Saigon, loses Viet Nam War.

1974

(J) Death of Duke Ellington; Corea, *Where Have I Known You Before;* Weather Report, *Mysterious Traveler.*

(M) "All in Love Is Fair" (Wonder); "Midnight at the Oasis" (Nichtern); "Sunshine on My Shoulders" (Denver-Taylor-Kniss).

(H) Nixon resigns presidency.

1975

(J) Davis, *Agharta* and *Pangea.*

(M) "Feelings" (Albert); "Laughter in the Rain" (Sedaka-Cody); "Philadelphia Freedom" (John-Taupin); "Send in the Clowns" (Sondheim); "Rhinestone Cowboy" (Weiss).

(H) Communists control South Vietnam and Cambodia; U.S.-Soviet joint mission in space; Franco dies.

1976

(J) Keith Jarrett, *Köln Concert;* George Benson, *Breezin';* "Wildflowers," week-long loft jazz festival in New York City; Ornette Coleman, "Dancing in Your Head."

(M) "Get Up and Boogie" (Levay-Prager); "I Wish" (Wonder); "I Write the Songs" (Johnston); "Afternoon Delight" (Danoff); "Fifty Ways to Leave Your Lover" (Simon).

(H) Death of Mao Zedong; Viking landing on Mars; Carter first president from Deep South in 125 years.

1977

(J) Weather Report, *Heavy Weather;* Hancock, *V.S.O.P.*

(M) "You Make Me Feel Like Dancin'" (Sayer-Poncia); "Sir Duke" (Wonder).

(H) Anwar Sadat conducts state visit to Israel.

1978

(J) Art Ensemble of Chicago, *Nice Guys;* Woody Shaw, *Rosewood;* Toshiko Akiyoski-Lew Tabackin, *Insights;* Anthony Braxton, "Composition for Four Orchestras."

(M) "Stayin' Alive" (Gibb); "Night Fever" (Gibb); "You Don't Bring Me Flowers" (Diamond); "Boogie Oogie Oogie" (Johnson-Kibble).

(H) Senate approves Panama Canal Treaties; Pope John Paul II becomes first non-Italian pope since 1523; U.S. and China establish full diplomatic relations.

1979

(J) Weather Report, *8:30;* Joni Mitchell, *Mingus;* The World Saxophone Quartet, "Steppin' With."

(M) "Hot Stuff" (Belotte-Faltermeyer-Forsey); "I Will Survive" (Fekaris-Perren); "The Gambler" (Schlitz).

(H) Shah of Iran deposed, 53 American hostages taken; Three Mile Island incident.

1980

(J) Johnny Griffin, *Return of the Griffin;* Air, *Air Lore;* Jack DeJohnette, *Special Edition;* Muhal Richard Abrams, "Mama and Daddy."

(M) "Magic" (Ferrar); "It's Still Rock 'n Roll to Me" (Joel); "Celebration" (Bell and "Kool and the Gang").

(H) Reagan oldest president to enter office; U.S. boycotts summer Olympics in Moscow; Mount Saint Helens erupts; major earthquakes in Italy and Algeria.

bibliography

jazz books

BERGER, MORROE, EDWARD BERGER, and JAMES PATRICK. *Benny Carter, A Life in American Music.* 2 vols. Metuchen, N.J.: The Scarecrow Press and The Institute of Jazz Studies, 1982. An extensive biographical and musical study.

BLESH, RUDI and HARRIET JANIS. *They All Played Ragtime.* 4th ed. New York: Oak Publications, 1971. Wonderful study of ragtime history, well illustrated, with musical examples.

BRUNN, H. O. *The Story of the Original Dixieland Jazz Band.* Baton Rouge: Louisiana State University Press, 1960. Historical study of the first important jazz group.

BUDDS, MICHAEL J. *Jazz in the Sixties.* Iowa City: University of Iowa Press, 1978. Comprehensive, in-depth study of the numerous jazz styles in the 1960s.

CARR, IAN. *Miles Davis.* New York: William Morrow and Company, 1982. An excellent biography; contains much analysis of Davis's solos, some transcriptions, and a complete discography.

CHARTERS, SAMUEL B. and LEONARD KUNSTADT. *Jazz. A History of the New York Scene.* New York: Doubleday, 1962. A very good history, well illustrated.

COLE, BILL. *John Coltrane.* New York: Schirmer Books, 1976. A good biography of Coltrane.

DANCE, STANLEY. *The World of Count Basie.* New York: Charles Scribner's Sons, 1980. Personal recollections and anecdotes by the Basie band members.

DANCE, STANLEY. *The World of Duke Ellington.* New York: Charles Scribner's Sons, 1970. As in Dance's work on Basie, this book contains much anecdotal information.

DAPOGNY, JAMES. *Ferdinand "Jelly Roll" Morton, The Collected Piano Music.* New York: G. Schirmer and Washington, Smithsonian Institution Press, 1982. The best transcriptions ever done of a major jazz artist, complete and annotated.

ELLINGTON, EDWARD KENNEDY. *Music Is My Mistress.* New York: Doubleday & Co., 1973. Useful autobiography.

FEATHER, LEONARD. *The New Edition of the Encyclopedia of Jazz.* New York: Horizon Press, 1960. Useful biographies.

FEATHER, LEONARD and IRA GITLER. *The Encyclopedia of Jazz in the Seventies.* New York: Horizon Press, 1976. A continuation of the earlier work.

GILLESPIE, DIZZY and AL FRASER. *To Be or Not To Bop. Memoirs.* New York: Doubleday, 1979. A fine jazz autobiography, though occasionally self-serving. Contains discography.

GITLER, IRA. *Jazz Masters of the Forties.* New York: Collier-Macmillan, 1966. A fine study.

GODDARD, CHRIS. *Jazz Away from Home.* London: Paddington Press, 1979. A useful study of jazz in Europe.

GOLDBERG, JOE. *Jazz Masters of the Fifties.* New York: Collier-Macmillan, 1968. A fine study.

HADLOCK, RICHARD. *Jazz Masters of the Twenties.* New York: Collier-Macmillan, 1965. An excellent study.

HAMM, CHARLES. *Yesterdays. Popular Song in America.* New York: Norton, 1979. By far the best history of American popular music.

HAMMOND, JOHN and IRVING TOWNSEND. *John Hammond on Record. An Autobiography.* New York: Penguin Books, 1981. Useful reminiscences of an important jazz talent scout and record producer.

HANDY, W. C., *W. C. Handy: Father of the Blues.* New York: Collier Books, 1970 (first published 1941). Important autobiography.

HENTOFF, NAT and ALBERT J. McCARTHY, eds. *Jazz.* New York: Da Capo Press, 1975 (first published 1959). Intelligent stylistic and historical analysis by 12 important critics and scholars.

HODEIR, ANDRE. *Jazz. Its Evolution and Essence.* New York: Grove Press, 1956. A fine though somewhat dated study of jazz style.

JEPSEN, JORGEN GRUNNET. *Jazz Records: A Discography.* Holte, Denmark: Knudsen, 1963-. An indispensible discography that begins where the Rust discography leaves off; new volumes to be issued.

JONES, LeROI. *Blues People.* New York: William Morrow & Co., 1963. Important sociological study.

KEEPNEWS, ORRIN and BILL GRAUER, JR. *A Pictorial History of Jazz.* New York: Crown Publishers, Inc., 1955. An excellent collection of photographs.

KINKLE, ROGER D. *The Complete Encyclopedia of Popular Music and Jazz 1900-1950.* New Rochelle, N.Y.: Arlington House, 1974. An essential reference work. Contains lists of popular songs, recordings, movie musicals, Broadway shows, major record company release dates, academy award winners and nominees, jazz poll winners, and biographies.

de LERMA, DOMINIQUE-RENÉ. *Reflections on Afro-American Music.* Kent, Ohio: Kent State University Press, 1973. Useful for a list of European music influenced by jazz and black music.

LOMAX, ALAN. *Mister Jelly Roll.* Berkeley and Los Angeles: The University of California Press, 1973 (first edition 1950). An often fascinating account, assembled from Lomax's interviews with Morton.

LYONS, LEN. *The 101 Best Jazz Albums, A History of Jazz on Records.* New York: William Morris and Company, Inc., 1980. A very helpful book, especially since most of the records are still available.

MECKLENBURG, CARL GREGOR HERZOG ZU, and WALDEMAR SCHECK. *Die Theorie des Blues Im Modernen Jazz.* Baden-Baden: Verlag Valentin Koerner, 1971. The most comprehensive analysis of the conflicting theories of the origin and status of the blues.

MEEKER, DAVID. *Jazz in the Movies.* New Rochelle, New York: Arlington, 1977. The only existing guide; quite thorough, though not enough information about the music itself.

MINGUS, CHARLES. *Beneath the Underdog: His World as Composed by Mingus,* ed. Nel King. New York: Alfred A. Knopf, 1971. Powerfully written autobiography; anecdotes and personal recollections.

MURRAY, ALBERT. *Stomping the Blues.* New York: McGraw-Hill Book Company, 1976. A compelling and unique discussion of African-American music—"The blues as such."

NANRY, CHARLES. *The Jazz Text.* New York: D. Van Nostrand Company, 1979. A sociological approach stressing large-scale historical trends. Balance of emphasis between the major and minor artists, but contains many errors on music theory.

NKETIA, J. H. KWABENA. *The Music of Africa.* New York: W. W. Norton & Company, 1974. Excellent survey of general trends, styles, and aesthetics.

OWENS, THOMAS. "Charlie Parker: Techniques of Improvisation." Ph.D. dissertation, Los Angeles: University of California, 1974. An extensive study that contains numerous transcriptions. (Available from University Microfilms, Ann Arbor.)

PLACKSIN, SALLY. *American Women in Jazz.* n.p., Wideview Books, 1982. Information on often neglected women instrumentalists.

REISNER, ROBERT GEORGE. *Bird: The Legend of Charlie Parker.* New York: Bonanza Books, 1962. Useful collection of personal reminiscences.

RUSSELL, ROSS. *Jazz in Kansas City and the Southwest.* Berkeley: University of California Press, 1971. The best study of the development of swing and the impact of the Kansas City style.

RUST, BRIAN. *Jazz Records 1897-1942.* New Rochelle, N.Y.: Arlington House, 1978. An essential discography of jazz up to the time of the recording ban.

SARGEANT, WINTHROP. *Jazz, Hot and Hybrid*. 3rd ed. New York: Da Capo Press, 1975 (first ed. 1938). The first serious study of early jazz. Contains fine analytical insights.

SCHULLER, GUNTHER. *Early Jazz, Its Roots and Musical Development*. New York and Oxford: Oxford University Press, 1968. Excellent discussion of jazz recordings before 1930.

SHAPIRO, NAT and NAT HENTOFF. *Hear Me Talkin' to Ya*. New York: Dover Publications, 1955. Useful first-hand accounts by various musicians.

SOUTHERN, EILEEN. *The Music of Black Americans*. New York: W. W. Norton & Company, 1971. An important history.

SOUTHERN, EILEEN, ed. *Readings in Black American Music*. New York: W. W. Norton & Company, 1971. Fascinating collection of original source material.

SPELLMAN, A. B. *Black Music: Four Lives*. New York: Schocken Books, 1966. Biographical information and interview excerpts on four jazz musicians controversial at the time: Ornette Coleman, Cecil Taylor, Herbie Nichols, and Jackie McLean.

STARR, S. FREDERICK. *Red and Hot, The Fate of Jazz in the Soviet Union*. New York and Oxford: Oxford University Press, 1983. A brilliant study of the spread of jazz into the Soviet Union; a fascinating example of how a non-Western culture reacted to and assimilated jazz.

STEARNS, MARSHALL and JEAN STEARNS. *Jazz Dance*. New York: Schirmer Books, 1968. The only extensive study of the history of jazz dance. Contains interesting speculations on the mutual influence of jazz and jazz dance.

STEARNS, MARSHALL. *The Story of Jazz*. New York: Oxford University Press, 1970 (first published 1956). A fine early history.

TAYLOR, ARTHUR. *Notes and Tones*. New York: Perigee Books, 1977. Several dozen musician-to-musician interviews with many of jazz's greats.

TIRRO, FRANK. *Jazz, A History*. New York: Norton, 1977. Extensive treatment of nineteenth-century prejazz music, but little on modern jazz. Many musical examples, excellent bibliography, a few transcriptions, much historical information.

WILDER, ALEC. *American Popular Song. The Great Innovators 1900-1950*. New York: Oxford University Press, 1972. An indispensable sampling of many great standards; analytical and insightful.

WILLIAMS, MARTIN, ed. *Jazz Panorama*. New York: Collier Books, 1964 (first published 1958). Fine collection of stylistic and historical essays.

WILLIAMS, MARTIN. *The Jazz Tradition*. New York: The New American Library, 1971. A fine history.

WILMER, VALERIE. *As Serious As Your Life*. Westport, Conn.: Lawrence Hill & Company. The only in-depth treatment of the new jazz to date. Excellent biographical information, numerous photos.

jazz periodicals

The most important academic jazz periodical in the United States is the *Journal of Jazz Studies,* whose title has recently been changed to the *Annual Review of Jazz Studies,* published by the Rutgers Institute of Jazz Studies in Newark, N.J., 07102. The other most important scholarly journal is *Jazzforschung/Jazz Research* (Graz, Austria), with articles in English and German.

In the past, the only publications dealing regularly with jazz were the so-called "fan" magazines. *Downbeat* was the most well known in America. *Downbeat* now calls itself a magazine of "contemporary music," although it pays more attention to current music that has something of a jazz flavor as well as to old-time jazz. There are many other publications in English on jazz as well—the *Annual Review of Jazz Studies* has published extensive lists of them—including *Cadence* (from Redwood, N.Y.) and a magazine dealing exclusively with "urban blues," *Living Blues* (formerly out of Chicago but now published by the Univ. of Mississippi).

Many foreign magazines on jazz are published, too. One of the most important foreign magazines in English is the British publication *Jazz Journal*. Other good foreign magazines include the French publication *Jazz Magazine,* the German publication *Jazz-Podium,* and *Coda,* from Toronto.

The fan magazines contain record reviews, interviews with jazz artists, articles on history, reviews of concerts, and nightclub appearances and, in *Downbeat,* articles of technical interest to musicians. The more scholarly journals tend to include technical analyses of musical styles, histories of artists, histories of jazz groups and eras, discographies, sociological studies, and occasionally extensive interviews. For a broad list of magazines, books, and articles, see Tirro's *Jazz,* listed above.

music theory books

BAKER, DAVID. *Jazz Improvisation*. Chicago: Maher Publications, 1971. Useful improvisation exercises, but little on the art of thematically constructing a solo. Also contains bibliography and discography.

BAKER, DAVID. *Advanced Improvisation*. Chicago: Maher Publications, 1974. Same as above, but for advanced students.

COKER, JERRY. *Improvising Jazz*. Englewood Cliffs, N.J.: Prentice-Hall, 1964. Useful theory and exercises, however, neither extensive nor thorough.

GARCIA, RUSSELL. *The Professional Arranger Composer*. Hollywood: The Criterion Music Corp. A must for both studio and jazz big band or small-group composers/arrangers.

JAFFE, ANDREW. *Jazz Theory*. Dubuque, Iowa: William C. Brown Company Publishers, 1983. A useful work on jazz theory, though its concentration is almost entirely on harmony.

MANCINI, HENRY. *Sounds and Scores. A Practical Guide to Professional Orchestration*. n.p., Northridge, 1959. A very useful guide—contains recordings of many of the scored examples.

MEHEGAN, JOHN. *Jazz Improvisation*. 4 vols. New York: Watson-Guptill, 1959-1965. vol. 1: *Tonal and Rhythmic Principles;* vol. 2: *Jazz Rhythm and the Improvised Line;* vol. 3: *Swing and Early Progressive Piano Styles;* vol. 4: *Contemporary Piano Styles.* A few extended treatments of piano voicings, but little on constructing an artful solo. Vol. 2 has a good collection of transcriptions. The treatment of left-hand chord voicings is very helpful in vols. 3 and 4.

PISTON, WALTER. *Harmony*. (4th ed. revised by Mark DeVoto.) New York: W. W. Norton & Company, 1976. Comprehensive study of classical tonality.

RUSSELL, GEORGE. *The Lydian Chromatic Concept of Tonal Organization*. New York: Concept Publishing Co., 1959. A fascinating, totally unorthodox approach to a theory of improvisation. Rather complex.

SCHENKER, HEINRICH. *Free Composition*. New York and London: Longman, Inc., 1979. (1st edition, *Der freie Satz,* published by Universal Edition, Wien, 1935.) The most important work on tonal theory by the century's most acclaimed theorist; Schenker's theory of harmony, voice leading, and diminution reaches its most mature form in this work.

STANTON, KEN. *Jazz Theory. A Creative Approach*. New York: Taplinger Publishing Co., Inc., 1982. Contains some useful exercises and ideas.

YESTON, MAURY, *ed. Readings in Schenker Analysis and Other Approaches*. New Haven and London: Yale University Press, 1977. Useful articles that can serve as an introduction to Schenker's thinking on tonal music.

index to enjoying jazz